Politicians and Public Services

Politicians and Public Services

Implementing Change in a Clash of Cultures

Kate Jenkins

Visiting Professor, Government Department, London School of Economics and Chairman, KJA Ltd.

Edward Elgar
Cheltenham, UK • Northampton, MA, USA

Published by
Edward Elgar Publishing Limited
Glensanda House
Montpellier Parade
Cheltenham
Glos GL50 1UA
UK

Edward Elgar Publishing, Inc.
William Pratt House
9 Dewey Court
Northampton
Massachusetts 01060
USA

A catalogue record for this book
is available from the British Library

Library of Congress Control Number: 2008926572

ISBN 978 1 84720 142 3 (cased)

Printed and bound in Great Britain by MPG Books Ltd, Bodmin, Cornwall

Contents

Acknowledgements

The major part of this book is a description of the work done by the Efficiency Unit in the British Government during the 1980s. I must record my gratitude to the staff of the Unit, in particular to Karen Caines, Charlotte Dixon and Angharad Rhys who worked with me during my time there and to Sir Robin Ibbs who, as the Prime Minister's Adviser, supported and advised us and oversaw our work.

Warm thanks must go to William Plowden who has worked with me on this manuscript as on so much else, to George Jones, Richard Dykes and Karen Caines who commented on the drafts as they were written, to Clive Priestley whose experience of the issues discussed here is extensive and to Peter Hennessy who persuaded me that the subject deserved a book.

Finally my thanks to the public servants and Ministers in countries across the world with whom I have spent many hours discussing the subject of this book over the past twenty years.

Kate Jenkins
London, 2007

Introduction

Public services and public sector management are the subject of political debate around the world. Users and voters are concerned with the outcomes; officials handle the inputs, the management and the finances, politicians deal with the policy and the political consequences of success and failure. The theme of this book is an exploration of why it is governments find it difficult to run public services effectively, why politicians repeatedly try to reform public services and largely fail, and why the public is so often dissatisfied with the services they use.

The efforts of the Thatcher government in the 1980s to put analysis and political attention into the process of management in central government are described as an example of how a significant change to the organisation of public services was handled. The introduction of executive agencies demonstrated the critical importance of the definition and communication of policies so that implementation could be feasible and effective. The largest organisations on earth are publicly run organisations. Britain is not alone in finding the task complicated and difficult both to understand and to manage. The efforts of the international agencies, the countries in the OECD group and developing countries to tackle the problem have all highlighted how great the difficulties are.

Executive agencies may have resolved some of the flaws in public sector management, but by no means all of them. In almost every country the government provides services essential for its citizens, whether it is a tyranny, a dictatorship, a single party democracy or a fully open democratic government. The services may be provided directly by the central government or through local or regional governments or organisations. They may be provided by NGOs, agencies or private companies, but the main decisions will be taken by a central, regional or local government and the funding will come, directly or indirectly from the public, from taxation, fees or other sources.

For any government the scale, scope and quality of public services are of importance and for most citizens what the government provides matters no less. The services may be only basic roads and drains in cities or it may be the full range of modern government. Few people in the world can escape entirely from the activities of the nation state in which they live. Public services, the economic and physical infrastructure, security, defence, social welfare arrangements and the regulation of economic and social relationships, absorb the majority of the resources which most states spend. People have little choice about how they pay for public services, what quality they provide or who provides them.

Despite their significance to both governments and their citizens the quality of public services is a constant source of comment and irritation. People are seldom satisfied with what the state provides; politicians offer improvements in public services as a major part of their appeal, whether they are justifying a coup or taking part in a democratic election. The organisation of public services varies widely from country to country – hospitals may be run by an elected Minister or by the President's wife. Roads may be built under licence and charged for by tolls or built by state employees and completely free to the user. Schools may be run by churches or by a secular state, they may be free or expensive, available to all or to only a few, they may provide a good, bad or indifferent education. The courts may have a long history of judicial freedom and academic excellence or be corrupt, untouchable and damaging. How the services are run is fundamental to whether they provide what the citizen has been promised or needs.

Criticising the government is one of the commonest occupations on the street, in the shop, in the café, or the local bar in countries all round the world where speech is reasonably free and there is a semblance of democratic choice. Some governments do provide adequate services, but any citizen will be able to provide an enquirer with an impressive list of failings. Although there are significant gaps, by 2005 some two-thirds of the world's countries had what has been described as a democratic system for elections which provided its citizens with an opportunity, although with significant exceptions, to choose between different parties to form a government. As the number of governments elected by democratic election has spread rapidly in the final years of the twentieth century, the pressure on politicians to provide some of what they promise during elections has increased.

The expansion of government activity in size and scope means that it is more important to resolve the unsatisfactory state of many public services. Badly run, corrupt or over-bureaucratised services have an increasing impact on everyone's lives and a disproportionate effect on the poorest citizens. The political issue is becoming a managerial one – whether a government in power is capable of running the public sector efficiently and effectively. The late twentieth century policy debate about what a government should or should not do for ideological reasons is being supplanted by the practical issue of whether it has the institutional capacity to do what it decides is necessary or desirable.

There have now been several decades of expanding government activity and the application of management principles to public services around the world. The scale of public services has increased in many countries but whether the quality has matched the political promises is a matter of debate. It would be easy to accept the traditional view of the citizen in the street that all politicians are thieves and rogues and should never be trusted with anything. In many countries the experience of government fits that bill rather closely. But that view of the public sector would be grossly unfair to the numbers of people, both politicians and public service employees, who work long and hard to try to improve the quality of what their public sector provides. There are Ministers, deeply committed to the quality of education or health, and senior and junior officials who take public service seriously. There are farming communes in southern Mexico where new farming methods are producing remarkable results, supported with small-scale loans and grants administered locally. The elderly in Kent in England have a card supplied and paid for by the local authority which enables them to purchase social care directly, making their own choices about what they need and when they need it. Such public services are exemplary, but they tend to be the exception rather than the rule.

The first chapter of this book considers some of the ways post-war governments have tried to deal with managing public services. The principal argument is that underlying the obvious challenges of managing large, dispersed organisations is the extent to which policies for public services are in the hands of people with conflicting priorities. Politicians have political priorities and political timescales which can be different from those of a well managed organisation – or of the customer for whom the service is provided. These conflicting priorities throw many public service organisations into a tug of war between what they are expected to provide and what political imperatives demand that they do.

Chapters 2 to 6 describe, from a viewpoint within the United Kingdom Government during the 1980s, the process of analysis of what was wrong with management in central government, the origins of the ideas and the objectives behind proposals to set up executive agencies, the nature of the political and official debate about whether such a structure would be practicable and the political view taken about the recommendations.

Chapter 7 considers the implementation process which transferred some 70 per cent of central government employees into new management structures over a period of five years, and Chapter 8 reviews the reaction of commentators and political theorists to the changes during implementation and after completion of the programme.

Chapter 9 discusses the wider context of public sector reform internationally and the development of the debate among commentators of the development of programmes of state reform. Chapter 10 returns to the United Kingdom experience to consider why the state of the public sector continues to be a cause for concern and political debate twenty years after the Next Steps Report. The final chapter discusses the responsibilities of politicians and public servants for the condition of the public services and the lessons to be learnt in constructing a way forward for the management of public services.

There is unfinished business and a challenging and changing economic, social and political environment to be considered. Public services need skills and flexibility to face a constantly changing world. There will not be a single answer, much less a 'reform' that will solve the difficulties; and first it is necessary to understand what the problem is and where the answers may lie.

1. The management of public services: what goes wrong?

Most modern governments face difficulties in meeting the expectations of their citizens. The public sector takes up between a third and a half of the finances of most developed economies. It tends to be referred to as if it is a single homogenous whole although it is made up of widely differing institutions. It can absorb people and money like blotting paper. Its scope extends beyond activities which are technically 'services'. The provision of personal services, personal, domestic and international security, defence, economic and social development, transfer payments and regulation take up the lion's share of what many governments do. They operate either through their directly managed organisations or under some form of agreement or contract with other organisations or through other tiers of elected authorities.

The most well-intentioned politician finds bringing promises to reality difficult. A familiar plaint of many a disillusioned Minister is: 'I pull the levers and nothing happens'. While it is difficult enough for officials to explain to a senior and distinguished Minister that pulling levers is no longer, if it ever was, the way to get a decision implemented, the remark itself explains how far from understanding management most politicians are. I have heard frustrated ministers use the same phrase on three continents and in many countries. The internal workings of the public sector baffle most people – politician, business person or citizen – who are not part of the inner circle which runs the government day-by-day and year-by-year. Its scale, the scope of the tasks that are performed and the way those tasks are carried out are frequently shrouded in an obscurity which is difficult to penetrate from outside.

Elections are exciting events for politicians; during an election campaign politicians in most countries are closer to their electorates than at any other time. They speak, argue, listen, lose their voices and have occasionally to dodge flying eggs or worse. Above all they promise. They promise improvements, changes, more money, less taxes, different priorities. They issue manifestoes with crafted plans for what their government would do if it gets elected. And the day after the votes are counted, the results announced and the parties are over, they enter a different world.

On gaining office, most modern governments, especially if they have been in opposition for several years, find it difficult to meet their own expectations of what they should do. The scope for policy changes, for new expenditure, for shifts in priorities to meet their own objectives and the promises they have made to their electorates, is almost always far less than they supposed from their position as an opposition party. The reality of government is invariably worse on the inside. Money has been pre-empted, decisions are circumscribed by factors which are invisible outside government, changes take more time than was expected and the public expects fast results.

But the politician faces a serious challenge: poor government can be an economic disaster and an electoral liability. Elections can be fought and lost on lack of security, bad hospitals, poor policing, inadequate education or unchecked corruption. Elections are won on promises of fewer taxes, better performance, better services and reform, but with the limitations of established policies, committed forward expenditure and the need to keep the system running at all costs, however badly, the scope for action can be severely limited.

Government is a complex business; part of the politician's task is to reduce that complexity to manageable proportions without losing sight of the significance of the complexity. Most politicians are willing to listen to advice on how to manage the operations for which they are responsible, and there are many possible sources of help and advice. Politicians in government turn first to their advisers both from the permanent public service and from their party machine and then, as the policy solutions have to fit with the complexity of their management task, they also turn to organisational theories, business models and academic advice.

They ask for restructuring, reform, for the old officials to be cleared out and new ones appointed, for business people to be brought in, for cut backs or expansion. But a core of difficulty almost always remains, caused by trying to match political skills, rhetoric and promises with the steady slog of managing large organisations. Planning and decisions have to take account of routine activity, huge budgets, rising costs and changing demands. Many of the solutions that are used are organisational: new structures, different and frequently more expensive people or different management systems. As many governments take greater control over the lives of their citizens and the cost of running public institutions grows, the need for solutions becomes more urgent.

MATCHING SKILLS: POLITICIANS, POLITICAL APPOINTEES AND OFFICIALS

Most public services are overseen, directly or indirectly by elected or appointed politicians. The services are funded mainly from public resources;

the scale and quality of the service is decided by reference to political decisions, election promises and available money. Politicians determine the scope of services, approve the finances and occasionally become involved in the detail of the organisation. In most democratic countries they are elected both to ensure that political priorities and policies are implemented and also to oversee public services and ensure that taxation is properly spent. Public participation in the running of public services is variable; in some countries there is a culture of participation as a public responsibility, in other countries it is sporadic or non-existent, managing government is left to politicians. In some countries public involvement is the last thing the Government wants or is prepared to allow.

Many national politicians come new to the task of taking major decisions for large organisations; they may have been in party politics all their lives or come from a professional, academic or military career. Relatively few will have had experience of running a large organisation at a senior level, much less a public service, unless they have survived in a long established government or returned to a ministry where they have worked before. One common characteristic of most elected politicians is the belief that, whatever and whoever has gone before, they can do better. The adversarial nature of a democratic election encourages politicians to promise improvement or a new approach, to promise to do a better job than the last lot, even when previous attempts to do so have failed. In an election promises for the future are made and public services loom large in the assurance of better things; the next election will bring recriminations as well as more promises and the cycle revolves again.

There are governments which superimpose another cycle – the revolving Minister. The United Kingdom may be an extreme case, but few ministers survive in the same job for any period of time. In 2006 in the United Kingdom no senior minister had been in the same department for more than three years apart from the Prime Minister and the Chancellor of the Exchequer. The Home Secretary, responsible for security, immigration and most of the criminal justice system, had had no job in the previous nine years for more than 20 months – he had worked in nine major Departments. In the Home Office there had been four different Home Secretaries in the previous five years. Officials in the Departments he left and in the new one must have been wary of how they adjusted to another short term minister.

Decisions taken by inexperienced Ministers can be damaging. Poor or ill-considered decisions have a direct effect on the running of public organisations, and can waste huge sums of money. Organisations tend to defer to where the power lies – there is nothing unusual in that – but when the centre of power is a long way away from the operational centre and communication is poor it is difficult for the person with the power to understand the impact of his or her decisions. Most politicians have very little idea of what lies beneath the surface of their ministries and will have no grasp of what the impact of a particular decision might be. Unfortunately the same is true of many senior officials who have less excuse.

The policy may be complex but the sums of money involved can seem unreal to people used to more normal budgets. There may be a tighter and harder fought argument about spending $2 million on the car pool than $50 billion on aircraft, partly because the amounts of money involved are easier to comprehend for a politician with little experience of the costs of government procurement. But, however inexperienced, the senior politician is responsible for that $50 billion and may be answerable either to the head of the Government or to a parliamentary or congressional committee. Understanding the management of money is an essential part of his or her job as a minister even though it may not be in the list of necessary qualities for a successful one.

Dazzled by the numbers and the scale of the public sector, politicians, since the nineteenth century in the United Kingdom and the USA, have reached for private sector businessmen to help on the grounds that they know how to run things. Businessmen accept the invitation. However shabby the Government may appear to be, a role as an adviser, a chief executive or even a Secretary of State appears to be regarded by many as an accolade or as a means of access to power. They murmur into the cameras on taking office about making a contribution or even putting something back. And with monotonous regularity the businessmen retreat gratefully back to business after a while, where the personalities are more controllable and the exogenous factors less devastating. In the United Kingdom they have had occasional successes but, as in any organisation, the most innovative changes after a few years leave little mark, unless the changes have been unusually skilful.

Political appointees are a familiar part of the political landscape, both as senior officials and as policy advisers. They are an often undervalued part of the process of government: they can contribute by articulating political objectives and injecting new ideas, new ways of thinking and new management ideas into organisations which can be hidebound and inert. But they too have to deal with understanding the complexity of the policies and the organisation with which they are working if they are to be effective.

In most governments there is a critical working relationship between politicians and senior officials. The policy maker who is a political ally of the Minister will have one approach; the appointed official, whose career is in the Ministry not with the politicians, will have another. It is a difficult relationship with confused boundaries and responsibilities which follow personalities and individual skills rather than organisation structure.

Where the skills are not complementary or sufficient there can be gaps. As James Wilson observed, in the US State Department when Kissinger was Secretary: 'Policy was under Henry Kissinger's control; the department was under nobody's control' (Wilson, 1989). There are Ministers who can be highly competent at running a department, although they are difficult to find, and there are officials who are fascinated by politics and policy and profoundly bored by organisation and management. Both can find space for their skills in most governments; but the confusion of roles and the pressures of power tend to allow political rather than organisational expertise to be paramount. The Next Steps Report for Mrs Thatcher commented: 'we observed confusion between Ministers and Permanent Secretaries over their respective responsibility for service delivery'. There was no clear understanding of who was running the department (Jenkins et al., 1988).

THE STRUCTURE OF GOVERNMENT: THE INNER CIRCLE AND THE MACHINE

A new Minister is unlikely to have much idea what lies beyond his or her office or what is involved in making changes to the patchwork of activities that make up the Ministry. They will see advisers, experts and senior officials. They will have an office, a car if they are lucky, and a political role. But the life of the ordinary civil servant or the chain of control or even the site of many of the offices of the ministry will be beyond most ministers' horizons. The structure of governments can vary widely; there is no single pattern or model. Ministries, departments and their associated agencies, parastatals, private sector contractors, local and regional governments all form a complex system which develops as government grows, making the task of politicians more difficult and increasing their dependence on advisers. When, for example, the Federal Government in Brazil introduced 'social organisations' in the 1990s, in an attempt to gain some better control over the sprawling Ministries of the Federal Government, in spite of extensive discussions and consultations, many Ministers remained baffled about the purpose and the expected benefits of the change; how the ministry worked was not within their view of their role.

The link between Ministers and the organisations they are accountable for can be tenuous. Most governments have an unmistakable fault line between the centres of government – the political structure and the senior officials – and the operations of the public sector, especially the organisations responsible for the services directly provided by the government. The dividing line can vary. On one side one might find, broadly speaking, the politicians in power either in or connected to the central government, senior officials who may or may not be appointed by the politicians, but who work with politicians on the twists and turns of the political management of the government and on the development of their policies. This group is surrounded by external advisers in think tanks, research institutes and universities and by pressure groups and lobbyists who all have an interest in what happens and who does it.

In shorthand these groupings are often referred to by the place where they operate, Washington, Paris, Whitehall, Pretoria, Brasilia, Delhi. The place names mark one of their distinguishing features – a relatively small community with close internal links, many of whom know each other well, at the centre of national life – aptly described by many observers as 'a village'. In every case the media play an increasingly important role. Journalists dominate the communication of information and political messages, their timetable can dictate how and when policies are announced. They are normally clearly within the circle around Ministers and politicians, concerned with personalities and policies and seldom with much current experience of life outside the political 'village'.

The second group – beyond the fault line – is very different; there is no political glamour. The offices are away from the centre of the capital, if they are in the capital at all. The Minister seldom, if ever, visits. But here is where the work is done that directly affects the citizen – where those levers do or do not connect. The tasks often, but not always, involve dealing directly with the citizens of a country: transfer payments, licensing cars, building roads, running hospitals, the secret police, the military, mapping the country – the list in most countries is almost endless, the common threads are the links with the centre of government. The connection might be a close one with policy and operations regularly monitored and directed from a central organisation, or delegated with main decisions taken by a local, regional or national manager or director. The money will come directly in a budget based on decisions taken in the central group or from fees which the organisation has power to raise directly.

Major areas of public policy may also be under the direct control of local elected groups and officials. Local and regional government has a different feel to it from that of a central or national government. It tends to be less formal and more directly aware of its voters. Local issues figure largely in elections, irate citizens can shout at the governor or the chief of police in the street, and the rubbish on the corners or the closed school are the concerns of everybody. In most cases the shuttered school or the uncollected garbage is a long way from the Elysee or the White House or even the regional government but elected governments ignore or misread local events at their peril.

Public service organisations have a different timeframe from the group at the centre of government. There will be critical dates for introducing new policies, but the year will be dictated by holidays, budgets and recruitment drives. Staff may expect to work there for decades, not a few years, indeed many will consider they have a right to be there for life – and so do their children. For some, the job they do will be compelling – they may be the national expert on mapping, or an international expert on explosives or infectious diseases. But the vast majority will be carrying out clerical tasks, some by hand on browning forms, others on screens as part of huge computerised systems. They will be recording, assessing and deciding issues which directly affect peoples' lives. They will normally be modestly paid and spend much of their day on the telephone and the computer; they may consider they have a career or perhaps just a job. They will be only vaguely aware of the Minister or indeed what is going on at the 'centre'. But what they do and how they do it can materially affect how people live their lives, how national politics works and in extreme cases whether a minister or a government survives.

The link between the clerk and the Minister is weak with rapid changes of minister the connection becomes almost invisible but the need for experience and comprehension of how the organisation works is essential. Unless the people taking decisions understand the nature of the organisation and how it deals with changes, any decision or instruction, however well meant, will go awry. Inexperienced politicians who want to announce changes immediately, in response to crises and who fail to heed warnings frequently have to deal with expensive mistakes subsequently. To be successful they need enough understanding to judge how far the warnings are accurate assessments of what might happen, or reflect the tendency of big organisations to warn against changes, especially those devised elsewhere. The pattern of political initiatives that produce little change can simply be a consequence of not understanding the nature of the organisation, but the irate taxpayer who has had bad treatment turns rapidly into an irate elector. Politicians become scarred by trying to do what seemed necessary and right but failing to get the results they expect.

THE BUREAUCRACY AND THE MACHINE

Politicians operate in a public arena in many democratic countries, but government organisations can be much less visible. Even in the most laissez-faire economies the impact of government institutions both as regulator and service provider is pervasive. But most of the public see only the tip of the iceberg of government. The regulations, the internal rules, the operating instructions and the way in which they are drawn up, approved and enforced is largely unknown. The quality of service provided and the details of the costs and constraints within which public organisations operate will often be a mystery. In many countries there will be upwards of a quarter of the labour force working in the public sector and even after some decades of following the international fashions for cuts, controls, and privatisations, the bulk of government functions in most countries remains unchanged: finance, health, education, defence, security, local and national administration.

The public sector and public services are relatively recent inventions. Indeed, modern democratic governments are recent inventions, and have only a toehold in many technically democratic countries. Long experience of an extensive and powerful public sector rests mainly with the older democracies and the old empires. Early public sector activities were tax collection, internal and external defence, communications, the protection of economic interests and latterly, drainage, sewerage and water. In the nineteenth century industrial developments and growing populations focused attention on the needs of vulnerable populations, for whom the old agrarian system had broken down and who were at the mercy of unprecedented developments in manufacturing and working practices while living with disease and extreme poverty in overcrowded and filthy towns. Until the twentieth century most social welfare services were provided by charities and religious groups; government did what no one else could or would do – and only then when it faced serious political pressure.

While Europe and North America faced many of these problems in the nineteenth and twentieth centuries, many parts of the world have similar patterns of social need in the twenty first century. The sprawling cities of Latin America, Africa and Asia dwarf the horrors of nineteenth century London or early twentieth century Chicago and the inhabitants of those cities are far more visible than their counterparts in Europe would have been as films, television and travel widen awareness of the world. The twentieth century saw a vast increase in the scope and the scale of government activity.

In many countries the patterns of political activity can be reasonably well understood. Even in the tightest dictatorship the relationship between ruler, supporters and people can be observed and in open societies the government is normally subject to constant scrutiny and comment. The government bureaucracy will be different. In most places little will be known about how it functions, what determines what its employees do, what the internal power struggles are and what idiosyncrasies dictate its assumptions and actions. For most of the population, eager to follow the machinations of politics, the activities of the bureaucracy will be regarded as dull and unimportant. Most bureaucracies prefer it that way.

How the public sector bureaucracy works will determine whether or not a government's policies are effective. In any system, whether it is led by political appointees or by career bureaucrats, at the end of the chain will be employees or contractors of the state who will make the payment, dig the road, let the contract, lock up the prisoner, or drive the truck. Someone has to decide what has to be done, in detail, to make the policy happen and someone has to tell the payment clerk or the road digger exactly what to do.

It can be an organised chain. In many countries the structure will be institutionalised with boards, directors, highly paid senior staff and recognised trade unions. It is slowly becoming the case that there are some measures of outcomes to replace the old dependence on subjective judgement from the top. But many of the important but implicit assumptions of what constitutes success for a bureaucrat can be political: the avoidance of embarrassment, a contented Minister, eager willingness to agree to political proposals for new policies and staying out of trouble. Successfully serving the public is a relatively recent measure of success. It is difficult to define and still more difficult to measure. There is a deeply entrenched view, found both in bureaucrats and professional politicians, that government should give people what it thinks is good for them rather than what they want. Local government can be different. There, the measures of success are more obvious and the recipients closer to hand. But often while the payment clerk and the road digger can see what is wrong and have to deal with irate citizens, the people who make the decisions at the other end of the chain are far away from both and have priorities of their own.

The person to whom all the activity is directed is normally the paymaster – the citizen. It is to the citizen of most democratic countries that the government is answerable for what it does. It is for the citizen that many of the services are provided and it is the citizen who may be able to decide whether the government stand or falls. In many active democracies politicians are painfully aware of the views of the voters. But as public services become more sophisticated in organisation, objectives and outcomes the citizen appears to become much less a part of the picture. Organisation and systems can become more significant than the outcome achieved at the end of the process. The cumulative effect of the activities of different parts of government on individuals is seldom, if ever, considered in policy making.

The impact of government on day to day life is increasing. As a consequence, changes to policies and processes can have a disproportionate effect on individual citizens. Writing in *The Independent* newspaper in London in September 1999 the columnist Eva Pascoe pointed out that the individual citizen had no hope of knowing what the government was doing; the problem was both a lack of information about public service changes and the scale and impact of them. She had missed a planning application which ruined the value of her house, a new parking control outside her house which made access difficult, and a government scheme to help in staff training which directly affected her business, all in the course of a two week holiday. Government was so involved with the details of daily life that understanding what was going on was important but probably impossible. Ms Pascoe's problems will have increased since then as the politicians concerned, in her local authority, in the national government in London, and the European Union government in Brussels have extended their reach and their intervention into the lives of citizens.

INCOMPATIBLE OBJECTIVES: POLITICS AND MANAGEMENT

Despite its political significance politicians consistently underestimate what is involved in the public service. National politics drive the group at the centre. Timescales are short, public perceptions of what is happening shift and alter from day to day with the flickering of television screens. The most compelling issue for many politicians is the next election, closely followed by any danger or embarrassment the government may be in from shorter term errors and misjudgements; uncontrollable foreign policy events and financial problems all loom larger than the carefully crafted policies developed in opposition.

In democratic countries underlying all political decisions is the electoral timetable. There may be another national election, a local or regional election, a gubernatorial election, a presidential election or simply a shift in the majority in the elected chamber. Even if the incumbent cannot be re-elected for constitutional reasons, the time available is limited by the end of the period of office. Political skills will therefore be the most valued: the capacity to be selected, handle elections, manipulate the party and its followers, announce popular and impressive changes, fight the battles and, above all, win.

On gaining office the politician, consciously or not, will be most aware of what will keep him or her there and project them to further political gain. There will be policy promises to be met, on the assumption that the present group knows better how to manage things and has a better plan for the future than the last one. At most there will be a period of anything between three and seven years in which to make the changes, so most politicians deal in promises rather than outcomes. They are unlikely to be around to see the results. But most will have an urgent need to be able to demonstrate that they are able to have an effect, and that they have a portfolio of ideas for instant action culled from past experience or a party manifesto.

Politicians with little experience of running organisations are faced with responsibility for huge amounts of public money, with a complicated range of people who may be affected by any decision, and a web of statutory controls which make taking any decision more confusing. In most cases there is no one right answer and no simple measure of success. The implementation of a change in policy or a new plan involves layers and layers of any organisation. There must be changes to working habits and changes to the distribution of finance, normally against a timetable which makes political but not operational sense. The changes frequently have to be made by people numb from the impact of repeated 'reforms' or outraged that there should be change at all. In the background is the ever present possibility that the politician who set it all in motion may lose interest, be moved to another job, change the policy or be voted out at any moment.

While political interest may be significant in institutions which respond closely to the interests of political leaders, there are many public organisations, further from the political system, which conversely depend on their own internal culture for priorities and leadership and develop a reluctance to do anything which is not consistent with internally recognised behaviour. James Wilson's example of the State Department in the 1980s where serious and repeated security lapses occurred: 'as the result of an organisational culture which simply did not assign a high value to security' (Wilson, 1989) is but one example. In that case, as in the Pentagon during the Iraq war, the system did not respond to political direction because individuals did not recognise the validity of instructions from political appointees (Woodward, 2006).

An apparently minor operational failure, a sudden natural disaster or a disintegration of a service under pressure can cause rapid and unexpected trouble for a government where political priorities have distracted attention from management detail. In the United Kingdom in 2006, a backbench opposition MP, Richard Bacon, took the trouble to read detailed evidence about the release of prisoners who were illegal immigrants. His questions triggered a chain of events which led to the dismissal of the Home Secretary, one of the most senior ministers in the Government, for an operational failure which had led to the release instead of deportation of foreign nationals who had completed prison sentences for serious crimes. The political appointee who was in charge of the Federal Agency responsible for disaster relief in the USA went in a blaze of recrimination when, facing a range of internal problems, senior management failed to deal with the very public emergency caused by Hurricane Katrina in 2005. Ministers can be sacked for many reasons but public service failures come high up on the list and single events can have a startling national impact.

Problems with poor communications and extended lines of control are inevitable in most large organisations. But politicians, the policy makers and the managers who work with them, take into account other pressures: the arguments from interest groups, the possibility of a backlash from senior management, the complacent inertia of a monopoly service and,

incessantly, the attentions of the media seeking the flaws in the policy proposals. Decisions may be taken for reasons that have nothing to do with the
merits of a case and cannot be foreseen – they may depend on a constituency interest, a negotiation in Brussels about something completely
different, or the fact that the Minister had flu and missed the crucial
meeting. Businessmen shake their heads and retreat. Ministers angle for
another job and the organisation continues its uninterrupted way but with
its view of 'political meddling' reinforced yet again.

In the United Kingdom the established Civil Service used to have a well
oiled process for dealing with expected changes. Work would begin before
an election if a change in the government party seemed likely. The idiosyncrasies of possible ministers would be studied and possible approaches to
changes in policy would be ready immediately after a General Election,
giving the misleading impression that any policy change could be swift and
straightforward. The advance preparation tended to encourage inexperienced politicians and political appointees to believe that the notion that 'we
decide and you do it' was a rational and professional approach to the development of major public policies. It ignored the complexity of government.

It was an attitude particularly common during the 1980s in the United
Kingdom with politicians who failed to understand the assumptions underpinning the traditional professional relationship between politician and
civil servant. Civil servants assumed that politicians understood that what
they considered their constitutional role was that of an independent and
apolitical adviser with an obligation to implement what ever decision was
taken. Politicians thought they were being merely obstructive and unhelpful. It became necessary for individual survival for civil servants to ignore
or deny any difficulties in policy proposals because disagreement, however
carefully phrased, was manifestly unpopular. It would be a brave and stub-
born official who was prepared to defend the complexities of the constitutional, much less the management task, or to provide reasoned judgements
about what could be done, by when and at what cost when it was clear that
their jobs and their careers were at stake. Absurd decisions, badly planned,
carried costs and misery with them.

ACCOUNTABILITY

Political accountability should be at the heart of any democratic system. But
service failures have an immediate effect on individuals while the consequences for those in charge come later and do little to compensate the victims
of failure. Although individual politicians and officials may suffer for policy
or operational failures, many succeed surprisingly well in protecting their

personal position, even if there is a major political storm, and the serious consequences of poor public services for social welfare remain. The examples are legion: poorly educated children, dirty, under equipped and dangerous hospitals, corrupt police forces. Mismanagement of the consequences of Hurricane Katrina in New Orleans in 2005 claimed a few official scalps but left hundred of thousands of people in a desperate plight while the rest of the world watched in horror. A new and much vaunted Family Credit system in the United Kingdom was badly planned and badly executed. No senior official or politician suffered and millions of invisible families were thrown into financial misery and debt and in some cases acute problems which led to suicide. A badly executed change to passport regulations in the UK led to vast queues, cancelled holidays and general chaos throughout one summer. The consequence was not apologies and a better service but a huge increase in the cost of a passport – the public paid directly for the errors of the Ministers and officials who were responsible for the trouble in the first place.

The resignation of one or a few people is normally the only penalty for wasting vast amounts of money and causing inconvenience or misery to hundreds of thousands of people. In the United Kingdom the much vaunted punishment of standing up in the House of Commons and explaining the mess, and occasionally resigning does nothing to compensate for a wrecked family, a ruined life and hundreds of millions of pounds wasted. Few commercial companies or senior private sector managers would survive if they were responsible for the disasters of public policy. Poor schools, worse hospitals, bad transport and under equipped defence services can continue for a surprising length of time without carrying serious political cost. Many ministers appear unaware of the damage their decisions can and do cause.

Politicians and officials are protected from the consequences of their poor decisions on the population; particularly the ministers and officials in Finance Ministries who wield more power than they like to admit and seldom, if ever, face the consequences. Citizens have only the weakest of recourse to those responsible for the damage wreaked on them; holding individual ministers or organisations to account costs money, takes time, and by the time a decision is reached, the people responsible may have moved on.

PUBLIC SERVICES AND THE POLITICAL DEBATE

The weary cynicism with which the electorate face the enthusiasms of politicians for reform in government should cause little surprise. The gap between rhetoric and reality is as great as ever. In 2003 in a worldwide survey of views, citizens regarded politicians as the least trusted profession and a majority, even in the most well established democracies, considered that their government did not act in accordance with their wishes (Stoker, 2006). What is surprising is that politicians still appear to believe that the public services can work miracles and they can find the answers which have eluded all their predecessors, as though a change in political decisions and their own leadership was all that was needed.

In the 1990s Clinton and Gore attempted to change the US system of health care and the process of Federal public administration. The first foundered and the second faded. Cardoso and Bresser Periera in Brazil wanted to restructure the sprawling, inefficient and expensive central government based in Brasilia but found they had to change the constitution first. Zedillo in Mexico contemplated changes to the Federal administration but put greater emphasis on electoral reform as a first stage. In the United Kingdom in the 1980s, the Thatcher government wanted to free up the market economy by privatising, deregulating, encouraging small firms and shuffling regional policy while reforming the health service, changing the education system reforming industrial relations and restructuring central government.

Britain has a long recorded history of government, both local and national which can be observed at work for at least fourteen hundred years. The activities of the monarch and the senior officials, the collection of taxes, the record of legislation, the development of local government are all recorded and accessible but the people and the system which made it work are almost absent from the record. There are shafts of light on the detail: Chaucer's Tales on the way to Canterbury in the second half of the fourteenth century is one source; another, the seventeenth-century diary of Samuel Pepys as a clerk in the Navy office, is treasured for the unforgettable picture it gives of life in London in the mid-seventeenth century, but it is also one of the few detailed glimpses available of office life within seventeenth-century government. The details of social welfare pressures and failures have become better understood as analysts have explored what happens in practice at the point of contact between client and professional (Hunt, 1998; Day and Klein, 1987). The development of systematic and open audit has opened up much that was inaccessible in the workings of public sector organisations (National Audit Office Reports, Audit Commission Reports, Ombudsman Reports).

The debate about public services is not a recent phenomenon. Although the consequences of increased size and rising expectations carry their own problems, it has been a truism for centuries that public services are not as efficient as they could be. Two examples stand for innumerable cases of government institutions failing their citizens. In the first, four hundred years ago, Sir Walter Raleigh complained bitterly about the incompetence of the local taxation office in the West of England in recording taxable wealth in 1593: 'Our estates that be £30 or £40 in the Queen's books are not the hundredth part of our wealth'. In that case, Professor Tanner who recorded it, commented dryly 'it was not in practice possible . . . to break down the tenacious custom which governed the entries there' (Tanner, 1928).

In a second case, the historian C.V. Wedgwood argued that a major cause of the long drawn out agony of the European Thirty Years War in the seventeenth century was the incompetence of government 'The routine of government was ill-organised; politicians worked with inadequate help; honesty, efficiency and loyalty were comparatively rare and the average statesman seems to have worked on the assumption that a perpetual leakage of funds and information was inevitable' (Wedgwood, 1938). A description which could stand in the twenty-first century.

It is entirely possible that people are eager to complain about public services precisely because that is what they are. Most services are monopoly providers and most citizens have no choice about where to go. The services would have both to meet public expectations and work like clockwork for the complaints to diminish. They would certainly need more exemplary management than operated in the sixteenth century tax office or seventeenth century Europe or in many late twentieth century state organisations. The United Kingdom Government has undergone repeated upheavals in the past twenty-five years, in what has appeared at times to be a desperate search for the best way to run its public services. The example of restructuring in the United Kingdom in the 1980s, described in the following chapters and known as 'Next Steps', demonstrated how painful the process of devising, planning and gaining consent to a change can be, and how unexpected the pressures are which drive decisions.

Political parties have long recognised the need to improve public services. Political manifestos in Britain have referred to changes and improvements at almost every general election in the past forty years but the promises are vague and the changes are frequently marginal. It could be argued that it doesn't really matter; as long as the roads are built, the air traffic control systems route aircraft effectively, pensions are paid, and the police are available and not too corrupt, people should not have to be concerned about how competent the systems are. But the generalisations hide inequity, petty corruption, wasted opportunities and high costs. The 'large and complex task', as the post-war Conservative manifesto described government, has grown steadily since 1945. Walter Williams, comparing Washington and London in 1988 observed: 'Complexity and expectations have far outdistanced government's competence to cope with a vast array of problems' (Williams, 1988).

Public discourse tends to focus on those in the public eye: the politicians, advisers and journalists who conduct the modern political debate. The scandals of failure and the occasional success are recognised but the system that produces the outcomes and the people involved are seldom part of the discussion. The role of ministers and officials in making the operations of government work effectively are critical for political success; they have to bring the right skills to the task if the state is to be able to make a reality of political promises. The themes this chapter has opened up: the scale and challenges of managing public services, the skills of those involved and the consequences of incompatible objectives and inadequate accountability will be explored later in the book. The following chapters consider the United Kingdom's experience of reforming management in government over forty years. It has been argued that the United Kingdom has done more 'reform' than most other countries but the question whether government is better for it is still hotly debated. The experience of the introduction of the Next Steps Report and executive agencies, described in detail, is an example of how careful analysis, political support and committed senior management can produce a significant change, even in the most conservative of organisations.

2. The United Kingdom Government: the pressure for change

This chapter discusses the background to the approaches taken by the British Government to improve the operation of directly managed public services during the 1980s. Later chapters focus particularly on the origins of the development of 'executive agencies' as a new structure for public services provided by central government under the direct control of Ministers.

In the 1980s the British Government led by Margaret Thatcher, with a radical agenda to reduce the size and cost of the state and pressure from acute financial problems, introduced major changes to the scope of government. The intervening quarter of a century has seen further changes in Britain and similar changes in many other countries. What was viewed in the 1980s as a right wing attack on the consensus-based, liberal post-war structure of government has become accepted as the norm. As the political rhetoric of shrinking states, the virtues of private ownership, and the incompetence of public officials has mellowed over the intervening years, the experience of the changing structure of the state is now commonplace in many countries which have no political tendencies to what was known as 'Thatcherism' or 'neo liberalism'.

The need for reform in government has a long history in Britain. Improbably, rioters in London in the 1780s are said to have shouted 'administration reform' as they smashed windows and hurled stones at the wealthy in Piccadilly. The Government has steadily increased the size and scale of its activities since the nineteenth century when the conditions of the working classes, especially in the big cities, driven by the industrial revolution, gave rise to political pressure for greater public provision and the regulation of public services. The development of more complex central government, the new structure of local government and the introduction of a more professional Civil Service created a system which could take on the increasing scope of nineteenth century government. In the twentieth century the domestic impact of two major wars radically altered the role of government and public expectations of what it could and should provide. The twentieth century saw the development of a huge system of social and economic welfare, reaching virtually every citizen, at every stage of their lives. At the centre of this system is a bureaucracy that takes its instructions from the small group of Ministers and officials who run the government from London and manages its workforce of around half a million to provide a wide range of services.

This chapter describes some of the changes over the past half century in the way the business of government in the United Kingdom is managed. I have described only some of the major changes and, in particular, the shift to an acceptance of the need for better management. I have sought to give a sense of what it was like to be directly involved in the development of new ideas and the persuasion necessary to get them accepted in the context of one of the more successful changes – the introduction of executive agencies. There have been other, more formal descriptions of what happened in the years in which the British system of government was radically changed but the formal record gives no sense of the background of hard work, the bitter arguments, the sense of hopelessness, and the lack of personal responsibility, which led so many of the best of their generation to leave the public service, and above all the virulent opposition which was mounted to the changes proposed and the risks taken by those who devised or supported the changes. By understanding what happened inside the system, how individuals reacted and responded it is possible to make more sense of the outcome. In later chapters I will also discuss the attitude of those involved in implementation and of the observers who watched what was happening within Whitehall, from the sidelines, or from the Ministerial chair in the Departments most concerned.

THE HOME CIVIL SERVICE

The task of managing the explosion in government activity in the second half of the twentieth century lay with two groups – the politicians in Parliament and local government, who decided what should be done, and the officials who managed and operated the services. At the apex of this activity, for over a hundred years, have sat the senior officials of the Home Civil Service, a carefully selected group of people with the responsibility of seeing that what is called 'the business' of Government runs smoothly and efficiently. That 'business' includes the work of politicians in Parliament, and the swirl of gossip and activity which surrounds them, and is recorded night by night by the media. It is also the decisions about government policy, the shape and content of legislation, taxation and how to spend it, relations with international groupings, responding to Parliament and managing the information flow from the centre of government. Closer to home for most of us are the licensing of cars, the regulation of companies, the collection of taxes, the provision of services, the control of personal relationships, the application of law, the state of the streets and the host of other actions which directly affect individual lives.

The institutions responsible for these activities are, still, directed primarily from a central bureaucracy based around the street in the middle of London, which lies along the site of the old royal palace of Whitehall. It is close to Parliament but for all Parliament knows of what goes on, it might just as well be hundreds of miles away in Runcorn or Penzance. It is secretive by nature and instinct and is extraordinarily cut off from the community it serves. 'Whitehall' has its own rules and quirky habits. It likes to call itself a 'village'. It gathers its offices together so that the area is close and familiar. Thirty years ago the Ministry of Health and the Ministry of Education were banished for reasons of economy and social benefit across the river Thames to the ancient suburbs of the Elephant and Castle and the Waterloo Road. Economy and social benefit were not sufficiently strong advantages to outweigh the problems of being separated from the comfort zone of Whitehall. The successor Departments are now safely back in smart new buildings within a stone's throw of Parliament Square with no troublesome water separating them from their peers. One erstwhile government office block, optimistically called 'Alexander Fleming House' now contains luxury apartments. The other, 'Hannibal House' is, in 2007, a crumbling eyesore. For all the expensive attempts to move central government out of London to what is still referred to as 'the provinces', it is in Whitehall that the senior civil servant makes or breaks his or her career.

Secretaries of State, the senior ministers who are members of the Cabinet, have constitutional responsibility for all the activities which are within the control of Departments. They take decisions on policy, they can intervene in management decisions and they are the public face of the Department. The size, structure and scope of Departments varies over time; a new government, or a ministerial reshuffle of posts and people can include renaming or reordering the responsibilities of a Department. The 'machinery of government', a Cabinet Office term of art for the structure of the central government, is kept firmly in the hands of the Cabinet Office and the Prime Minister who can make changes at any time. The senior officials who work with ministers are responsible for advising on policy, managing the Department, overseeing the implementation of policy and the use of the resources which are approved by the Treasury for the purpose of the Departments' activities. The Permanent Secretary, the archaic title of the official head of the Department, is accountable to Parliament for the money that has been spent. The Secretary of State is not accountable for expenditure but, together with the Department's team of junior ministers, is technically accountable to the House of Commons for all other aspects of the Department's work. The main lines of accountability are clear but day by day it is easy for responsibilities to become confused and areas to be ignored altogether. The work done on the Next Steps Report in the 1980s demonstrated a serious level of confusion about the boundaries of working responsibilities between Ministers and officials at senior levels.

The process of creating a modern government service in Britain has been traditionally marked by the publication of reports recommending modest improvements. Reports of this kind in Britain tend to be attached to the name of a distinguished member of what is called with irony 'the Establishment', or 'the Great and the Good', even though the thinking and the work – not to mention the writing – is normally done by other hands. In Britain the distinguished names are assumed to make acceptance of what might be unpalatable recommendations less painful.

The foundations of the modern British Civil Service were laid in 1870 when Gladstone introduced an Order in Council – a process of legislation linked to the mediaeval institution of the Crown's Privy Council – to begin the laborious process of implementing a radical reshaping of the Civil Service recommended by the Northcote Trevelyan Report of 1854. The main aim of the report, produced in response to widespread disquiet about jobbery, incompetence and corruption in the public service was to eliminate political appointments, to establish appointments on merit and to set up a professional career for civil servants. These changes took longer to implement than merely the laying of an Order in Council. When the report was published it was greeted with almost universal hostility and it was over forty years before its full purpose was achieved. In mid-nineteenth century England, the Civil Service and positions within it were part of a system of patronage and were the perks of office, not a service for the State, the Government or the community.

THE FULTON REPORT

The most significant piece of thinking about the Civil Service, between the Second World War and 1980 was the Fulton Report of 1968 – produced by a committee chaired by the Vice Chancellor of the University of Sussex, then seen as one of the more glamorous 'new' English universities. It is a model of careful analysis, clear thinking and sensible solutions. The report identified a crucial principle which it argued:

> applies to any organisation and is simple to the point of banality, but the root of much of our criticism is that it has not been observed. The principle is: look at the job first . . . The service must avoid a static view of a new ideal man and structure which in its turn could be as much of an obstacle to change as the present inheritance.

The Fulton Committee asserted that the most senior level of the Civil Service, which had been known as the 'Administrative Class' for a hundred years, had to change radically to meet the new challenges of a growing Civil Service. Above all the senior Civil Service would need to grapple with the new skill of management. The nineteenth century view of a suitable background for a gentleman entering the Public Service was hopelessly inadequate for managing modern government.

Recruitment to the Administrative Class of the Home Civil Service in the 1960s was focused on young graduates from the oldest and most prestigious Universities of Oxford and Cambridge. They were predominantly men and joined the Civil Service with degrees in Classics, History or English with a sprinkling of Politics and Economics. The outcome of the selection process was not surprising. The entrance examination put a heavy emphasis on the written and interpersonal skills produced by the highly specialised and testing tutorial system which operated in only a few places other than the two 'ancient universities'. Candidates from less expensive and specialised higher education institutions found the entry process tested skills they had had fewer opportunities of developing.

On entering the Civil Service it was made clear to new recruits that they would learn their professional skills 'on the job'. The prejudice against specific training for the work of the Administrative Class was deep-rooted. Many senior civil servants took the view that if you were intelligent enough to get into the Civil Service you could acquire whatever specialised knowledge was necessary in the course of your work. No technical or specialist training would be of any use – and little was provided. When I joined the Civil Service in the late 1960s training was regarded as light relief, one of the benefits of being a young recruit, an 'Assistant Principal', rather than a serious opportunity to learn relevant or useful skills. The people who were running the Civil Service at the start of the twenty-first century were recruited under this system.

The recommendations of the Fulton Report – wider recruitment, the restructuring of the Administrative Class, professional training and a Civil Service department – were indeed, as the Cabinet Minister Richard Crossman waspishly observed, hardly exciting: 'The Report is perfectly sensible but, oh dear, it lacks distinction!' (Ziegler, 1993). Most people who read the Fulton Report had missed the difficult bit. Crossman was wrong; had the section of the report which recommended accountable management, looking at the job and the need to develop accountable units been taken seriously the consequences might have 'lacked distinction' – but the changes would have been every bit as revolutionary as the Next Steps Report was to be accused of being in the 1980s. The response of the system to the Fulton Report was simply a reflection of the inability of people with the culture and priorities of the political and administrative elites in Britain to recognise the need to think about how the policies they devised might be implemented. Management, except in crisis or war, was a problem for someone else.

There was another consequence: once the recommendations about management had been ignored, what was left could encourage people to believe that training, some new organisations and some modest reconstruction could provide the fundamental change the Civil Service needed. The uncomfortable consequences of 'looking at the job' were airily ignored. This view appears to have been shared by other governments and their advisers, who increasingly came to view training as something preceding change not there to support it. In many parts of the world, following the United Kingdom example, training became regarded as the solution to the problems of government. It was cheap and easy to organise and involved none of the difficult changes that substantive reforms would demand. And, of course, in an unchanged working environment, most training was completely ineffective. Speaking at a conference in southern Africa in the early 1990s, I mentioned my reservations about the Fulton recommendations, only to be challenged later by a senior official. He was, he said, staggered to hear anyone criticising Fulton. In Zimbabwe then they still regarded it as 'the bible for civil service reform' – nearly thirty years after it had been written and for a very different setting.

The Fulton Report, like other attempts to change the structure of government, is said to have been sabotaged by the senior civil servants (the 'mandarins'). Philip Ziegler in his biography of Harold Wilson, the British Prime Minister who commissioned the report, discussed the extent to which the Civil Service undermined the report's recommendations: 'Under pressure from the mandarins the terms of reference had been whittled down . . . it was no more than the shadow of a shadow by the time it had worked its way through to implementation on the ground' (Zeigler, 1993). The relatively modest recommendations which were taken seriously and the slow process of implementation was an important lesson for later efforts at reform.

THE MANDARINS AND REFORM

Senior civil servants grew up in an enclosed world of common education, office behaviour and reward mechanisms. The working habits of the senior Civil Service based in Whitehall in the 1960s, 1970s and much of the 1980s were those of the universities and pre-war London. The high esteem in which the Civil Service was held and the nature of the selection process for

entry meant that the senior ranks had in them people of very high intellectual ability – as measured by academic standards. They were generally what
would be regarded as 'very clever'. But they had little experience of challenges which used other skills. The written word was the medium of discussion and decision, papers were drafted with infinite care by a number of
different hands, meetings were only of significance if the record – 'the
minutes' – were accurate, in the sense of providing a 'view' or a decision to
'take forward'. Indeed the 'art' of minute writing was regarded as being the
skill of producing the 'right result' rather than necessarily an accurate
reflection of what happened at the meeting. Telephones were for arranging
meetings, not resolving issues. Most civil servants worked at their desks,
writing in longhand on sheets of paper stored in brown card covered files –
papers on the right, short notes, 'minutes', on the left. Their working days,
especially in the middle ranks, were ordered and orderly. They would take
a regular train in the morning, attend the occasional meeting, lunch with
colleagues in the canteen or a modest restaurant and then return to the files.

People who joined the Civil Service were normally pre-disposed to this
kind of life. The selection procedures, even when modestly modernised,
tended to select people who would fit into the austere and controlled atmosphere in most Departments. Even in the areas dealing with operational
issues, where the rough and tumble of seeing the public intruded, senior
managers followed the same calm and reflective pattern. Into this world,
even when the pressure and the pace of work increased as the demands of
politicians and the 'outside' world expanded, little had changed how work
was done. Minutes were written properly and carefully, recording actions.
Increased work meant more minutes, not new ways of working.

The Government's original terms of reference for the Fulton
Commission, which were modified by 'the mandarins', were to review the
whole working of the public service, a massive task and, for civil servants
at senior levels, a very threatening one. Restricting the terms of reference,
a classic bureaucratic move, was a signal of deep opposition to change. The
final words 'to examine the structure, recruitment and management including training of the Home Civil Service' might sound all embracing but it
did not stray onto the dangerous ground of policy and could be confined
to what would later be described as 'personnel'.

The Civil Service was used to handling all kinds of changes, from radical
tax returns, to setting up a health service or rethinking housing policy.
What had been inviolate, apart from during the war years, was the way the
work was done. Fulton's final report, even with more limited terms of reference, effectively suggested changes to what would now be described as the
culture of the Civil Service. If there was a reaction to stop the report at all
costs, it was not necessarily malign or manipulative in origin. It could have

been the automatic defence mechanism of any entrenched organisation, selected and developed on one basis, to proposals for changes. Senior officials faced with proposals to disrupt long standing working methods which would affect them every time they entered the office, were more likely to oppose than support the changes.

The senior Civil Service tends to be cast in a Machiavellian role, plotting to defend their interests and their corner. Occasionally this view is justified. Power once held is difficult to give up, and civil servants as the executive of government are well placed to be obstructive. They are, like most entrenched professional groups, normally and genuinely convinced that their way of doing things is best for everybody – not just themselves. They may also be cynical or tired of repeated and unsuccessful attempts to change. The long memories of civil servants are sometimes a major stumbling block to change. All these factors can make the task of those who want reform particularly difficult. But there is nowhere to turn for the process of implementing changes to government but to the Civil Service itself.

The Fulton Report had all the substance in its analysis and recommendations to be ground-breaking. But, like so many of its predecessors it recommended improvements without attending as carefully to the crucial question of implementation. It contained 158 recommendations but the significant change lay not in the detail of the list but in the 'principle' which the report enunciated. It was possible to implement the recommendations without achieving the underlying purpose. The implementation of the report, rather like the Northcote Trevelyan Report a hundred years before, ground on within the back offices of Whitehall long after it was relevant or useful. Fifteen years after the report was adopted, I found a middle ranking official hard at work with a tinkering adjustment to pay scales. His reason for doing it was to implement recommendations in Fulton: 'it's not necessary but we just have to get it done'. This dogmatic approach to implementation meant that the purpose behind many of the changes which were recommended by the Fulton Report was missed. If there is a substantial delay – and there almost always is with government reports – recommendations can be out of date before the decisions are taken to implement them and even more so when the implementation takes place.

As part of the response to the Fulton Report, the management of the Civil Service was put into the hands of the newly formed Civil Service Department in November 1968. Policy, pay, relations with the trade unions, the rules and regulations governing the Civil Service were moved from the Treasury to the new Department. The professional title 'Head of the Civil Service' was given to the Permanent Secretary and there was a technical link to the Prime Minister as the Minister responsible, although there was always a departmental Minister of State as well, known as the Minister for the Civil Service. Although they now had their own Department of State and still retained the social and intellectual position of a senior and respected professional group, most senior civil servants took a gloomy view of their position. As one Deputy Secretary said to me at a party 'before the war I would have had a carriage and pair – now I can barely afford the tube fare'. It was not an indication of a good grip on pre-war standards, the cost of transport, or of the 1970s London underground fare but an example of the perennial senior Civil Service conviction that they are undervalued and underpaid.

THE EXPERIMENTS OF THE 1970s

Civil Service management remained a matter of interest after the change of government in 1970. The new Conservative Government had recognised the need to modernise the Civil Service and published a policy statement *The Reorganisation of Central Government* in 1970. It had a familiar ring. Government was to be organised using a:

> functional approach. . . . In practical terms this means the application of the functional principle as the basis for the allocation of responsibilities: government departments should be organised by reference to the task to be done or the objective to be attained and this should be the basis of the division of work between departments . . . executive blocks of work will be delegated to accountable units of management, thus lessening the load on the departmental top management.

The accountable units of management did emerge, of which the longest lasting was probably the Manpower Services Commission, but the application of the functional principle was confined to a transient reorganisation of ministerial responsibilities. The need to improve management itself was ignored. The policy statement provided a theoretical basis for reorganising several departments but its fundamental objective of reducing the size of government and improving the quality of what remained achieved little that was long term. Innovative attempts to improve policy were made but the next major attempt to improve the Civil Service and its management had to wait until the new government in 1979.

The changes which did emerge during the 1970s, many as a consequence of Fulton's recommendations, provided a sense of progress, but with relatively little to disturb the normal pattern of life or the attention that was given to management. The old Administrative Class was abolished in name, new grades were introduced to describe the new hierarchy, a 'Civil Service

College' opened, uneasily balanced between its instinctive urge to be an academic institution and the need of the Civil Service for practical, operational training. The training of fast stream recruits to the Civil Service, most of them straight from university, fell victim to the confusion in the role of the original college. At the beginning of the 1970s, assistant principals, the most junior grade in the Administrative Class, could expect at least six months of formal training in their first two years in the Civil Service, unrelated to the job they were doing but conforming to a central syllabus of induction, statistics, and economics. The academic bias meant that there was little or no connection between the subject matter and the specific skills those being trained needed in their jobs – a recipe for wasted effort.

In the experiments of these relatively 'early' years, the acceptance that there was something that needed to be learnt and could be taught was a breakthrough. The subsequent compulsory financial and management training for the most senior civil servants introduced in the 1980s was largely a consequence of this modest recognition that there was a serious gap in technical skills in the 1970s. Unlike the assistant principal training, the financial and management training was specifically linked to the developments of the new Financial Management Initiative (FMI), which those on the courses would have to work with on their return.

The 1970 Conservative Government had given much thought to improving the quality of policy making. Two innovations produced valuable work and provided a basis for later developments. The establishment of the Central Policy Review Staff (CPRS) in 1970, designed primarily to advise the Cabinet on policy issues, was an example of how the process of government could be invigorated. A small group of mainly younger people from the Civil Service and from outside government advised the Cabinet collectively on major policy and financial issues. The Civil Service was defensive but courteous, and individual civil servants were exemplary in their recognition of the value of another set of brains on some intractable, and in some cases, neglected issues.

But the CPRS used the same approach as the senior Civil Service, careful semi-academic analysis, intense high level thinking, and a few moderately radical ideas. When they tried to look at issues outside the confines of the normal working boundaries of Whitehall, the results were mixed. The admirable *Joint Framework for Social Policies* published in 1975 (CPRS, 1975) pointed out organisation-driven gaps in social provision: 'Ministers need to ensure that their priorities are adequately reflected in policies that are actually being carried out and that in practice these policies are having the effects intended' – a succinct statement of the problem that Fulton observed and which remained unresolved into the next century. The CPRS report also produced a working methodology which held for several years and is recognised as an important contribution to developments in the better co-ordination of social policy (Bogdanor, 2005).

The work done by the CPRS on population statistics and their implications for social welfare planning were important in emphasising the significance of variant assumptions about population figures which could and should be made in planning. On industrial policy and on public expenditure the CPRS contributed useful ideas and suggestions. Its most public fire was reserved for the Foreign Office, an even more entrenched bastion than the Home Civil Service, and where the defence was more skilful than the attack. A massive report was produced (CPRS, 1977). Some changes took place; the Foreign Office assured the world the changes would have happened anyway, and the CPRS retired, weakened.

The CPRS experience demonstrated that radicalism when it is useful, and solves a problem, can be welcomed – the British Civil Service, like most civil services, are used to changes in policy, and for the senior grades policy changes are their raison d'etre. But radicalism that demonstrates as part of its thesis that people have been foolish, venal or incompetent, even if the outcome would be better, is seldom welcomed. In the 1970s an ex-civil servant Leslie Chapman found how little interest there was in improvement when he demonstrated the many inefficiencies he was able to record in the Property Services Agency (Chapman, 1978). His book created a short-term cause célèbre but in the long term little happened within Whitehall as a result of his disclosures. The temporary political excitement lasted until the next scandal, and it contributed to a general sense of unease about public service management rather than a serious attempt at change. The CPRS report on the Foreign Office was another such attempt to change the way an institution worked and not just what it did. The dilemma was that unless the radical is superbly briefed – or is an insider – the insider is always in a stronger position. In the CPRS study, the Foreign Office itself did the briefing. This provided another lesson in the politics of reform which was a useful background to the changes of the 1980s.

Politicians seldom got involved in the activities of the Civil Service. The flurry of interest created by well publicised reports like a Royal Commission or the CPRS report on the Foreign Office were almost the only occasion when politicians were concerned unless at a change of government. Party manifestoes did contain some references to what were known as 'machinery of government issues' – normally the structure of departments in Whitehall – or promises to run an efficient and economical government machine: 'too much Government. There will be less, it will be more efficient and less costly' (Conservative Party Manifesto, 1970). The policy document which followed soon after the 1970 election *The Reorganisation of Central Government* did set out substantial restructuring but, as Peter

Hennessy put it 'the revolutionary elements were . . . allowed to expire because of neglect' (Hennessy, 1989). Neglect was an important tool in preventing substantive change.

The CPRS was responsible for another important innovation which was aimed at improving how ministers took decisions. Cabinet decision-taking, as government became more complicated, became less well informed and less the result of serious collective discussion. A minister who proposed a change would suggest it to his or her colleagues at a Cabinet Committee. If other departments had an 'interest', that is to say a departmental role, their minister would be provided with a partisan brief on the point of 'interest' for the Cabinet meeting. The Prime Minister or the committee chairman would have a chairman's brief from the Cabinet Office, describing the proposal and setting out the reason for it appearing on the agenda of the relevant committee or cabinet. Occasionally, a well informed department would brief a minister because the issue was of political or national importance. What was missing from this elaborate process was independent information on the merit of the proposal itself. The Treasury was concerned about the cost, the Chief Whip about the politics, and the Cabinet Office about the absence of consensus.

The CPRS developed the 'collective brief'. A paper set out the principal proposal, discussed its merits and its weaknesses, and suggested some trenchant questions to ask to open up what were seen as important issues. The Director of the CPRS attended Cabinet Committees to see that the questions were asked and answered. But most cabinet ministers were not interested. The outcome of government decision taking had become a partisan battleground, not a discussion of collective policy. There can, however, have been few who equalled the relaxed attitude of one Secretary of State who set off for Cabinet clutching his red folder of papers and returned it with a brief word of thanks to his private office after the meeting, remarking that it was more interesting than usual. On opening the folder his staff realised that it contained the Headquarters telephone directory, and not their carefully drafted briefing for the meeting.

Another development which attracted attention was Programme Analysis and Review (PAR). There has been learned comment on this design to organise the process of longer term policy improvements by systematising the selection and analysis of issues to be reviewed in large areas of government policy (Gray and Jenkins, 1985). By the late 1970s, the process was a nightmare and an object lesson in the importance of stopping a good idea before it has got out of hand. Subjects were selected by a laborious process of meetings, consultations and debate. Everyone went to the meetings. So many attended that the meetings had to be held in the main conference room in the Treasury and the main objective appeared to be to agree to reviews everywhere else to avoid attention being drawn to one's own Department.

Some of the reviews were distinguished and innovative. They absorbed the time and the energies of able civil servants, the analysis was excellent, and the data collection and preparation extensive and professional. But the reviews fell into the familiar trap of being too long, too detailed and difficult to implement. They were expensive to do and when the reports were done, more often than not they were sidelined. Commentators refer to the 'experiment in PAR' rather patronisingly as a failed attempt at reform. The idea of a formal review with some collective interest was a precursor of many later policy reviews. PAR failed because it was the victim of its own process. The system overwhelmed the purpose; it was a classic case of strangling in its own red tape – assisted by a determined attempt by the Treasury to take control. A lighter more flexible process managed by people with the power and skill to adapt it, and the wish to use it effectively, could have survived longer and been more influential. There was no shortage of areas that needed radical review. PAR was stifled by its own methodology.

By the end of the 1970s the changes which had been introduced following the Fulton Report and the 1970 White Paper had become institutionalised. The old Administrative Class was no more – in theory. Permanent secretaries had become Grade 1s and the old Assistant Principal, glowing and eager straight from Balliol, had become an 'administration trainee'. The Civil Service Department although still jostling with the Treasury for control over the pay and conditions for the Civil Service, was headed by a senior permanent secretary. The Civil Service College was training on a scale never seen before. The Government itself was in trouble. Industrial disputes, inflation and the state of economy were causing grave concern, so much so that the International Monetary Fund (IMF) had been called in to help, but the institutions of the Civil Service looked secure.

The governments of the 1970s had tinkered with 'big' Departments, with pay restraint, with a review of employment in the Civil Service and there had been strikes by civil servants. There had been modest changes but by the end of the 1970s, tensions were building up as the government's relations with the wider group of public service employees exploded in the public services disputes of 1978. Trade union power and the benefits they expected from a Labour Government were under severe pressure during the economic disasters of the mid-1970s; fury boiled over into repeated and unpleasant strikes. The election in 1979 returned a new Conservative administration with a different view of what the structure and the functions of the public service should be.

Both Heath and Wilson, the Prime Ministers of the 1970s, had tried reform. But their reform was primarily organisational: new ways of managing the senior Civil Service, new support for Senior Ministers, better analysis, more training. The approach was one of finding ways of doing what was done already better rather than a radical break with the traditional system. Many of the difficulties facing the governments of the 1960s and 1970s had been caused by the increasing power of the trade unions. In 1968 the labour government had retreated from a sensible and practical reform of industrial relations (*In Place of Strife*, 1969) in the face of virulent trade union opposition. Throughout the Heath administration from 1970 to 1974 major industrial disputes, particularly in government-owned organisations, were a constant feature of life. The near anarchy in some industries brought acute power shortages, a three day working week and a 'who runs Britain' election in 1974 to their inevitable outcome – another change in government.

The pressure on government of either party was to solve the immediate dispute, not to resolve the underlying problem. Industrial changes moved faster than trade unions or governments adapted. The Government increased intervention in the car industry, shipbuilding, steel, the railways and the mines while demands for better education, housing, transport and health care mounted. The request for support from the IMF as the economy appeared to be collapsing, in 1976, was the nadir of government. In 1974 the nation had been reduced to living by candlelight because the power generating industry was crippled by strikes; in 1979 as the election was called, bodies lay unburied in local authority mortuaries and rubbish piled up in the street because local government employees were striking for higher pay as inflation mounted and the government struggled to keep expenditure under some semblance of control. The 1979 election was bitter and hard fought, the results were close and the new government looked, at that stage, no more secure than its predecessors.

THATCHERISM AND THE 1980s

Elections and a change of government always bring excitement, gossip and a frisson of the unknown into the corridors of Whitehall. An unknown Prime Minister and a relatively new team of ministers can always produce some surprises. Civil servants had security of tenure, they might be discreetly retired but never sacked; they were part of the Establishment and protected by it. Government and senior civil servants might mistrust each other but they expected to work together; many had been to the same schools and universities and shared similar interests and social networks. What would now be described as 'networking' was crucial to the operations of the senior levels of government. New entrants to the administrative class were eased into a system where everyone, irrespective of rank was on first name terms. They could telephone each other without preamble for advice or assistance. Jenifer Hart's description of her first years in the Home Office in the 1930s was still valid into the 1970s – a small group where many knew each other from social or family ties and expected to help smooth the career of those they knew well, without, of course, impairing the 'free and open competition' laid down in the nineteenth century as the basis for preferment in the public service (Hart,1998). Samuel Finer observed a similar phenomenon in 1950 when he commented on 'the rich interaction between a small group of people at the top who knew each other well' (Finer, 1950). The result of the election in 1979 was to change much of the old comfortable consensus.

The 1979 Conservative election manifesto was unequivocal. The condition of the country demanded radical changes. The winning party argued that the government machine had proved itself unfit to manage the public sector. Ideology was significant. The Tory party had moved to what was then seen as the right: the scale and scope of government was not merely incompetent, it was in principle wrong that so much should be in the hands of the state, that taxes should be so high and that people should find it possible to live 'off the state' without earning their living. This breach with the post war consensus about the Welfare State and the economy represented a significant shift in the political landscape.

The new administration in 1979 was determined to rein back the power of senior civil servants. Any new government coming into power brings with it a collection of policies designed to distinguish it from its predecessors. The post-Heath Conservative party had been planning for major changes and its new leadership was determined to make visible reforms to the organisation and effectiveness of government. Their promise was to reduce 'waste, bureaucracy and over government.' It was not to improve the quality of the services the government provided but to provide them better and cheaper – 'efficiency' was to become a guiding principle. The 'taxpayer' had become an important part of the political landscape.

The size of the Government was an obvious and relatively easy first target. Apart from the move of the Post Office from a government department to a nationalised industry in 1975 there had been little major change in the scale of the Civil Service since the early 1950s. The transfer of the Post Office out of the central government to the nationalised industry sector had reduced the number of civil servants by some 300 000 but the postmen remained in the public sector. The proportion of the employed population in the total public sector had crept up from 23.7% in 1961 to 27.1% by 1971. By the end of the 1970s the evidence that the public sector was not well managed was overwhelming. Strikes, always a good indicator of poor management, were a regular feature of life in the public sector, although not in the Civil Service, and had been a major contributor to the fall of the Heath government in 1974 and the Callaghan government in 1979. The Conservative Government under Mrs Thatcher were determined not to meet the same fate.

Efficiency was hardly a new discovery of the Thatcher administration, although sometimes it was presented as if it were, but the way it was handled gave the topic a new feel. There have always been debates and discussions about how to manage the public service better. Under Heath discussions about measurement and outputs had begun in earnest but not got very far. Individual civil servants had made progress in some areas and there had been genuine improvements in the ways in which some services were run. But the Thatcher administration brought sharpness and focus to the issue which had not been there before. Hugo Young in his book on Mrs Thatcher asserted that:

> No government has been elected whose leader was as deeply seized as this one of the need to overturn the power and the presumption of the continuing government of the civil service, to challenge its orthodoxies, cut down its size, reject its assumptions . . . and teach it a lesson in political control. (Young,1993).

The issue of responsibility for the competence and effectiveness of the Civil Service became a personal one for the Prime Minister, not simply the subject for academic or theoretical debate. The new Prime Minister made her position abundantly clear. In her view the public service was too big and too ineffective and she was going to see to it that the position was going to change 'I was determined at least to begin work on long term reforms of government itself' (Thatcher, 1993).

The Civil Service did not know what had hit it. The Government took what was optimistically referred to as a 'robust approach'; it almost appeared to relish its own capacity to create difficulties. The relationship between the politicians and their staff developed against a background of irritation, cost cutting, pressure on numbers and challenges to the established order. The change in absolute numbers reflected the government's sustained determination; 730000 civil servants employed in 1979 were reduced to 580000 by April 1988. The absolute figures masked bigger changes. Some Departments, notably the Department of the Environment, were cut substantially while others running demand-led services increased in size. The Prison Service, the Benefit Services and the Employment Services all saw their numbers rise as demand reflected social and economic needs as well as policy changes.

Politically 'the cuts' were regarded by some as the hand of a right wing government getting back at the poor and the working classes while letting the rich off its super tax. The tension in some parts of the Civil Service was palpable. The principle that the Civil Service would do whatever the Government wanted was used against the establishment of the Civil Service itself. The senior Civil Service normally relished new policies, but the added elements of financial stringency, attacks on its professionalism and an unpredictable government made this an uncomfortable time within Whitehall.

The Civil Service was in shock and deeply resentful. The Government asserted that civil servants were incompetent, expensive and, by implication, lazy. The old working relationships appeared to have been swept aside and the new approach had an aggression and an abrasiveness not normally part of the culture in Whitehall. Criticism of the Civil Service was hardly new and Treasury assaults on Departmental expenditure were the normal stuff of life. The public expenditure system was based on negotiations which produced an outcome, preferably with battle honours about even. But the normal niceties of negotiation had been pushed to one side. The new cuts to be made in numbers and costs were presented as fixed and while Departments were, in theory at least, left free to find the cuts themselves, the Treasury took a great deal of detailed interest in the substance of the changes, no doubt to assure themselves that the reductions would really happen.

The government remained convinced that fundamental changes to the Civil Service were essential and the Prime Minister constantly returned to the theme of 'dealing' with the Civil Service. There was little new in her view that the Civil Service was a problem; Labour ministers too had complained vociferously about the obstructionist tactics of the Civil Service. Leslie Chapman, an official in the Property Services Agency (PSA), had demonstrated how defensive and negative the normal internal procedures were. His saga of how he tried to deal with problems in the PSA – responsible for the Government estate – was influential with Mrs Thatcher in the debates within the Conservative Party about the Civil Service (Chapman, 1978). The substance of the Prime Minister's complaints had a new twist. It was not that the Civil Service ran its own devious system or that the professional *amour propre* of the mandarins stopped government policy in its tracks. It was the assertion that they did not do their job properly that hit senior civil servants hard.

The accepted and comfortable view was that the British Civil Service was the best in the world. It served governments with 'consummate skill' – a favourite expression of the Civil Service – whatever their political flavour, and it was seen as being constitutionally responsible for the stability of the state. For a Prime Minister to challenge that rosy view was deeply shocking. For this challenge to happen at the same time as numbers were being cut and budgets sliced back was difficult for the Civil Service to accept.

Mrs Thatcher's relationship with the Permanent Secretaries who did not work closely with her was a good indicator of why Whitehall was approaching crisis. The comfortable world of the mandarins who had made good was broken in on by someone who argued, was not good at listening and had to be challenged rather than debated with. Most were deeply uncomfortable. One much recorded incident at a dinner with the Permanent Secretaries was indicative of the gulf that lay between them. The Prime Minister asked why the lights were left on at night in the Victoria Street job centre, a question which should present no problems to today's Permanent Secretaries, but left their predecessors uncomfortable and contemptuous. These issues were not what Permanent Secretaries dealt with. The Prime Minister was using shock tactics of a brutal kind, whether consciously or not, and her power and position protected her. Of the dinner in question she has recorded 'this was one of the most dismal occasions of my entire time in government' (Thatcher, 1993), a stark indication of the quality of her relationship with the most senior officials in Whitehall and of their approach to working with her. In recalling the occasion some of those present demonstrated precisely the kind of arrogant insularity tainted by sexism for which they were renowned.

THE ROLE OF MANAGEMENT

The early retirement of Sir Ian Bancroft, the Permanent Secretary at the Civil Service Department and professional Head of the Civil Service, and the abolition of the Civil Service Department in 1981, demonstrated that the Government was serious. Much of the Civil Service was genuinely baffled. At senior levels their job was to discuss major policy issues. The management of resources and the management of government services were dealt with 'elsewhere'. For many of them the 'point' of questions about management was unintelligible.

That bafflement was shared by many members of the Government. The only department of the Government where there was strong ministerial interest in how it was run was the Department of the Environment under Michael Heseltine. He was determined to introduce more modern management into the sprawling empire covering a huge range of central and local government services in the gaunt buildings then in Horseferry Road. He introduced a management information system for Ministers (MINIS) which became a byword in Whitehall for its size and detail. It took some years to produce information in manageable quantities and to persuade people to use it, but it was the first serious attempt to use an information systems approach to make it possible to understand what was going on within a Department – and to use the system as a preliminary to managing it more effectively. MINIS was regarded with considerable reserve in the rest of Whitehall.

A reforming government in Britain had an operational problem, especially if it wanted to take on the Civil Service. Any reform had to be implemented by the Civil Service which traditionally prided itself on carrying out the policy of the government of the day, whatever it was. It had seldom had to turn the knife on itself in quite so dramatic a way. There have been many attempts to bring in 'outsiders' to do things the Civil Service was not trusted or seen as competent to do. The Heath experiment with businessmen, Derek Rayner's time at the Procurement Executive and Victor Rothschild at the CPRS had been useful in a limited way but the power and stability of the organisation was huge. It could and did outlast any individual, however effective.

The main mechanism for applying cuts in expenditure and staff was still the Treasury. It used the established channels of control which did, in that unconvincing phrase, 'go with the grain' of the Civil Service. More significantly, what had to be done to meet the new Government's objectives was an extreme form of the normal processes of central resource control. Departments were used to having difficulties with the Treasury. These 'difficulties' were the old world but in a more acute form. What was needed was some way of making it possible to handle the depressing and discouraging process of managing reductions and cuts. What is now known as 'Human Resource' policy was then in the all powerful hands of Establishments. The 'Director of Establishments' was an influential figure in most departments. He (invariably) was responsible for the careers of all the members of the Department. His time was primarily spent on the most senior staff and on nurturing the bright young stars. This role was the closest most Departments came to having a central management function. It was a relatively late development and a radical departure from tradition when the two resource functions – Establishments and Finance – were finally brought together in the mid-1980s.

In the early 1980s the issue for Establishments was how to persuade people to leave careers which they had always believed they would be in for their whole working lives. Most of them had no experience of working 'outside' the Civil Service and at senior levels would expect to retire on a comfortable pension, with perhaps a modest honour, a sense of status and of having a valuable career behind them. The outside world, especially if they had been in the Civil Service for twenty or thirty years was frightening. For civil servants career insecurity was unknown.

The only easy routes open were 'natural wastage' and early retirement. Natural wastage – not replacing people who left their jobs – could reduce

numbers, especially in the clerical grades which had a tradition of relatively high turnover, but there was a price to be paid in inefficiency. Early
retirement had been used before, but sparingly and only in 'special
circumstances'. In the new world, early retirement was positively encouraged. If the alternative might be forced redundancy, retirement with a full
pension – the same amount as if one had worked to 60, the normal retirement age – suddenly looked like a good deal. It worked only too well.
The gossip was that the doors had to be shut down at the Ministry of
Defence (MOD), to prevent the entire staff leaving immediately. Early
retirement suddenly become the solution to all problems. 'How old is he
or she' would be almost the first question a harassed Establishment
Officer would ask, wondering if the newly available golden handshake
would remove a long standing problem. The numbers who left the Civil
Service were surprising and the costs were astronomical. They were
always justified by the easy calculation that it would cost more to keep
people in employment. The financing was an unintentional masterstroke.
The cost of an early retirement package was carried on the central pension
vote, the gain from a reduction in staff counted in a Department's
'savings'. So anyone who left cost nothing and the benefit to a department's budget was immediate.

Problems arose when essential staff wished to go or new staff were
needed. The development of a more selective approach to retirement and a
tight 'head count' control had proved to be the only way of managing the
situation. Headcount control was highly inefficient and much criticised. In
the early stages no distinction was made between types of head. Although
the cost might be different, the loss of a competent and irreplaceable clerk
was often more serious to the smooth running of an organisation than a
senior manager. It took several years before the systems developed the
greater sophistication of proper budgets in place of the two tier controls of
costs and head count. Only with a budget covering all expenditure was it
possible to distinguish between the sensible allocation of resources and the
costs of changing the balance of staff.

The second solution, efficiency, was an old favourite in a new guise.
Inefficiency in the Civil Service was hardly a new discovery. In 1970 Mr
Heath had brought businessmen into the government to increase efficiency.
Derek Rayner, a senior director at Marks & Spencer and, later, Chief
Executive and Chairman, had had experience in the Ministry of Defence
as director of the Defence Procurement Organisation. In 1979 the Prime
Minister appointed Rayner as her personal adviser on management with a
very different task. The significant signal to Whitehall was that the Prime
Minister was to take management sufficiently seriously to have an advisor
on 'Management and Efficiency in the Civil Service'. Not only was Rayner

to advise the Prime Minister, he had a small staff to help with taking action, an exceptional role for an adviser. The next chapter discusses the management innovations that Rayner and his staff introduced and which were developed by the Efficiency Unit, the successor to the Rayner Unit.

3. Management and the Civil Service: the Rayner approach

In 1980, management was not a glamorous subject. It ranked low in the list of topics the senior Civil Service was interested in. It was down with premises and cars as a task for people who could not cope with a thinking job. Management was for them, not for us. Senior civil servants were kindly to managers as long as no one expected them to do the managerial jobs. One senior official was told in an appraisal interview that he would do a very good job of running the National Health Service but he would not make a Permanent Secretary. There had been flurries of management fashions before, training courses included sensible advice from older executives on remembering to tell your staff when you wanted them to work late and from an accountant on how to read a balance sheet. The innovations following Fulton and the 1970 Heath government White Paper had produced some changes, but the Civil Service, as an institution, was not managed. It was controlled and administered but not managed. Many people in the Civil Service seemed not to have grasped the point about management: it was a means of achieving objectives, using resources effectively and improving the way organisations worked. For the public service it had the potential of breaking out of the circular routine of cuts in resources and inadequate services using outdated systems.

RAYNER AND SCRUTINIES

Rayner set out to demonstrate that using some simple techniques and a good deal of common sense it was possible to turn the carnage of the cuts to good effect. The first two years of reductions in expenditure had mainly taken the form of a percentage reduction on all costs. It made surprisingly little difference; with a bit of tightening here and a little early retirement there, fairly comfortable organisations could cope. Year three was a bit more difficult and by year four it became clear that the relatively easy days of 1979 were unlikely to return. The Rayner philosophy of 'scrutinising' activities to streamline and simplify them was one way of beginning to look systematically at how Civil Service organisations worked. In Marks &

Spencer Rayner had developed a process which he called a 'scrutiny' which was designed to encourage people to look at what they did critically and with fresh eyes to try to find more effective and simpler ways of doing things. Within the Civil Service the focus was to be on the process, not on the policy. The policy was to be taken as given; the change was to be in how the policy was delivered – the management process.

While the theory owed something to organisation and method techniques, its application to areas of the Civil Service which had seen little of such methods was new. The scrutiny was simple to grasp and could be carried out without special skills or extensive training. It had much more to do with sensible management of the 'go and find out what is going on' school, linked to finding out what was preventing sensible solutions. It was simple, quick and with the Prime Minister's support, highly visible. There was no disguising the urgent pressure for reductions in costs and numbers, but there was also a significant emphasis on the possibilities of finding better ways of managing the outcomes as well. Reductions in resources did not need to be an entirely negative process; increasing effectiveness could and should be part of the process of reducing costs.

The senior Civil Service was dismissive of scrutinies. The Permanent Secretaries who knew nothing and cared less about the size of the Department of Employment's electricity bill were not, as some of them asserted, going to be reorganised by someone whose specialism was selling underwear to the nation. Derek Rayner proved, however, to be as good at getting at administrative and organisational stupidities on a large scale as he was a retailer. He was not new to Whitehall and he had some understanding of how to get under the skin of the major Departments. He was one of the few people in business or the public sector who was genuinely fascinated by what people wanted and how to supply it. One of his staff recollected sitting with him by the skating rink at the Rockefeller Centre. Rayner sat absolutely silent for thirty minutes while his assistant wondered miserably what frightful sin he had committed. At the end Rayner turned to him with a furrowed brow and asked if he had seen any consistency in the clothes the skaters were wearing. He could not pick out any pattern – he had been trying to work out what he could sell to them.

It was this obsession with customers which led him to insist that scrutiny teams must talk to the people working with the customers because they would know most about what was preventing a better service. One day in a benefit office with an appalling record of delay in making payments he noticed a woman working a cheque printing machine and went over to talk to her. He asked to be shown what the machine did and noticed that it printed two cheques for each recipient. Why? The rates had gone up but no-one had the authority to alter the setting on the machine, so two cheques, two envelopes and two sets of bank charges was the solution. The approach – using the knowledge of people directly involved – was of crucial importance in building up the analytical approach for later scrutinies.

When Permanent Secretaries heard that the first Rayner scrutiny was to be the Treasury typing services, they considered that their initial reactions were justified. The Treasury was the most powerful department. Its typing services were constantly blamed for delays and mistakes. It was typical of much of the senior Civil Service that they would complain but do little to put it right. Their view was that if scrutinies, for all their publicity, were to look at areas like typing pools this was a project about candle ends, not about things that really mattered. But the typing pool was a classic instance where a relatively small and undervalued service can damage the effectiveness of a more significant operation. Moreover, for Rayner, the Treasury typing pools were a sighting shot for bigger issues. It would be useful to demonstrate that the Treasury typing pool could be better managed and provide a better service but it was in the big operational Departments where billions of pounds were spent and thousands of people were employed that the real impact of scrutinies could be of value. While the Treasury typing pool would test the effectiveness of the process which was being developed, it was in the operational areas, like Social Security, Unemployment Benefit and the Inland Revenue, where service to the public was poor and costs were high, that the real gains would come.

Rayner's scrutinies followed a standard pattern even in the early years: a small team of civil servants from the Department concerned, but normally not from the area being scrutinised, between two and five members, an emphasis on information and a fast report, decisions, implementation and results. The Rayner Unit in the Cabinet Office provided three pages of type-script which guided the early teams. What was new about scrutinies, and provided much of the excitement for people doing them, was that the teams were specifically told to challenge, to ask difficult questions and to be radical in their solutions. A good scrutiny team was left free to follow their evidence and to pursue any issue provided their analysis stood up and their evidence was sound. For the scrutiny teams, often young and inexperi-enced, the imposing figure of Sir Derek Rayner with his direct line to the Prime Minister was a support and a challenge. If the team could persuade Rayner and Clive Priestley, the civil servant at the head of the Unit, of their arguments the report would have a far better chance of success.

The reports were deeply unpopular with much of the Civil Service and with some ministers. Unless they were carefully handled, a scrutiny of a sensitive area was seen as central meddling in the affairs of a Department, and indeed many of the early scrutinies were done under pressure from the central Departments rather than because the Department concerned thought they would get any benefit from them. The scrutinies were closely associated with 'the cuts', which had become a political catch phrase, and were regarded as generally a precursor to lost jobs and declining services. The early scrutinies focused on reductions but emphasised the potential of service adaptations which could mitigate the impact of reduced resources.

One of the classic instances of recommendations which appear simple and obvious but carry a history behind them emerged from the 1982 Scrutiny of the Payment of Benefits to the Unemployed by a team from the Department of Employment led by Ian Johnston. Johnston was a pattern scrutiny leader. He had joined the Department of Employment as an assistant principal in 1969 after gaining a PhD at Birmingham, spent a year as private secretary to the Permanent Secretary, the legendary Dennis Barnes, worked on the industrial relations issues of the Employment Protection Act 1974, spent some time as a labour attache in Brussels and worked at ACAS on conciliation. The scrutiny was an interlude in a career which continued at the Manpower Services Commission (MSC) and as Deputy Secretary in charge of training policy and then moved on outside the Civil Service into higher education.

Ian Johnston was given the task of rethinking the process of payment of Unemployment Benefit, paid to people out of work with a record of national insurance contributions which entitled them to a modest payment for a limited time, as long as they were unemployed. Each person was required by the rules of the insurance scheme to demonstrate they were not working by 'signing on' at government employment offices once a week during normal working hours. They had to attend an office at a specified time and literally sign a declaration that they were 'available for work'. In the 1980s the level of unemployment meant that hundreds of thousands of people went to employment offices each week. Unemployment was rising steadily and the network of local offices was unable to cope with increasing numbers.

The scrutiny team suggested that little would be lost if people signed on fortnightly instead of the traditional weekly signing. This was a classic scrutiny recommendation. The change could have an immense impact on the capacity of a local employment office to handle its increasing workload and reduce the need to recruit more staff and open new offices as unemployment increased. Fortnightly signing was not a new idea, but it had always been rejected as 'politically difficult'. Concern about the number of fraudulent claims had always been a factor in the requirement to 'sign on'. Less frequent visits to the employment office were regarded as risking higher levels of fraud which had always created political criticism. Ian Johnston and his scrutiny team presented their findings and proposals at a meeting with the Prime Minister at Downing Street and the decision was taken on the grounds that the gains outweighed the disadvantages. It was a case where the scrutiny gave a management issue the political weight to make changes which were sensible but had seemed too difficult to achieve before.

Scrutinies were damaged – in the sense that they were disliked and mistrusted by much of the Civil Service – by their close association with job cuts. In the early years the political imperative to reduce numbers was intense, and remained an important factor for several years. Job reductions were carefully recorded in the early reports and monitored in the decisions taken on implementation. For scrutiny teams the taxpayer became a real figure: public money was 'taxpayer's money'. There was a constant background litany that money was scarce. It had to be used effectively and could not be relied on as a constant as it had been in the past. The association with job cuts was a major factor in the Civil Service trade unions' dislike of scrutinies throughout the 1980s. There were consultation procedures within all scrutinies. In some cases the trade unions played a constructive part, particularly in the service wide review of personnel processes; in others, notably the Next Steps review, they chose to play little part at all.

THE SCRUTINY 'PROCESS'

Doing a scrutiny was difficult and often stressful. A relatively young civil servant would be pulled out of a job and given the subject of the scrutiny and told to get on with it. If they were lucky there would be terms of reference and even a team but frequently the team leader had to deal with all the basics, from finding an office to a discussion with the Permanent Secretary about the purpose of the scrutiny. The trade unions had to be consulted, the Efficiency Unit brought into the picture and, frequently, scrutiny team leaders might find themselves writing their own terms of reference. The selection of the rest of the team might be determined by internal politics, availability or the significance of the topic.

One team which reviewed the Urban Programme, a DOE led programme to spend limited sums of money in run down inner cities, had members from five Departments all of which had an 'interest' in the Urban Programme. Technically all the members of the team worked together. In practice there was a great deal of undercover pressure from the main Departments involved. This pressure surfaced when decisions about recommendations had to be made and when individual Departmental policies had to be blended into a practical report. In that case little of value emerged – the conflicts of Departmental interest prevented any radical or useful outcome. Departments could expect too much from the scrutiny process; in an Inland Revenue scrutiny of a revenue issue affecting millions of taxpayers the Department concerned was sure the study could be handled by two junior members of their staff with no support.

When the work on a scrutiny started, the first task was to find out what the terms of reference meant. Conflicting views were common. To one senior official 'personnel' might mean holidays and welfare for junior staff, to another the full range of establishment power wielded by the Director of Establishments. The Rayner Unit guidelines were clear. The terms of reference should define the area to be studied and any crucial issues involved, but the team should regard and be allowed to regard the terms of reference as a guideline not a straitjacket. If compelling evidence took them beyond the terms of reference, it was legitimate to follow the issue but it would be sensible and prudent to discuss with the Department concerned any issue which appeared to be outside the terms of reference.

The first three weeks of the total of 13 weeks allowed for a full scrutiny were spent producing a study plan. The plan set out what the terms of reference meant, who was going to do the work, how they would approach the task, whom they would talk to and what information they needed. The team had to include a first attempt at what they thought were some of the key issues. The great gap in the analysis was not ideas – there was never any shortage of 'key issues' – the gap was in basic information. Especially in the first five or six years the question 'what does it cost' was normally met with a blank stare. Cost information was rare and inadequate. Staff costs could be estimated, programme and other costs could be gathered but in most cases, no robust, unallocated, management related cost information could be obtained at all. Most scrutiny teams spent much of their time dealing with the inadequacy of information.

The second issue that needed careful handling were the people themselves. Civil servants, who had worked in an organisation for many years, suddenly found their humdrum daily activity under a spotlight held by a group with little experience and a licence to question and challenge. For the first few years scrutinies could be an uncomfortable and worrying experience for the organisation under review. Subsequently the Efficiency Unit modified the process to give the management a role throughout the review and responsibility for implementation. This change put an obligation on a scrutiny team to work with the management and persuade them of the practicability of the scrutiny recommendations while convincing the Unit that their proposals were radical and innovative.

A scrutiny team worked under pressure. For some of them, for the first time in their lives they could be working in close contact with senior officials and ministers. They would have to come to difficult conclusions and defend them, and take personal responsibility for the outcome. Doing a scrutiny was not easy. Just asking questions was frequently unpopular and if the analysis came up with critical or difficult issues the team could come under considerable strain. Part of the Rayner Unit's role was to see that these stresses did not become overwhelming. A bit of quiet investigation, a discussion with the scrutiny programme manager, and, in some cases, a phone call to the permanent secretary involved might be needed to ensure that the team could work both free of immediate pressure and also without a sense that their career might hang on the outcome.

Scrutinies for all their political support were still a small part of the Whitehall machine. They were innovatory because they dealt with the nuts and bolts of how departments managed. Traditionally attention and interest in both Civil Service and political offices was focused on policy. The development of political ideas, the construction of new policies and the fight for new approaches through the Whitehall and Westminster jungles was what most senior people spent time on. Even in the tax collecting departments, the Inland Revenue and Customs and Excise, the senior officials concentrated on taxation policy rather than the day to day operations. The declared interest of the Prime Minister had changed some of that emphasis but many Permanent Secretaries found it difficult to maintain an interest in how roads were built or what their architects department did.

The results of the scrutinies produced a not unexpected crop of stories: the farm grant that cost more to pay out than it was worth, the cost benefit assessment used to justify huge investment based on assumptions twenty years out of date. They also produced evidence that there were better ways of achieving the same results – and even of improving the service provided for no extra cost. The people doing scrutinies were young, at least by Whitehall standards. They were encouraged to be radical, to challenge and to question, and they had the protection of a central organisation. Unusually they were generally serving civil servants with some knowledge of the organisation they were dealing with which gave them an extra edge both with their colleagues and with their ministers. It was a sign of the value to be gained by using internal talent – people who knew where the problems might be – to find solutions.

LASTING REFORMS

The work of the Rayner Unit was not limited to fighting fires in isolated parts of the Whitehall empire. There were two principal objectives: to use examples from scrutinies and the experience of the teams to build a constituency in Whitehall which would be enthusiastic about management, and to embed changes which would lead to wider management reforms across the Civil Service. Rayner's 'lasting reforms' heralded in the 1982 statement of government policy established the critical building blocks of management reform. Reviews of 'service-wide issues' challenged the existing rule bound culture, the introduction of financial management and budgeting – the Financial Management Initiative – challenged the senior Civil Service to introduce a management structure which could use and develop financial information and greater delegated powers to manage more effectively. The measurement of outputs and performance would inform the process of making informed choices about priorities which would improve the effective use of resources. Rayner, like so many before and since, observed that a benefit of his lasting reforms should be to:

> bring about the changes and the education and the experience during the career of a civil servant which would (enable) him to manage the substantial amount of work that would unquestionably come his way (quoted in Hennessy, 1999).

The Rayner Unit's superb and undervalued work on the dreary quality of government forms, was a classic of the treatment every government needs regularly. Over five years 27 000 forms were removed from use and a further 41 000 were redesigned. It was an example of looking at the unfashionable and neglected areas of the Government and achieving results which had a lasting impact, although, like so many improvements, it would need revisiting.

Common rules bound the Civil Service and constrained what Departments could do individually. Rayner's team grouped Departments carrying out scrutinies of common issues together into 'multi-department reviews'. The reviews were overseen by the Rayner Unit, but carried out by scrutiny teams in Departments within their own areas. One of the complications of life in the Civil Service was the strength of the concept of 'service wide issues'. Rules were standardised and centralised. The Establishments Officer for the Department of Employment was expected to follow the central rules, in addition to the Departmental rules, which filled five foolscap sized folders and covered every conceivable situation. Rayner tried to deal with this all pervasive bureaucracy by encouraging Departments to look at what they needed to run their own operations and then adapting the central rules to take account of any necessary variations. The management of the collection and publication of Government statistics was treated in this way, as was the review of personnel policies and the review of consultancy services.

The value of the Rayner theory of building links across Whitehall was exemplified in the Personnel Management Review. It was chaired by John

Cassels, who was then Second Permanent Secretary at the Management and Personnel Office (MPO), which had replaced the Civil Service Department; he went on to be the Director of the National Economic Development Office and Chairman of the Manpower Services Commission. The reviews were carried out by teams from seven Departments with a final report of service wide principles by the central team. It was instrumental in some of the developments in process and practice in the Civil Service which made it a good, if not an outstanding, employer.

The reviews brought together many of the people who were to play a part in later developments in management in the Civil Service. I led the Department of Employment team, Karen Caines, later a principal author of the Next Steps Report who was to join the Efficiency Unit at a critical time, was part of the central team, together with Marie Shroff who went on to be Secretary to the Cabinet in New Zealand. Sandy Russell, later Deputy Chairman of Customs and Excise, was leading the work of the new Financial Management Unit as work on better financial management was taking shape, building the links between financial information and effective human resource management.

In addition to work on the scrutiny programme and the lasting reforms, Derek Rayner was Mrs Thatcher's personal adviser. She asked his opinion, and he gave it openly and freely. She had then a sense for potential trouble although it finally let her down, and Derek Rayner provided a sounding board as to whether something would work. She was invaluable in supporting the Rayner Unit if there was serious disagreement about a scrutiny. A word from the Prime Minister, even it if was merely an expression of interest, could undo a logjam or encourage someone to think again.

By the mid-1980s Whitehall was adjusting to a regime of continued resource constraint. The next phase was to use the building blocks of management changes which were in place as a basis for development. The pragmatic solution to a problem is not often the stuff of political theory and much of what happened may appear, especially with hindsight, incoherent or damaging to the constitutional or political theorist. In the longer term, as solutions shake down, they may prove to be impractical or of short term value or the right answer. A flexible system should be able to try out different solutions, and accept what works most effectively or reject what does not without blame. By the mid-1980s what was emerging was not the significance of any one or a combination of 'initiatives', but the possibility of changing how things were done. The development of a modest degree of flexibility was an important basis for wider changes later.

THE EFFICIENCY UNIT

By 1984 scrutinies were improving in substance and in their outcome and were becoming more accepted. Scrutinies were seen as one possible way of finding more innovative solutions to some of the problems posed by the pressure on resources. Derek Rayner had left Whitehall to become Chairman at Marks & Spencer and had been replaced by Sir Robin Ibbs, a senior director at ICI, who, like Rayner had had earlier experience of Whitehall, as Director of the Central Policy Review Staff (CPRS).

The CPRS had been abolished by Mrs Thatcher in 1983 on the grounds, not unjustified, that its work was not relevant to what she wanted to do – and an embarrassingly frank report had been leaked to the press. It was an understandable move but it left the centre of Whitehall dangerously weak in analytical capacity. Some members of the CPRS moved into the Downing Street Policy Unit, the Cabinet Office secretariat were given a more substantive role, but the CPRS role in putting an independent view to the Cabinet on the merits or demerits of a case, aside from departmental and political arguments, was lost.

Ibbs took over as the Prime Minister's Adviser on Efficiency and Effectiveness in Government and the oversight of the renamed Efficiency Unit. The Unit was led first by Clive Priestley who had been recruited by Lord Rayner and then by Ian Beesley, a statistician from the Civil Service. There were between six and eight other members drawn from government and the private sector – a model the Unit was to retain until the end of the 1980s. The Unit was working on a range of scrutinies and the development of the reviews of common functions across departments.

I joined the Unit in 1984 as the deputy head and manager of the scrutiny programme. Among other things waiting for me was a draft report on the stolid subject of the techniques used by Whitehall to control numbers, provide operational advice and improve internal efficiency. A study had been completed on the process of control of staff numbers, 'staff inspections', and the methods of reviewing operational areas. It also contained the first of many studies of the use of consultancy. I had for two years been responsible for this area, among other things, in the Department of Employment, where there were about 50 000 staff and a constant battle over the numbers as demand grew for unemployment benefit and manpower services as unemployment increased.

The staff inspections system was a straightforward piece of old style central control. Every few years a group of diligent men would appear in the office, review all the management processes and report on how many staff were needed to carry out the functions. They would then report to the Chief Inspector, whose role was to see that inspection reports were implemented. Some reports were excellent, others extremely pedestrian, but they had one overwhelming defect. They removed responsibility from management to oversee their own organisations and keep their staff numbers down. There was an unspoken assumption that the inspection would 'take out' 10–15% of staff, so any prudent manager made sure that the 10–15% could be removed without damage.

The Efficiency Unit report explored the implications of the introduction of the FMI into departments. Based on a series of reviews, using the Rayner 'multi departmental review' system the Efficiency Unit's report was the central review, collecting the general lessons from individual reports. It recorded the changes in Departmental management which were already, in 1983–4 in place in some departments. Most significant was the gradual transfer of day to day control of programme expenditure from finance departments to the new 'line manager':

> they will be responsible for organising their money and manpower, authorising and monitoring their own detailed complements and expenditure and, at the margins, they should be able to switch expenditure between manpower and other resources.

Many of the issues which became so familiar to the 'Next Steps' team lie buried in this report – the role of top management in strategic resource allocation and planning, the need for training and the role of the centre. Of the Central departments the report said crisply:

> it is particularly important in this area of the development of management skills that the centre should not be seen to be dragging its heels in developing its own organisation while encouraging departments to be more innovatory' (Jenkins et al., 1984).

The final report recommended that inspectors should be advisory and the responsibility for the control of staff numbers should pass to 'line managers'. It was the first confrontation with the Treasury that the Unit had had since I had joined it. For the Treasury, staff inspectors were the foundations of 'numbers control' – a logical argument in theory but, as with much Treasury theory, it ignored the impact of the control. The Treasury could not consider the possibility that switching responsibility from the inspectors to the managers might achieve better results. In a modest way these discussions were one of the forerunners of the 'executive agency' arguments. The Treasury, like most Ministries of Finance, preferred existing controls, whatever their weaknesses, to moving in the direction of more effective but different methods. The Efficiency Unit proposition that staff inspection should be advisory and managers should take responsibility with budgetary control for their own use of resources was several steps too far.

The upshot was a compromise. The argument had demonstrated the lack of what would now be called 'joined up working' between the 'central departments' who shared responsibility for management issues in the Civil Service. Staff inspectors were the responsibility of the Treasury, reviews and consultants the responsibility of the Management and Personnel Office, the modest successor to the defunct Civil Service Department, and scrutinies were the responsibility of the Efficiency Unit. Better co-ordination was to be achieved by formal machinery linking the three areas. A Unit – the Joint Management Unit – was set up headed by Valerie Strachan who later became Chairman of Customs and Excise. With the grim determination of officials with a badly constructed remit the Joint Management Unit had regular meetings of a 'co-ordinating group' run by Valerie Strachan. The members were Robin Butler, then Second Permanent Secretary in the Treasury and later to be Head of the Civil Service, Anne Mueller, the Permanent Secretary of the MPO and myself as the Head of the Efficiency Unit. The secretary to the group was, among other things, an authority on Lord Byron and was writing his PhD. The purpose of this curious coterie was to bring together the representatives of the different views and to produce some coherence. The Treasury was beginning to take some tentative steps towards more flexibility in the margins of financial control; the use of targets, the beginnings of performance indicators and measurement and discussions about merit pay were taking place at the same time.

The Efficiency Unit was beginning to work with the Treasury on the development of procedures for contracting out services. The first steps had not been well thought out. The people responsible tended to be both dogmatic about the principle and hesitant about the practice. It was possible to feel that areas for contracting out were chosen for their minimal importance and maximum irritation factor. One Permanent Secretary, with a beaming smile, recounted his success in reducing sandwich prices in the canteen and at the Ministry of Defence an elderly Brigadier complained bitterly about 'these contractors' – if you didn't put into the contract that the floor was to be polished every day it didn't get done: 'we've never had to worry about things like that before'.

The early experience with contracting out demonstrated to the Efficiency Unit that defining the details of a service for a contract specification was not going to be easy. It was a new skill for most civil servants for whom traditionally everything had been supplied 'in house'. Many of the early contracting out schemes were for support services – such as cleaning, porterage or security. There were instructions on what had to be done, but as with other Civil Service activities, outcomes were seldom measured or costed. Before, it had been possible to telephone and complain that the wastepaper baskets had not been emptied; now, unless someone had thought of it, the contractor could say: 'its not in the contract'. The discovery that to be precise about how often the linoleum was swept was as necessary for a good cleaning job as a detailed specification was necessary to build an aeroplane came as an unwelcome shock to many. Much time was spent making mistakes and learning how to deal with the consequences. In addition there was a significant impact on staff who might be affected by a contracting out decision. People became worried and anxious about what was happening. The messengers who delivered internal post – a crucial job in a paper run organisation – would gather in knots in the corridor anxiously discussing what was going on and whether their jobs, hitherto always secure, were likely to last.

The process of developing a contract specification opened minds to the possibility of finding new ways to do things. This pressure was important in a static and hidebound organisation. While it jolted people out of a comfortable rut, which is never popular, it gave people who wanted to do things differently and better, a chance to make substantial changes. I visited a hospital in South Wales where the catering contract was going out to tender. The hospital catering managers were young and energetic but they, like most of their contemporaries, had entered a world where the established ways of doing things were immutable. While they had accepted the difficulty of making changes as part of their job, the requirement to draw up a contracting out specification, although initially just another chore imposed on them by regional office, had fired the young internal team to think radically about what they had been doing in running the catering. They discovered that by better management they could improve quality and reduce costs by a third. Cleaning floors and improving the catering are seldom seen as the stuff of serious government but they are an important part of management – especially in a hospital. Even this modest process was an important signal that things which had not changed for decades might begin to move. If the food in the canteen improves, the whole office notices quickly; if the floors are dirty or the messengers upset, everyone throughout the office knows about it.

In 1985 the National Audit Office (NAO) decided that the time had come to review the success or otherwise of the Rayner programmes. Audit by the NAO was a curious process. A worried man from the NAO appeared in the office and asked for help in finding the figures. We had already given him complete freedom in the office to look at anything but he had decided it was too complex to work out on his own. The outcome was a report to the senior committee of the House of Commons, the Public Accounts Committee (PAC). Normally the committee's main function was to cross examine senior officials on mistakes, scandals and misuse of funds that had been uncovered by the auditors. The report on the Rayner Scrutinies was an unusual one for the members of the Committee.

At a stately session of the PAC, where members of the committee appeared to find it difficult to cope with a change of role, Sir Robin Ibbs and I discussed the NAO report. The Committee was not its normal mode of aggressive challenge, asking difficult questions and pin pointing weaknesses. They were faced with Robin Ibbs, not even paid by the Government and only very part time, and me, a more junior official than they were used to grilling, and they could not really find anything to complain about. The NAO report had been complimentary about the scrutiny process and the results it had achieved and endorsed the financial savings from scrutinies.

MAKING THINGS HAPPEN

One of the ideas triggered by the NAO review was the question of what makes a successful scrutiny. The point was not simply how to make scrutinies successful in the sense of their quality or their acceptability, but to understand what the constituent parts were of a successful policy decision which led to effective implementation and outcomes which were expected. The Efficiency Unit's report in 1985, *Making Things Happen*, suggested adaptation of the scrutiny process by including a phase of implementation which emphasised the significance of the role of the Permanent Secretary. This report proved to be an important precursor to the work done for the 'Next Steps' review two years later.

The Unit reviewed the history of several well known scrutinies – the Forensic Science Service, VAT registration and de-registration and the Payment of Benefits to the Unemployed. The team from the Efficiency Unit consisted of Graham Oates, on secondment from KPMG, Andrew Stott from DHSS and me. We each took a separate scrutiny to review and with help from the Department concerned dug out the past files. I sat in a dank room down at the dull end of Horseferry Road in London surrounded by dusty files. Somehow in only a few years the files had developed a dog-eared look. But unlike the Public Record Office, no one had had the chance of 'weeding' them. Short breathless minutes from junior officials, crisp notes from the Permanent Secretary's private office and notes of apparently boring meetings jostled with records of different drafts of reports, responses and ministerial statements. But the message was clear: if the Permanent Secretary took a grip on what was happening, there was some genuine action. If the scrutiny was delegated, however high its political profile, it was less likely to be implemented fully and successfully – the boss had to be and to be seen to be, behind implementation, and the most effective boss in implementing policy was the Permanent Secretary.

The Efficiency Unit report of the review recommended that implementation needed to be pursued with the same sense of urgency as had been applied to the 90 days allowed for a scrutiny; there should be a tight timetable and a final report. The whole process should take a maximum of two years and Ministers should be in the lead in seeing that the scrutiny was taken seriously while responsibility for effective implementation should rest with the Permanent Secretary.

This work led to the development of a systematic approach to scrutinies within the Efficiency Unit. The new proposals were set out in the Unit's report, *Making Things Happen – the Implementation of Scrutinies*. As always with Efficiency Unit reports, it went first to the Prime Minister before publication and was published with a foreword from her. It was greeted surprisingly warmly in Whitehall. The idea of focusing on the implementation of scrutiny recommendations, bringing people involved in the outcomes more into the review process, and giving them a recognised role, instead of leaving them outside, were welcome developments.

The review process changed very little. The scrutiny continued to be based on the ideas first promulgated by Derek Rayner several years before. It had to be a review of a definable organisation or area of policy which was in need of improvement, and the team had to ask the simplistic questions that are often the most effective way of opening up difficult issues. They were still urged to ask: what does it cost, who does what, what are you trying to do, with what result, is there another or better way of doing it?

To this familiar process the new Efficiency Unit review recommended adding a stage for careful planning and monitoring of implementation. Implementation was given a timetable, like the other stages in a scrutiny – the final implementation report had to be provided within two years of the start of the review. The report had to be produced by the 'action manager', the person responsible for the area throughout the review and implementation, and had to be sent to the Minister responsible for the scrutiny and to the Efficiency Unit. We were tying in the outcomes to the review process so that 'doing a scrutiny' was not simply focused on a review, however radical, but on the final outcomes with the manager and the Minister clearly responsible for what happened.

The new role for the Minister was significant. Until this stage ministers had been barely involved in scrutinies unless they took a particular interest in the subject matter – and that happened rarely. Now there was a specific responsibility to be followed up, and, what would be of interest to many young and underemployed junior ministers, the chance to be involved directly in something that had the Prime Minister's interest. Some of them took a close interest; it provided them with an opportunity to be concerned with the detail of the scrutiny and it emphasised to those responsible for implementation that there was political interest in what they were doing.

To make the changes clear and coherent we employed a designer to put together a simple folder which showed the stages of a scrutiny and the roles of the main people involved. It meant that the process was much clearer and everyone involved knew what their functions were, including the Permanent Secretary and the Minister. The inevitable criticism – Whitehall fed on criticism – was directed to the fact that we had used three colour printing and laminated the folder rather than to the substance. Effective communication of information was regarded in Whitehall as an unnecessary and rather flamboyant extravagance in the mid-1980s. Unlike the previous photocopied sheets of typescript the new folder was read – and not just in Whitehall. I have been shown treasured copies in countries as different, and as distant, as Colombia and Swaziland.

It was, however, dismaying in producing what was supposed to be helpful advice on how to get the job done, to discover how many people clung to the process as a lifeline rather than a guide. It was difficult to persuade people to think out for themselves what the most effective approach would be to their subject; they wanted a clear, definite process to follow. Rightly or wrongly, the Efficiency Unit gave them a process. It was designed to cover only what was really important and was always introduced as a guide not as rules. Despite our best endeavours, it was regarded by many as providing immutable rules and for some the rules were tiresome. As with so many systems people focused on the rule not on the reason for it.

THE FMI AND BUDGETS

What has been described as the Efficiency Strategy progressed on a wider front than the work on scrutinies and wider reviews alone. The Treasury was beginning work on the changes to systems and structures which were to be of crucial importance later. The Financial Management Initiative (the FMI) was managed by a small group, organised jointly by the Central departments with the by now classic mix of enthusiastic civil servants and private sector experts. The Unit was announced in 1982 and started work rapidly. Its task was to see that all Departments developed their own internal management systems using output and performance measurement, delegated responsibility for the use of resources, and information systems and expert advice to support the new approach. It was heavily influenced by the work at the Department of the Environment initiated by Michael Heseltine. What was innovative about the FMI was the approach the Unit took to the establishment of the new systems. Departments were not supplied with an established pattern set by the centre, they were to develop their own system. Provided this conformed to a few rules on compatibility it was left to each Department to determine how its system developed. Of all the management initiatives this one was arguably the most fundamental. It forced senior officials to undertake some management tasks. At one memorable meeting a senior Permanent Secretary flipping through the many tables of his top management information was heard to mutter: 'Do we really do all this?'.

Each Department produced an information system of sorts, though most of them fell into the same traps and had to be hauled out. The systems were too complicated, too detailed, full of unnecessary information and needed several years before they worked smoothly. But they were used. The information was both new and innovative and, in most Departments, it reflected what people said they needed to manage properly. The FMI process demonstrated clearly the virtues of decentralisation. Of course, some information systems went seriously wrong. Scale was an early problem; the information systems in the Ministry of Defence, notoriously, were so voluminous they had to be taken around on a trolley. At the Department of Employment the first information system report was solemnly published – and sold six copies. But in most Departments, over three or four years, people began to use the figures and to adapt the structure of the information to fit what they needed. As greater budgeting and delegation emerged in the mid-1980s, Departments were already becoming used to working with the information they would need to operate fully accountable budgets.

The central FMI Unit completed an admirable task and had the good sense to wind itself up. It must have been tempting for the staff to want to reach for the next thing and for the central Departments to build on success. But they had the sense to stop when the job was done. It was a model of how to introduce a new initiative, to know when to stop and to be allowed to go.

The natural progression from the FMI's management systems was the development of more delegated budgeting. The Treasury led and organised a review, based in a number of different Departments on how to introduce a delegated budgeting system. The Efficiency Unit provided advice about methodology and the Treasury ran the project; once the central Departments were all working together a great deal of progress could be made quickly and sensibly. The review of budgeting was followed by a central report from the Treasury and the introduction of pilot delegated budgets in some Departments.

The succession of innovations laid the groundwork for better management of resources and, eventually, for improved service delivery. Budgets gave people a grasp of what was happening within their part of the organisation as well as more control over how resources were used. It meant they were able to respond more effectively and in an informed way to changes in policy or direction. Inadequate information had always been a serious weakness in public sector organisations. It was a significant part of the cause for that familiar complaint of politicians that they 'pull the levers and nothing happens'.

Although by the 1960s the public service and its functions were growing, the skills of the senior Civil Service, as Fulton had emphasised, had not changed to match the demands. What Fulton missed, possibly constrained by his terms of reference, was that the management systems had to change as well as the skill base if the process of managing the Civil Service was to modernise. New skills, without a system to use them on, atrophy quickly. Financial information and budgets put in place systems to allow greater managerial skills to develop, greater accountability for actions and results, and greater responsibility, as it became possible to delegate decision taking to more effective levels. These changes had been trailed in the 1982 White Paper on Efficiency in Government and were an important part of the thinking of Derek Rayner and Clive Priestley as Head of the Rayner Unit. The first part of the 1980s saw the ground being prepared; the mid- and late-1980s took the process of reform one stage further.

The ideal of an efficient organisation providing a competent service was not new. But as the cost of the public sector rose inexorably during the 1960s and 1970s, resources became more difficult to manage. Public servants lived with constant last minute cuts to running costs, capital programmes, to anywhere where money could be easily found and removed. The Treasury was an embattled institution, with, in the mid-1970s, the IMF baying at its heels. Costs appeared to be possible to cut but not to control. All the familiar signs of penny pinching were there. Reused envelopes, recycled paper long before it became fashionable, elaborate and detailed expenses claims. The austerity of senior civil servants was a byword, eating in office canteens, experts on the cheap restaurants of Soho and Victoria, with few perks, and apparently little desire for them.

Financial management was based on the vote accounting system of the Treasury. It recorded expenditure by programme and sub-programme in great and accurate detail, but it did not relate expenditure to output or outcome. Attempts at control were often counterproductive; the damaging consequences of cutting off flows of expenditure in an arbitrary way appeared not to be understood. During the 1970s capital expenditure had been cut repeatedly. The consequences could be seen in the state of government buildings and installations where conditions were frequently deplorable; the more serious effect of the decline in investment in the health, education and transport sectors became more evident in the following decades while the lack of investment in the nationalised industries came to light during the privatisations of the mid-1980s.

The way that money was used, the effectiveness of the expenditure, and where the decisions were best made were the main themes of the efficiency drive. Scrutinies, the FMI and delegated budgets had put the building blocks in place for the next phase. Using these tools had focused attention on the need to understand and analyse resource use. They had begun the process of providing information which would make it possible for the first time to link what was spent with what was provided and to link what was done with the type and quality of the services the public received.

Scrutinies had also pulled Ministers – usually junior ministers – into the management processes of Whitehall. Despite what had been happening in Whitehall over the two decades since the Fulton Report, politicians were still effectively outside the system of management in government. Many of the crucial decisions were taken by Permanent Secretaries – the officials with financial and management responsibility for Departments. Politicians were involved closely in the development of policy and the financial support for policy through the public expenditure system but their role in management was minimal. This carried the consequence that their understanding of the implications of policy issues and the way in which policy might be carried out was often very slight. Scrutinies had their strengths and weaknesses; their analysis could be over simplistic, indeed sometimes crude, but a successful scrutiny did demonstrate what happened when poorly developed policy was implemented and how much care was needed in practice in ensuring that it was possible to implement policy in a way that would produce the desired results. The implementation role brought Ministers into the questions of how policy worked in practice and demonstrated what happened when the practicalities were ignored.

The next chapter considers how the Efficiency Unit took the process of management reform further. The Unit's investigation of progress in improving management and the identification of obstacles to better management led to more radical changes in the structure of central government.

4. Improving management in Government: the Efficiency Unit investigation

The Efficiency Unit in 1986 had a staff of eight to ten with members from both the private sector and the Civil Service. The main tasks were running the scrutiny programme, encouraging greater attention to management in specific projects and carrying out reviews of management issues for the Prime Minister. The scrutiny programme was the principal activity and occupied most of the working time of the team. The Unit was housed in the attics of the old eighteenth century Treasury building designed by William Kent in the 1720s. The rooms overlooking the Park were white panelled and thickly carpeted. The other offices had spectacular views of Whitehall's remaining chimney pots. One room had furniture economically recycled from the CPRS Directors' office and pictures from the Government art collections. The narrow passages held the filing cabinets; access was either up the back stairs, stone, narrow and winding, or through a large windowless room containing, bizarrely, a large table tennis table.

It looked like old Whitehall. Messengers delivered post every two hours. There were computers but they were so elderly and temperamental that few could understand them and only someone from the suppliers could repair them – at several days notice. New working methods were needed as badly as elsewhere in the system. But even in the Efficiency Unit there was strong opposition to the most basic changes. Grumbles and complaints greeted new computers on every desk, even though they were relatively fast and reliable. There were targets for individuals and for the Unit programmes, a linked internal computer system for all the staff and a systematic process of reviewing performance. The Unit had a budget of about £350 000 and, unusually, flexibility in how it could be used. It took at least three months, even in a small committed organisation for the complaints from the team, about introducing more systematic management of how the Unit worked, to subside and the advantages to be felt to outweigh the disadvantages.

While the Efficiency Unit was making painful progress with its internal arrangements, the rest of Whitehall was finding changing its working methods more difficult. In many Departments there was, as always, confusion and poor morale; the new management systems were being developed but few people were using the information they provided to achieve any substantial changes. Although scrutinies were going well, in some of the less successful ones the teams seemed to be going through the motions rather than thinking hard about more radical solutions.

ENCOURAGING INTEREST: TARGETS AND SEMINARS

The stagnation was not only in scrutinies. One of the functions of the Prime Minister's Adviser was to persuade senior management to take resource management more seriously. Each year senior Ministers and departmental managers were asked for their targets for improving their use of resources. In many Departments Senior Ministers and Permanent Secretaries were at a loss. They had no idea where to start with a target for improvement. The Unit was either gazed at blankly or given relatively trivial targets, like changing the window frames to reduce heating costs, in a Department with responsibility for national energy efficiency. What was more disturbing was that while it was possible to discuss domestic issues like the cost of the travel and subsistence budget or the departmental printing bill, it appeared not to occur to the most senior officials and ministers that a similar process could be applied to their major programme expenditure.

There would be stately discussions about the cost of repainting the building while billions of pounds were being spent on government programmes. Effective cost and resource management were not seen as part of resource control. Even where reasonable targets were produced, the second stage, a careful request for a progress report halfway through the year, with the reminder that the Unit would be back for the annual discussion, would often produce upheaval. Once the Unit had been seen off with some targets, the Department had turned to the next issue and forgotten all about them.

After several years two developments could be observed. First, the more astute officials were using the target process to increase internal pressure for their own projects. Within a Department, the Minister's Private Office would be responsible for preparing the papers and the plan for handling a meeting with the Adviser to the Prime Minister. This task was not easy if the subject was not a mainstream topic for the Department. A senior official with a subject he or she considered needed more attention would offer a suitable target to the hard pressed private secretary who was trying to put together material for the meeting. The Minister might pick up the subject of the target and become interested in it, or the Permanent Secretary might ask some questions about the substance or about progress.

At the very least the officials would know that the Unit would return to ask about progress once a target was in the Minister's list.

The second development was that the Treasury became interested in the process; they were eager to see the targets produced by Departments. As the targets were technically targets for improving value for money, they could provide the expenditure divisions of the Treasury with more insights into what was happening within the 'spending' Departments. It was a measure of how poor relationships were between the Treasury and the spending Departments that the Treasury came to the Unit rather than to the Departments for information. The Unit had to maintain that the information belonged to the Department and the Treasury had to go there for the information. If Departments had thought that the Unit gave 'their' information to the Treasury, co-operation would have come to an abrupt end.

This process had two objectives for the Unit: first, at least once a year there was activity at a senior level which focused on aspects of management and, second, the Minister had to demonstrate a grasp of how his Department was run. However trivial senior officials and Ministers might think our activities, few of them were prepared to be openly dismissive of the Prime Minister's Adviser. Two Cabinet Ministers were aggressive about what they considered interference in their private fiefdom but most were courteous, in public, and as far as possible appeared to try to be helpful.

The widespread use of targets through the public expenditure system is an indication of how effective a contribution to improvement sensibly used targets can be. The idea of targeting improving value was difficult and more complicated than the simple activity targets which were well established; the very fact that it was difficult to work out what a value for money target might be did make some people think about the issues involved.

As with so many useful ideas, targets have since become a nightmare. A good target needs careful construction to ensure that it is aimed at the right point in a system and that the consequences of concentrating on the target will produce the right result. Used as a means of detailed control, over-simplistic targets result in target chasing, distorted activity and time wasting. By the end of the 1990s much of Whitehall was using targets in a way which actively impeded good management. Even the normally admirable Audit Commission produced a telephone directory sized list of targets, many of them simple activity targets, which effectively killed off their value.

The second area in which the Unit tried to bring pressure on Departments to take management seriously was the development of seminars on 'value for money' with the Prime Minister. Mrs Thatcher was genuinely interested in the way Departments were managed, and because, by 1986, she had been in office for seven years, she had a good working knowledge of what went on. The purpose of the seminar was once every

18 months to 2 years to focus the attention of the Secretary of State and his Permanent Secretary on the management of the Department as a whole rather than on the individual policy issues which normally absorbed them, particularly when dealing with the Cabinet and the Prime Minister. A two-hour session would be booked with the Prime Minister. The Secretary of State and the Permanent Secretary would be there, together with the Adviser, Sir Robin Ibbs, myself as the Head of the Efficiency Unit and the Cabinet Secretary. No one else was allowed in, so the Permanent Secretary had to be able to answer any question which might arise. Most Departments had assumed they could bring a bright young under secretary with them to do the presentation so the Minister could peacefully listen without being involved in the detail.

Inevitably the quality of the discussions ranged from constructive to dismal. But the Unit's objective was that for six to eight weeks before the meeting the senior officials of the Department concerned had to concentrate on understanding their management role and on the presentation to the Prime Minister. The pressure of the meeting forced uninterested officials to consider resource and personnel issues within their Department, and it gave those who were concerned with these issues a rare opportunity to raise them with their minister and with the Prime Minister.

Efficiency Unit members reported with hilarity on the degree of activity before a seminar and on the number of phone calls asking for advice, help, practice sessions and run throughs before the event. In one notable case a desperate Secretary of State announced that he had never used an overhead projector and could not possibly both make his presentation and change the slides. He wanted to bring a deputy secretary to do it, as the Permanent Secretary also lacked this high level skill. But the rules were upheld. Although I changed the slides, the Secretary of State had to cope with the presentation without additional support.

OBSTACLES TO CHANGE

However modestly useful these levers were to try to persuade an uninterested senior group to take management seriously there was still no buzz attached to the changes. The whole point was, after all, to try to change the way Whitehall worked, to use resources effectively and to improve the end result. What was happening seemed to be a group of people going through the motions required by organisational change but without any alteration in attitude and approach. As a consequence improvements were mainly marginal. People could legitimately ask what the point was of all the upheaval.

The Efficiency Unit was not alone in its concern about what was happening. The most senior Permanent Secretaries were themselves worried that the Civil Service appeared to be stagnating rather than making progress. In 1986 a group of them met several times in private to discuss what was wrong and what might be done. These discussions opened up some of the issues which were later to become part of the background to the Efficiency Unit's report on improving management. They also raised an important point: the public stance taken by the government that the public sector was being reformed and becoming more managerial, was not borne out by what was happening. Progress was infinitely slow, and no one had a satisfactory answer as to why the changes which had been put in place were not producing results.

The Unit was concerned about the way in which Departments were run. In most cases it was a matter of over concentration on politics and policy and a neglect of management, not as a consequence of wilful or lordly neglect but partly that most senior officials were comfortable with policy and had no experience of management. Many of them genuinely thought that management was of secondary, or even marginal, importance. The pressures of political and policy issues more than filled their overcrowded days. Most senior officials did not know what questions to ask about management issues – nor indeed what the answers should be.

Some changes had produced improvements. Inside the Unemployment Benefit Service, modest delegated budgets had been introduced in 1984. An unemployment benefit office, given its own budget for maintenance could transform a dingy public office into something bright and welcoming, using the same sized budget, but with better value by purchasing locally, and taking decisions themselves. In one case, the grim pre-war hole in a run-down part of Birmingham was given carpets, instead of linoleum, chairs and desks instead of safety grilles and counters and gentler lighting. The 'claimants' become customers or clients, the atmosphere relaxed and the number of violent incidents fell sharply. The decisions were made by the local staff who wanted to improve their relationship with their clients and to have a better working environment. The clients were delighted – they said they felt as if they were being treated properly and not like animals. On a smaller scale, just being able to buy a new fluorescent tube instead of waiting six months for 'works' to supply and fit one made not only a difference to the light levels but gave the staff some feeling of responsibility for their work. It was an example of how much could be done to improve the way people were treated and how a public service was provided, as a result of a mundane change in an internal budget rule. There was an improvement in the quality of service, at little cost, as a result of sensible adaptation of an unnecessarily restrictive rule.

After considerable debate within the Unit it was concluded that the only approach that might open up the wider issues was to look at how the management reforms were working in practice and to identify anything blocking progress. I had been struck by a comment made by an MOD research scientist at a lecture I gave, who said she felt as though she was working with a block of cement on her head. The weight of the organisation above her, apparently committed to stopping her doing things, felt overwhelming. I had heard criticisms of the culture which prevented sensible changes all over the public service. The system was not lively, it did not encourage ideas and innovation; it stifled initiative and left the highly intelligent people who worked there feeling jaded and undervalued.

SETTING UP A REVIEW

In the summer of 1986, after I had taken over as Head of the Efficiency Unit, I wrote a short note for Sir Robin Ibbs to send to the Prime Minister suggesting there should be a study, to be done as a scrutiny, aimed at trying to find out what the obstacles were to better and faster progress with management reform. Many of the right things had been done but there was little evidence of substantial progress. The Prime Minister responded positively; the terms of reference set out the scope of the review but made it clear there were no preconceptions about what the answers might be. The Unit was asked:

- to assess the progress achieved in improving management in the Civil Service
- to identify what measures have been successful in changing attitudes and practices
- to identify the institutional, administrative, political and attitudinal obstacles to better management and efficiency that still remain
- to report to the Prime Minister on what further measures should be taken

At this stage, and indeed until much later in the process, the Unit regarded the review as a means of looking in a low key way at management systems which might come up with some suggestions for removing obstacles to progress. As an Efficiency Unit scrutiny it had a public profile and it needed careful preparation to make sure that as many people as necessary were involved, and that the process was planned to work smoothly.

The first resource was the Efficiency Unit. All the Efficiency Unit team were involved in the evidence gathering: the members of the main team were myself, Karen Caines, who had taken over from me as Deputy Head of the Unit, and Andrew Jackson. We were all Civil Service administrators with, between us, several decades of experience in Whitehall. Karen had a background in DHSS, had spent two years in the Civil Service Department and had an invaluable network of contacts; she also had a rare combination of experience as a senior civil servant and an understanding of management. Andrew had joined us from the Home Office as a principal. They could not be faulted on their knowledge of the Whitehall jungle. The other members of the Unit, Graham Cawsey from IBM, Richard Hirst from the Ministry of Defence and latterly David Tune from the Australian Civil Service added their experience as the review progressed. Throughout the scrutiny, as with all Efficiency Unit work, the management of communications, ideas, progress and debate were discussed with Sir Robin Ibbs at our weekly meetings with him. His involvement and support were of critical importance throughout the progress of the scrutiny, drafting the report and the process of achieving its final acceptance.

For this scrutiny the team was not the only resource the Unit used. It was important to follow the process the Unit imposed on everyone else, so Sir Robert Armstrong, the Head of the Civil Service and Secretary to the Cabinet, the 'Mandarin's mandarin' according to Peter Hennessy (Hennessy, 2001) found himself, probably for the only time in his official career described as the 'action manager'. Robert Armstrong was a tower of strength throughout the whole process. He was not known for his interest in management issues and was generally regarded as the archetype of a classic mandarin, but while the work was going on and throughout the discussions that followed he was helpful, constructive and interested although occasionally wary of the drafting of some of our proposals.

In addition to the Secretary to the Cabinet, other Permanent Secretaries were interested in what the Unit was doing. The five most senior formed an internal group with whom I had regular individual meetings to discuss ideas and information and latterly to test possible solutions. Sir Kenneth Stowe, who carried the burden of the unwieldy Department of Health and Social Security, was concerned with how Whitehall was working; after he moved to the Cabinet Office early in 1987, he worked closely with the Unit. Sir Brian Cubbon at the Home Office, the doyen of the permanent secretaries, and Sir Clive Whitmore at Defence, the largest and most resource-intensive Department, were involved in discussions regularly. The Unit went outside the Civil Service, primarily to people who had already been involved in government, particularly to Lord Rayner at Marks & Spencer who retained his interest in what was going on in Whitehall and was always ready to spend an hour or two or a relaxed lunchtime making sharp suggestions and swapping stories. Some of the nationalised industry chairmen who could help with ideas on what to look for and where to go were helpful. They were particularly good at suggesting areas where there might be evidence of why and how modernisation in the public sector was stalling.

We have subsequently been asked why we did not look at overseas experience or involve any of the academic experts on public administration. We were at this stage concentrating on whether there was any problem inside the Civil Service as it responded to the changes which the government had put in place. We had decided to use our own process; time was very short, and it did not occur to us that such an inward looking and modest review would gain from further consultations. We had no view at that stage of what the outcome might be.

THE FIRST STAGE: THE STUDY PLAN

Once the team was established and a group of advisers informally involved, we had to produce a plan. Unlike other scrutinies this one would not have a simple defined area of operations to review. The terms of reference were clear but the canvass was huge. It would be necessary to find a way of testing impressions by more careful study which would show whether the original sense of unease was justified, and that the general impressions gathered from discussions and scrutinies were right and reflected accurately what was happening.

Other scrutinies had had some element of the testing of assumptions. Few Ministers or Permanent Secretaries would agree to a review of part of their Department unless they had some sense that all was not as it should be. It might be that costs were running out of control, as with legal aid, or service levels were poor, as with agricultural grants, or the vaguer but familiar plaint: 'it doesn't seem to be working well, I don't really know what's going on'.

The Unit assessed earlier reviews of the Civil Service; they tended to follow a similar pattern. A committee of 'the great and the good' would be convened and then evidence, in formal terms, was invited openly or by specific invitation. Formal evidence was recorded, painstakingly reviewed and formal conclusions drawn out. On reviewing the earlier reports there seemed to be a significant gap. Most reports had received advice from their advisers on the Civil Service, from politicians, from commentators and from academics. What was missing was the view of the Civil Service itself – the half a million people who worked as civil servants for the central government. Curiously the Civil Service did not seem to value and tended not to use its own internal capacity, other than in a supporting role. Their 'views' were represented by trade unions often enough, but the voice of the employees themselves was seldom heard. As the Civil Service continued to recruit the best graduates from universities and school-leavers, there was a swathe across the Civil Service population whose views would be both informed and intelligent and had been so far unheard.

At this stage the most the Unit was trying to do was to shake up the way internal management systems worked. With hindsight it would have been invaluable to have had views of users of the services as well as those of providers but our initial focus was entirely internal. Although it would have been valuable to have been able to consider service quality there would have been little support for such a move. Opinion polls in 1986 would have been regarded as even more frivolous than the Unit's lamination of the 'Notes for Guidance' for scrutiny teams. At this stage we did not see service improvement as the significant issue it later became.

Time was short. The normal scrutiny timetable and process were to be kept to as far as possible: the Unit had to include the people who were responsible, go out and see what was happening, gather relevant data and accept only propositions that could be tested independently. Above all, we had to go out and see for ourselves, not sit in Whitehall and think and read behind a desk – and all within 90 days. It would need tight organisation and all the capacity of the Efficiency Unit, not just the central team. The first stage was a study plan; it had to be supported by a precise management plan if all the necessary meetings and research were to be fitted in, evidence collected, recorded and collated and the timetable met. Karen Caines took responsibility for organising the management of the scrutiny and developed an admirable process which could be reviewed and updated weekly. She kept constant track of what was happening and what issues were emerging. Once work began it proved to be a constant challenge to keep up with the pressure of events as new avenues opened up and had to be explored. Karen Caines' system was essential in keeping us all in touch with what was emerging.

The Prime Minister was not involved; once the terms of reference were agreed, her office left the Efficiency Unit to carry out the scrutiny. There were no formal progress reports in the first few months; the Prime Minister's office was told informally of the directions the work was taking, and left the Unit alone, whether because they were not really interested or had more pressing things to worry about. It was for the Efficiency Unit to devise their own approach and develop their own views.

The first move was to inform the Civil Service, through the Permanent Secretaries meetings, that the scrutiny had been commissioned. They made it fairly clear they thought it a pedestrian topic, unlikely to come up with anything of substance. One or two thought the Unit might make some simplistic recommendations about better planning or targeting, or be more involved in the long running saga of the best use of staff inspectors. The team was given open access to Departments to talk to anyone and to go anywhere. I suspect this generosity was as much in the interest of a quiet life as because they thought there would be any benefit to be gained from the review. The few senior Permanent Secretaries who were more involved took a mild interest in what was happening. The Treasury made it clear they regarded it as a bore rather than a threat.

The first stage, the study plan, was difficult enough. The plan was the first public statement of how the Unit expected to work. It was the first time we had emphasised that this review was to be genuinely internal, drawing not on outside experience or the views of the great and the good but on the views and perceptions of the Civil Service itself. One of the issues that had to be recognised was that it was only under informal circumstances and conditions of personal anonymity that many civil servants were prepared to talk. The effect of years of working under the Official Secrets Act, together with the tradition of reticence about personal and political views to protect professional impartiality and career prospects, had developed an ingrained reluctance in many civil servants to give a personal view about any matter affecting the operations of government.

Partly because of the 'confidentiality' surrounding much of government, only the people working within the Civil Service had information about how the system really worked – everyone else was either guessing or relying on hearsay. The Civil Service had been described frequently and at length by observers, but seldom by those working in it and least of all by junior staff who day by day coped with the consequences of the way the organisation was managed, the rules and the impact that implementing those rules had on their clients. The decision to do little outside the Civil Service was deliberate. It was not a grand review of the organisation of the Civil Service; it was conceived as an investigation into why greater progress with improvements in the public service had not been made. Therefore, the Unit planned to look inside at the internal procedures and processes, not outside for other ways of doing things. The aim was modest.

There were limitations in using the scrutiny technique. The process had been devised to deal with institutional inertia. It was deliberately rough and ready, aimed at shaking traditional approaches to difficult issues. Many scrutiny teams had found it difficult to balance a critical look at how a programme was organised and delivered while accepting the policy as a given. It was easier to make recommendations about policy changes rather than to understand the detail of how operations should be organised if the current policy was to be implemented effectively. In the longer term my view was that effective policy would have to recognise the possibilities as well as the constraints of the practicalities of implementation, but we were a long way from persuading politicians as well as most civil servants that implementation as well as policy was important.

There was a danger that the Efficiency Unit could behave or be thought to be behaving as though scrutinies were the only way to look at difficult issues. Scrutinies were designed to challenge assumptions about how organisations worked; it was important to concentrate on areas that could properly be treated in this way and not to use scrutinies in areas for which it was not the right tool. In the Next Steps scrutiny, there were a number of substantive issues to watch. The scrutiny could not look at the whole structure of the Civil Service – it was aimed at finding out why the changes were not producing results – but as a review done at the request of the Prime Minister, it would inevitably involve senior people across the Government, both politicians and the Civil Service.

As with all scrutinies, at the start of the review the team had to recognise they were amateurs in a world where almost everyone else was more expert. When all the evidence was in and analysed, if they had done their work properly, the team should know more about the subject than most other people because they had looked at the whole topic and not only the constituent parts. In recording and reporting the findings it would be important to be able to reflect what was said so that an accurate picture of the issues could emerge. Each meeting was recorded – one sheet of paper for each meeting was the limit. The notes were distributed to the team so that everyone had a sense of the direction of the project. Weekly meetings provided an opportunity to reflect on the outcome of the past week and the main themes for the next week. With a team, a study plan and lists of meetings, it was possible to start work.

GATHERING EVIDENCE

The study plan, produced after three weeks, set out the programme and what at that stage seemed to be the significant issues to be investigated. It was based on the terms of reference and set out what the team planned to do and how it would work. It formed the basis for discussions in the early stages. Meetings were inevitably short, making the study plan available in advance saved much explanation and discussion at the start of each meeting which could then concentrate on essential issues. It provided background for the meeting so that people could prepare their thoughts in advance and be ready with their main points.

Meetings were better than written papers. Face to face, it was much more evident what people thought, where they put their real emphasis, and it was possible to pursue new lines of thought and inquiry. The pressure of meetings was considerable. Normally two members of the team went to each meeting, one to record and the other to handle the questioning and discussion; the record would be more accurate and based on two people's view of what had been said. The timetable was demanding. Meetings were crammed into long working days, sometimes 10 or 12 separate discussions a day with a taxi waiting outside to go to the next meeting – extravagant for the Civil Service but far cheaper than a government car and driver. 'You have a taxi waiting?' said a Permanent Secretary with a budget of billions, 'Good Lord!'. The team travelled across the United Kingdom and talked to civil servants in a range of offices. It also drew on the evidence already gathered in other scrutinies.

The team carried out 150 individual interviews with Ministers and central government senior civil servants. Together with one other member of the team, I had meetings with twenty-one Ministers including most members of the Cabinet, and with twenty-six Permanent Secretaries, including all the Heads of Departments. There were meetings with twenty-six Grade 2s or Deputy Secretaries. In each of the meetings we set out the main questions: how effective was progress in improving management in the Civil Service, what measures had been most successful, what obstacles remained and what should be done next?

The responses fell into two main groups. The first consisted of the traditional response – general comments on the introduction of new initiatives, the FMI, the Public Expenditure system, the impact of political pressures and the influence of Ministers on what happened. The reaction was a reflection of the view that it was just how things worked and should be accepted as the natural order of things, with perhaps a few minor changes at the margins. The more 'modernist' second group came armed with evidence of the management changes they had introduced. In one case the meeting had to be rescued from a catalogue of the improvements to the canteen and the building maintenance contracts which the Permanent Secretary had produced. 'Oh', he said, 'You mean you want to talk about whether the whole thing works properly, whether this is all worth doing,' there was a long pause, 'but that's a very big subject indeed'. What he was really saying, but using Civil Service code, was that it was just not worth discussing, it was far too big a topic for him to talk about and nothing could be done. For him management was about small domestic issues and while he would play along with the current fashion by recognising there was a canteen somewhere and it should not waste money, 'the whole thing' was a very different issue.

Frequently with Permanent Secretaries the debate concentrated on their role and relationships with their Secretary of State. For most of them management of any kind depended on the expectations and the demands of this relationship. What became clear as the discussions continued was that there were a number of permutations to the relationship. In some 'he leaves me to get on with running the Department' effectively described what happened. In others it was a variant of: 'I can't do anything without his meddling, he thinks he runs this place'. This confusion was genuine – in part a consequence of the different backgrounds of Ministers and in part of the different interests of Permanent Secretaries. It was obvious that there was no clarity about the respective responsibilities of these two crucial roles. The division of functions frequently depended on the inclination of individual Ministers – and to some extent on the toughness of the Permanent Secretary.

In the discussions with Ministers there was a similar range of descriptions to those put forward by Permanent Secretaries when they were asked who managed the Department. The replies ranged from 'Oh, I leave that all to X, it's his job' to 'I can't take my eye off X for a minute – he has no idea of how to run anything'. The most worrying Departments were those where both Permanent Secretary and Secretary of State claimed to leave the management to the other – this was true of at least two of the major and several of the smaller departments. One Minister summed up the role of Permanent Secretaries: 'they are advisers, not managers – they have no experience of managing'. In the published report we referred to this problem – and no one questioned it:

> It is easy for the task of improving performance to get overlooked especially when there is, as we observed, confusion between Ministers and Permanent Secretaries over their respective responsibilities for the management of service delivery. This confusion is made worse when short term pressure becomes acute (Next Steps Report, paragraph 6).

Discussions with the Deputy Secretaries, the next rank below Permanent Secretary were more revealing. Deputy Secretaries could afford to be indiscreet, particularly if they were not likely to 'make' Permanent Secretary. Many of them took a relaxed view about their management role: 'of course management doesn't really matter, none of us know anything about it; it's how you handle politicians that really determine who gets on'. More junior officials provided a range of views: for some, the weaknesses of the existing ways of managing systems were evident. They had information systems and budgets but their lack of real responsibility was something which frustrated those who had a sense of what could and needed to be done. For many civil servants, a system which demanded intelligence of them as a condition of employment and then required them to act in a way which ran counter to intelligent ways of working was deeply irritating.

The issue which emerged repeatedly in the discussions was the lack of personal responsibility and accountability felt by middle and senior officials in the big Departments of State. Several meetings were held with people who had left the Civil Service during the mid-1980s when resignations of 'high fliers' were at what appeared to be an all time high. These groups were of people at Grade 7 and 5 (principal and assistant secretary) to Grade 2 (deputy secretary). All said much the same thing. No, they had not gone for the money, although that was a bonus; they had gone for the opportunity to take personal responsibility for what they did at work. The lack of real responsibility and accountability was deeply frustrating in the middle ranks of the Civil Service.

The meetings with most London-based civil servants produced similar results. In regional and local offices, discussions with staff introduced a different set of issues. The meetings were deliberately informal. With more junior staff the Unit arranged to see groups of them on their own with no senior managers present. Their preoccupations were more local. They were clear that for them the system had to be accepted – they were in no position to challenge it. Their main point was the complexity of the systems they had to operate and the impact of the rules which constrained, in an apparently inefficient way, what they could see could be done. The delay in gaining approval for minor activities and the sudden changes of plan dictated by the whims of head office figured in the discussions – but these frustrations would arise in similar discussions in any network organisation, whatever its function. Local and regional offices in Birmingham, Manchester and Leeds were visited as well as the large operations of the Inland Revenue at Telford, DHSS in the North East and the RAF at Brampton. In each case the discussion centred on the changes that the people there could see were necessary within their own organisations and their own working context. It was significant that few organisations had any arrangements for hearing the views of their staff, much less acting on them.

The ideas put to the team were surprisingly constructive. By 1986 the Government's most public intervention in the public service had been cuts in staff, some contracting out and the big privatisations. The changes to financial management, personnel management and training had reached few people outside the inner Whitehall core. Most junior staff found out what the Government was doing from the media or their trade unions. There was little effective internal communication. There was a record of trade union disputes with the Government across the whole of the public sector, as well as, exceptionally, in the Civil Service itself.

As the scrutiny progressed the team considered what the indicators of a successfully managed organisation outside the public service might be. This was not a search for simplistic private sector models to copy which would have been both absurd and ineffective. The interesting question was whether there were any common threads in the management of large organisations, whether they were in the public or the private sector, which might have some useful lessons. There were discussions with a number of chief executives, the staff of two private sector companies and one nationalised industry to see what lessons might emerge from their collective experience. The ICI Fibres division, the Halifax Building Society London Region and British Rail, Network South East provided a range of contrasts and similarities. Large organisations developed large bureaucracies in the private sector which were remarkably similar to the public sector.

Another strand of evidence was what had happened to previous reports on the Civil Service. Andrew Jackson reviewed all the previous major reports and what had happened to them. The experience of the original Northcote/Trevelyan report was instructive. That cornerstone of the modern public service had four main recommendations: recruitment by competitive examination; a division between intellectual and mechanical work; promotion on merit, and measures to unify the Civil Service, including common recruiting. It had taken nearly 40 years to put in place in the teeth of constant obstruction and lobbying. Much of the widely endorsed Fulton Report criticised problems that were still there in the 1980s. Its core recommendation 'look at the job first' together with the introduction of 'accountable management' and a distinction between planning for the future and operations, had made little progress in spite of the efforts that had been made to implement its recommendations, as the Efficiency Unit team were to discover.

FINDINGS

The gathering of evidence took November and December 1986. The Efficiency Unit arranged to meet over the New Year period, having read the evidence collected in a 200 page record of all the meetings, which each member of the Unit took home with them for Christmas. There were no conclusions at that stage, the task was simply to master the material so that the whole team could work on a similar basis. The meeting of the Unit and Sir Robin Ibbs took place in January 1987 in London; we reviewed all the evidence from the two hundred or so meetings. The team sifted the views of clerks, middle managers, Permanent Secretaries and Ministers. The messages were similar, and worrying. If the series of comments that had been put forward, separately and from all over the country, was a reasonable reflection of the views of this wide sample of the Civil Service, there was a serious and alarming set of issues that needed to be tackled urgently.

The evidence that had been gathered appeared compelling. Some progress with basic management had been made; people were more aware of the costs of their activities and had management systems in place, in most areas, which gave them some idea of what they were doing. The general view was that budgeting systems and manpower cuts were the most effective instruments in changing attitudes and practice. But the list of obstacles to progress was formidable.

Senior people did not take the delivery of government services seriously even though the vast majority of the Civil Service worked in these areas. The senior Civil Service still, even after years of 'Fulton', lacked the management skills and experience necessary for the responsibility they carried. Short term political priorities still tended to squeeze out longer term issues and even modest planning was a low priority. The financial systems, as well as the political pressures, still concentrated on providing the money rather than on achieving results.

Furthermore, the evidence emphasised how constrained people felt by the 'system' they worked in. There was a wide range of organisations, carrying out all the activities of government, with little need for common systems of management. Even the common systems of pay, defended in the interests of avoiding leap frog settlements were internally admitted to be unnecessarily expensive. A system run by rules and principles had become more important than its functions. The activities of government had been amalgamated under a system of centralised rules and central pay bargaining. The outcome by the 1980s was a huge organisation of between 500 000 and 600 000 people, with common rules which were not necessarily suitable for its constituent parts. The system was genuinely seen by its defenders as more important than what it was there to do and there was a strong sense that the risks of dismantling it were too great.

We reviewed and checked our findings. This stage in a scrutiny, known as 'emerging findings', was often difficult and in this case what was emerging was startling indeed. The logical conclusion was uncomfortable. If the team took what had been said to them and the collected data seriously the main conclusion was inescapable: the Civil Service was much too big and diverse to be run effectively as a single operation. We realised that the conclusion would be seen as breaking up the Civil Service. We had accepted from our first jobs in the Civil Service, and some of us had worked there for nearly twenty years, the principles of a single Civil Service with common rules of behaviour, management and practice. We knew that all Departments, however small or distinct were run with the same principles, the same documents and, in most cases, the same furniture. I had seen identical files and desks in one office in the South Pacific with a coral beach and palm trees outside the window, in the Unemployment Benefit Office in Gibraltar, where men in desert costume queued just as in Barnsley, London, Edinburgh or North Wales clutching the same UB40 form to claim unemployment benefit.

It was an amazingly pervasive culture, and, for many a comforting one. To break it up seemed unthinkable. At the most we had thought of changes at the margins, but a wholesale reorganisation was implied by the information we had. Common rules imposed on a large and diverse organisation tended to fit no part of the organisation well. It was the combination of size and diversity which caused the difficulty. It is possible to run a large organisation in a centralised and uniform way particularly where there is a similar product provided in a number of different places. The Passport Office or the Coastguard are expected to provide the same service everywhere. Many large organisations in both the public and the private sectors have provided a uniform service successfully. It may, perhaps deliberately, stifle initiative but it provides for both staff and customers a sense of familiarity and consistency which can be an important virtue for some organisations. But if the range of activities is diverse, uniformity can be damaging.

Recruitment and pay, two of the most important centralised functions in the Civil Service, produced real inequities. A job which was eagerly sought in the North of England could not be filled in London and the disparity in service quality reflected the effect on recruitment. Furthermore, the structure of the system meant that adaptations were difficult to achieve. The people doing the planning and the negotiations were inevitably concerned with the virtues of uniformity. But the lack of flexibility that a centralised pay system imposes on a decentralised management system means the overall effect on individuals and above all on service standards are disastrous. If pay levels fall, recruitment and retention suffer in some parts of the country and, in a labour intensive organisation, clients suffer immediately, not after the next pay settlement, as badly paid and badly managed nurses and clerks disappear. If pay levels are too high, costs are unnecessarily high and money is wasted. But the central negotiators are not on the wards or in the jobcentres and they do not see, much less feel, the consequences of their actions.

Central recruitment posed further problems. At the end of the 1970s most recruitment, above the clerical level, was done by the Civil Service Commission to a common set of standards, even though a local office manager for DSS needed a different set of qualities and skills from those needed in a Whitehall policy office. One of the most long standing justifications for the common systems was to allow people to move easily around the public service. The team tested the use made in practice of this principle. Although a handful of senior level moves around the main Whitehall Departments could be seen, there were relatively few examples of movement across Departmental boundaries elsewhere, especially in areas where, if the principle had value, one might have expected to see far more mobility. In one regional centre, which was an obvious place for such moves because of the proximity of a number of government offices in one city, the number of transfers between Departments in recent years had been in single figures.

The existence of central rules which could only be changed at the centre of the organisation prevented people from thinking laterally and intelligently about their jobs. Extensive rules encouraged bad habits, even though the original justification for the rules was understandable. The classic example was a financial rule which has since been modified. An elaborate year end rule which required spending precisely to a single point merely encouraged lean spending in the early months of the year and silly bonanza spending at the year end since money unspent would be clawed back out of the budget for the following year. The rule encouraged inefficient planning and spending and poor value. Although the purpose of the rule was understandable – to keep control of in year costs – its effects were wasteful.

But, in some ways even more harmful, was the belief created by this kind of rule that most rules were silly. When sensible changes and adaptations were made people refused to believe the changes had happened. Rules were not a rational part of life to be used to make things work, they were a classic part of bureaucracy: erratic and often irrational constraints on doing a reasonable job sensibly. The way budgets worked affected service levels; the structure of the rules prevented Departments from adapting their service to meet variations in demand. The Passport Office and the Driver Testing offices had peaks in demand which led to long and unacceptable delays. The financial regime prevented the temporary recruitment of staff to meet sudden but predictable increases in demand, even though revenue increased as demand increased.

The existence of central rules had a further negative. They were used as alibis by the managers within Departments to justify their own departmental rules. The scrutiny found 'marked differences' in the flexibility given to budget holders to move money between different sub-heads. When challenged, a Department would justify the differences by reference to 'Treasury rules' even though the only rule set by the Treasury in these cases was there should be no transfers between capital and running cost budgets.

Underlying this rule-bound system was a serious structural problem. An organisation responsible for a social security system will operate most effectively if its systems are designed for that task. Organisations running a conference centre, a major tourist attraction, a prison or a minister's office may all need different structures, and probably different staff for their very different objectives. But the government system in 1986 imposed virtually the same organisation on them all. It was not simply the similarities of office equipment, decoration or holiday entitlements. It was the full range of personnel, financial and managerial processes as well as an all pervasive system reinforced by common recruitment to a central model, common organisation of trade unions, pensions and welfare. Almost the only thing not held in common was child care facilities; a few brave Departments ran their own nursery facilities available only to their own staff.

This was a system which discouraged change or improvement. Any civil servant who was concerned with the quality of service their organisations provided, and there were many of them, could find that it was only by bending or even ignoring the rules that modest improvements could be made, even if the changes were modifications which might make it possible to provide the service the government had promised. The encouragement of local initiatives was rare and the absence of scope for making sensible changes was a disincentive and a discouragement to those who wanted to see improvements. The effect of this structure was to diminish the develop- ment of commitment to an organisation; being a civil servant was more significant than being a part of the Driver and Vehicle Licensing Centre or English Heritage or the Ministry of Defence. The Civil Service provided your employment terms and conditions, your status and your security. Success in your job was defined not by your achievements but by your status in a complex hierarchy.

A critical question for the Efficiency Unit was whether changes could be made to this elaborate structure without the whole system going out of control. This fundamental issue was debated throughout the period leading to the final report: could the levels of control be delegated from the central organisation without an overall loss of control?

At this stage the Unit was focusing on the views gathered from people working in the Civil Service and its constituent organisations. First, the common theme: 'I could do this much better if I could run it sensibly' is a familiar grumble within an organisation where the dead hand of head office, the boss or the supervisor stands between staff and what are seen as sensible decisions. But we had heard not the familiar grumble but a cogent and widespread discontent. We had also observed that, in the public service, the continuous flow of money to run organisations was always taken for granted. The private sector plaint about the Civil Service: 'you don't have to earn it' was absolutely justified. For many people, their job was nothing to do with money. Although money was apparently always in short supply for new light bulbs or a coat of paint, they always got paid, even if they didn't work hard. A sensible devolution of responsibility for budgets would encourage the constructive use of money as a resource. Some budgets were already in place in a few organisations, like parts of the Manpower Services Commission. A good budget should show full, man- ageable costs, and provide the information on which questions could be asked about priorities for expenditure and the value obtained for money spent. Only when a manager could make choices to decide what money should be spent and where, would their resources begin to feel real: it would matter that the choices were good ones and could be justified and accepted.

A new system could transform the process of filling in a form and calculating which year the photocopying paper would arrive. A good manager with the money could go out and buy the paper when it was needed, get the right quality and spend some petty cash on photocopies from the corner shop while waiting for supplies. A good fleet manager could do a deal with a supplier for cars at a substantial discount. A good local office manager could give a better public service by having the office open later in the evening at no cost by introducing staggered shifts, with fewer people when the workload was light. Small scale change could add up to a better managed organisation. It was argued that the possibility of introducing even these modest changes would give encouragement and opportunity to people who wanted to achieve improvements. The uniform system made any of these examples almost impossible without a major change in policies from head office or 'the centre'.

THE PROBLEM OF MANAGEMENT

More delegation of budgets and greater flexibility in the rules to give scope for improvement required better managers. The managerial weaknesses in the Civil Service were evident. The scrutiny team had been told, and had seen that top management – Permanent Secretaries and Deputy Secretaries – spent the majority of their time on support for Ministers through the political minefields of developing and legislating government policy. They did not spend their time managing their organisations. One senior manager claimed to spend 90% of his time dealing with Ministers and 10% on his department. It may have been reasonably well run, but it was not without its problems.

The view of the top of the Civil Service was that the criteria for appointment to senior jobs was that people were good at policy and at 'dealing with ministers'. Normally the people chosen had neither the aptitude nor the skills of management. As a consequence of their lack of experience, they evaded management issues, because they felt ill equipped to deal with them. But the organisation of the Civil Service was structured on the assumption that these same senior officials would manage the organisation and were accountable for what happened. The confusion of skills and function could create a vacuum at the top of a Department which was sometimes painfully evident. It was not clear where responsibility lay for management at the apex of major Departments of State. Some Ministers felt responsible for management, some Permanent Secretaries did and, as we had found, in some departments little senior level strategic management was done at all. Indeed, some Permanent Secretaries openly acknowledged that they had neither the skills nor the aptitude for management. This weakness at the top sent a clear message through the organisation – if you want to get on, be good at policy and writing; if you've given up or have been given up you will get a management job.

The financial controls were operated by the Treasury and there were good grounds for sympathy with them in their feeling that no-one but themselves took public expenditure sensibly. But their system of control denied responsibility for what was spent and how it was spent from those making spending decisions. Most people in the Treasury were wearily convinced by bitter experience that managing public expenditure was about 'control' not about management; indeed many of them took the view that management was about control too. A good central system was all that was necessary because the prime objective was the control of public expenditure. The Treasury's dismissive description of the other great Departments of State with wide responsibilities as 'the spending departments' summed up the relationship admirably. It was inevitably negative and confrontational. What was missing from this philosophy was a recognition that the 'spending departments' were carrying out government policy and the Treasury's role in public expenditure was the division of always limited resources to support that role.

We had tried for some years to persuade people in the Treasury that better management would give them more control than the shoddy crisis ridden system they operated at the time. Planned spending focused on outputs and good value would give a better outcome than tight control on inputs and little attention to the results. These arguments did not fall entirely on deaf ears but, as Nigel Lawson has made clear in his book on his years at the Treasury, misunderstandings were rife, not least because the Treasury in the 1980s had a defensive approach which was palpable and unhelpful (Lawson, 1992). At its crudest, some of our respondents had argued, the Treasury did not mind what happened on the ground, even if costs were unnecessarily high, as long as the expenditure plans came within the current planning total. This implied message that cost limitation was more important than value was damaging to large areas of the public sector. Repeated and blunt capital and running cost reductions had damaged the physical infrastructure: decisions were taken for short term expenditure reasons that had disproportionate and unforeseen long term costs.

We would return repeatedly to the control versus management issue throughout the whole of 1987. At this stage as the team contemplated its conclusions the view was that the Treasury would never allow flexibility. There was a conflict of views: the Treasury asserted that there was flexibility, the Departments claimed that when they asked for flexibility it was never granted. The evidence we had gathered was compelling. Across the Civil Service there were large areas with unnecessary rules, poor controls, depressed staff and an ineffective organisation run by people without the skills and aptitude for the job. It made a damning catalogue of reasons for making substantial changes.

CONCLUSIONS

The outcome of the discussions in January 1987 was a decision to take the preliminary views of what had been found to a wider audience. It was important at this stage to test the accuracy of these findings and the reasoning for the conclusions, before moving to any recommendations for changes. The analysis had to be systematic, sustainable and accepted by the people who had contributed to it as a recognisable description of reality. A short paper was produced on 'emerging findings' setting out fairly bluntly the outcome of the first stage of the scrutiny. A further round of meetings was organised to discuss what had emerged so far.

The first informal discussions were with a small group, primarily the Permanent and Deputy Secretaries who had been advising the team throughout the scrutiny. The process was one the Unit had used before. It was essential to ensure that people could recognise and accept the diagnosis. If there was agreement about the nature of the problem, about the factual descriptions of events, structures or the way a system worked, the answers to the problem could then be dealt with in an atmosphere of constructive response. No one could be expected to accept the possibility of solutions – to which there was not necessarily a right or a wrong answer – until there was agreement about the problem.

In this case the response was surprising. The first stage findings which were put to the meetings were:

- the developments in management over the past few years were seen as helpful
- senior civil servants were still selected for their policy skills, not their managerial skills and experience
- Civil Service priorities were set primarily by the short-term demands of politics; improving performance tended to be overlooked
- ministerial overload was now serious
- financial controls still focused on expenditure, not on results
- there was little external pressure for improvements in performance
- the Civil Service was too big to manage as a single organisation

These findings, supported by the evidence that was set out in the paper on 'emerging findings' were, on the whole, accepted by the people we met in the first round meetings. What was perhaps more startling was they were generally not surprised by them; as one Permanent Secretary said: 'that has always been the situation; I can't see what you are going to do about it'. This was the clearest impression left by discussions at this stage – the description was accurate but there was nothing that could be done to change it.

At that stage, like the Permanent Secretary, the team had no clear idea of what to do either. Ideas were beginning to stir as the process moved on to devising final conclusions after the 'emerging findings' meetings. One of my meetings was with the Chief Executive of the Manpower Services Commission (MSC). It was an organisation with a strong chief executive, an independent chairman and a defined function. It had its own constituency, reflected in a Board constructed, in 1970s corporate style, of representatives from the CBI, the TUC and a few 'independents'. I sat in the waiting room at the MSC before the meeting, wondering if this structure, with greater freedom from the grip of the Department of Employment, might be worth thinking about. At that stage it was no more than a thought; I had considered the possibilities of this kind of structure when I had been working on inner cities policy several years earlier. There, a single agency pulling together the work of several Departments had been one possible solution; it now seemed to be again a useful line of thought.

The first discussion meetings took place in January 1987; in February work began on what proved to be a difficult short paper pulling together our findings and conclusions. Everyone tried their hand at it but each draft was more tepid than its predecessor. It took several weeks to produce something useable – a clear signal that the ideas were still not properly sorted out. The debates and discussions and finally the drafting went on throughout February and early March. I had a series of individual meetings with Permanent Secretaries, with heads of major industries and with the Secretary of the Cabinet as our ideas began to develop.

The team had to find ways to make the Civil Service a better managed organisation so that it could make more effective use of its resources and provide an improved public service; a range of possible ways of achieving that were considered. Underlying the ideas was a simple principle which would be set out in the conclusions: an organisation is effective only if it is managed in the way that enables it to perform its function best. It did not make sense to run organisations with different tasks in the same way. And, as far as could be seen, there was no demonstrable benefit in the uniformity which outweighed this fundamental weakness.

The second proposition was that, to be properly managed, organisations need people to run them who have managerial skills. Without those skills, there has to be the safety net of an administrative system. By 'management' was meant people with the capacity to organise the resources of an organisation so that it could meet its objectives as effectively as possible. People, finances, planning, plant and equipment all need attention to arrange the operations of the organisation to optimise the outcomes within the parameters set by policy and objectives.

The third point was, then, even more uncomfortable: no one was really interested in improving the way money was spent or in improving the quality of services. The system – financial and administrative – almost always stopped where the rules stopped, at the inputs of the system. There were few figures which measured what the outcomes were and even fewer people who were interested. A local manager who found a cheaper way of doing something was more likely to be reprimanded for breaking the rules than congratulated for saving money. It was clear that while simple solutions would be best, there were three distinct areas which each had to be considered: the organisations in the public sector where services were provided directly to the public, the centre of Departments where the policy and the distribution of finances were decided, and the Departments at the centre of Whitehall which still controlled the systems that were used throughout the public service.

So far the conclusions were based on the findings of the scrutiny; as the thinking moved on to recommendations, it was important to have no substantive preconceptions about solutions. The outcome in general terms was becoming clear, but the method of achieving that outcome was open. By this stage the team was no longer a small group working on their own. As the work had developed and people began to understand the issues there was support in debate and discussions from many of the most senior members of the Civil Service. Discussions about the right structure were almost continuous but as the final recommendations took shape they were constantly refined to make sure that what was being recommended was a solution, not simply a change of organisation or structure.

5. Administration to management: 'a plan to shift the foundations'

In early 1988 the final shape of the report was still being developed and the nature of the review was altering. The Efficiency Unit and those working with the scrutiny team realised that the scrutiny findings implied that more than modest internal adjustments were needed. The conclusions raised more substantial and serious issues than had been expected. The recommendations could be far reaching and would need careful thought and extensive discussions. The final report is set out in full in the Annex. It is the report sent to the Prime Minister in March 1987 and published by the Efficiency Unit in February 1988.

The team had had to understand what was happening within the Civil Service, it had to draw conclusions from that view and then, and only then, to move to recommendations. In some reviews this staged approach is impossible – the solution is self-evident from the beginning. But if the process of thinking through the analysis is divided from the development of solutions there is a better chance that the problems can be identified and solutions which deal with the problems can be devised. Rushing to solutions can produce favourite hobby horses. It risks gaps in the coverage and a tendency towards theoretical rather than practical solutions.

At this stage, while the study team were working in a small group, their ideas on recommendations needed to be honed down and prepared for discussion with the Prime Minister before the issues were discussed with a wider group. There were three preoccupations. We had to decide the form of the essential changes. Those changes had then to be described in terms that could be quickly understood and implemented effectively. Earlier reports on the Civil Service, with the notable exception of the 1868 Northcote Trevelyan Report, had many recommendations with detailed prescriptions on the actions to be taken. This detail left little opportunity for people to find their own solutions or adapt recommendations to fit specific circumstances, a flexibility which had been recognised as an important part of improving management.

Fulton contained 158 recommendations; the Civil Service managed the recommendations by focusing on 'implementing Fulton' rather than reforming the Civil Service. Avoiding this trap was not easy. Simplicity in recommendations was, in one sense, not difficult. The Efficiency Unit had always adopted as a general principle that an elaborate set of recommendations which could not be remembered by any reasonably interested person would probably not be implemented. A Minister or an official reading a report had to be able to understand the principal points, think about the substance and discuss the conclusions without wading through a detailed document. The minimum of recommendations was essential although inevitably explanation of what each point meant was necessary. It was a difficult balance – more explanation meant that people did less thinking for themselves; less explanation ran the risk of deliberate or innocent misunderstanding.

The most difficult issue that had to be resolved was how to establish the process of implementation so that it would be effective and not die of neglect. Drawing on our experience of what made a successful scrutiny from the work done for our report *Making Things Happen*, we concluded that only someone with real power inside the system could hope to have any impact. Significantly, a Minister acting alone could not achieve the result we wanted. Although the power to decide to change the way the Civil Service worked lay with Ministers, the Prime Minister's view was crucial and the Cabinet collectively had to agree the need for the changes. But to make the system respond and for real changes to happen, the responsibility for implementation had to be carried by the Civil Service.

Furthermore, if the responsibility was to be carried by the Civil Service, the person chosen had to be a senior civil servant. Only a Permanent Secretary would have the weight to achieve substantial changes. The normal reaction of the Civil Service to any radical change would be to have an under secretary or at most a deputy secretary in charge. But in the Whitehall pecking order that could mean giving a Permanent Secretary and a minister the power to change the pace and force of implementation. There was always a risk that short term pressures of the day to day would weaken the drive for implementation. Although oversight should rest with the Prime Minister, a Permanent Secretary working directly for her was the only way to ensure a sustained level of implementation.

This decision to recommend a Permanent Secretary for implementation made the difference between success and failure. As the Efficiency Unit had found with scrutinies, changing the system meant challenging it; the normal processes seldom worked. The 'normal processes' were designed for smooth running. Consensus building had produced the present system, the same working methods would not move the system out of its present rut. The issue for the people working on implementation would be that for success to be achieved they had to behave in a counter cultural way. The Civil Service had a powerful culture. It would not be fair to say success was of no significance, but success had to be on terms comfortable for the people who took the decisions. The group who encouraged us to carry on with a radical report were safe – their careers were behind them and they were in most cases within a few years of retiring. Those who were not so free from pressure were more circumspect; rocking the boat was the ultimate sin. Anyone who was to be responsible for seeing a report like this one implemented had to be prepared to commit that ultimate sin and not to be concerned about the personal consequences.

THE REPORT: AGENCIES TO FOCUS ON THE JOB TO BE DONE

The report took its final form during the first weeks of March 1987, with recommendations sifted into the three main areas: focusing on the job to be done, having the right people and maintaining a pressure for improvement. In each of these areas, different actions would be needed in departments and at the centre. While the changes had to be simple to be comprehensible, they had to be sophisticated to work. By this stage no one was under any illusion but that the report being prepared would be regarded, and indeed was, a proposal for substantial changes in the structure of Government. To assert that Government should be providing services of as high a standard as possible was not new as a principle; the challenge to the gap between rhetoric and reality would be regarded as potentially revolutionary.

The first recommendation had a simple and unequivocal basic purpose: 'greater priority must be given to organising government so that its service delivery operations function effectively'. This recommendation was the essential one. The aim was not to set up agencies; it was to find the most effective way of providing public services. The description of what an 'agency' should be in paragraph 19 of the report is deliberately non-specific:

An agency of this kind may be part of government and the public service, or it may be more effective outside government. We use the term 'agency' not in its technical sense but to describe any executive unit that delivers a service for government.

There was a lengthy debate about the use of the word 'agency'. If it were to acquire a capital 'A' much of the flexibility of the main purpose would be lost. Bureaucracies reach for organisational solutions because they can be structured, organised, and reduced to a set of rules and patterns. It was a risk that had to be taken to try to shift the focus from policy to services, but it was a source of constant misunderstanding.

The words were chosen to reflect the driving principle: 'to describe any unit that delivers a service for government'. One could argue it should have been spelt out more clearly. The point could have been put at greater length (always easier than brevity) but how much impact that would have had on the management of the agencies it is difficult to say. The habit of making assumptions about what is expected, and to follow that assumption, is powerful in a large organisation; it is also often much easier than to go back to first principles and think out the best solution even when encouraged to do so.

THE FRAMEWORK AGREEMENT

At the heart of the new relationship between Minister and officials in the agencies would be a 'framework agreement'. The concept was defined as precisely as possible:

> these units need to be given a well defined framework in which to operate, which sets out the policy, the budget, specific targets and the results to be achieved ... the management of the agency must be held rigorously to account by their department for the results they achieve.

This gap was the most glaring we had observed in Whitehall management. For many areas the only statement of objectives and expenditure was the annual 'spending round' with the Treasury, focused on how much money would be spent. Policy was often handled by someone else who was not involved directly in negotiations with the Treasury. It was theoretically possible for policy to be developed in isolation from the financial constraints and for the two to be brought together only when the negotiations were concluded. Few Departments were as badly organised as that at the top, but at more junior levels the financial implications of policy were seldom considered in detail.

It was clear from our research that the task of defining the operational consequences of policy would be a difficult function for the Civil Service; the two skills of policy and management had to be used together to produce a coherent solution. The setting of effective targets and goals involved an understanding of how the people and the organisation would respond to specific pressures; the difficult or uncomfortable consequences of inadequate funding, or confused policy ideas had to be brought out into the open and resolved rather than ignored. Establishing the links between policy and operations, so that operational instructions were clear, was a difficult and demanding task which required a combination of skills which few people in the Civil Service possessed. Experience since the 1980s of the use of targets in Whitehall has demonstrated how damaging badly conceived targets can be in the hands of incompetent resource managers.

The first change was in the concept of a 'framework'. Hitherto there had been financial agreements with the Treasury about money and policy. The precise nature of what the money would buy had become more refined during the 1980s but was still shrouded in mystery from most people engaged in operations. There were careful procedures linking finance and numbers of people, and linking the numbers of people to functions. In some relatively rare cases the numbers of people were linked to a calculation of the processes carried out. But it was unusual for the numbers and the money to be linked to any kind of output or output measure.

The Next Steps framework was designed to force a Department to be specific in operational and outcome terms about what their policy position meant. For many agencies drawing up a framework was to be a difficult and long drawn out process. The answer to 'what does the Minister want to happen?' was often different from the answer to 'what does the Minister want?'. In a framework it was to be necessary to be specific about relationships, priorities and goals. For many institutions these specifics did not exist.

The tradition in many Departments had been a simple administrative function which translated policy into 'instructions' which were written – and printed – as though they were semi legal instruments rather than management documents. Some organisations were improving. The Manpower Services Commission (MSC) had clear objectives and goals. Its structure meant that the Department of Employment had to give consent to the objectives which the MSC set for itself. The new frameworks were to be the responsibility of the Department and the Agency working together to agree how to balance Ministerial policy, resources and operational reality. The formal agreement had to be specific about outcomes and concluded before work began.

The new framework documents were to be public. The issue of open government had been perennial long before 1986 and the team were well aware that the celebrated Official Secrets Act cases had not encouraged the Government to greater openness. Technically the colour of my office carpet (dark blue) was still an 'official secret'. The precise managerial requirements of the huge Benefit Service were of greater potential embarrassment to the government than my office decoration.

In making scrutiny recommendations there was a long established principle that a scrutiny provided an opportunity to think and recommend radical action which might not return for another ten years. Most of the recommendations of this report flowed naturally from the analysis behind the conclusions. The recommendation that the new framework documents should be public was the outcome of a discussion within the unit at a late stage. As the institutions were part of the public sector the basic management agreements which directed their work should, in principle, be public; there would be sensitivity about publication, but openness was sensible and logical and we took the view that agency framework documents should be generally available. It was always possible that, whatever happened to our report, such a suggestion might be removed or overturned, but if openness was not recommended, in the climate then current, it would have never happened.

The final paragraphs of the first recommendation dealt with the implications for Departments and Ministers. The report said that the concept of a 'framework document':

> applies therefore to the relationship with any organisation which is providing services for which the Department carries some responsibility, whether agency, nationalised industry, local authority or public body although the detail and the structure will vary with the precise relationship and the job that has to be done.

The section continues:

> the Department's task is to set a framework, tailored to the job to be done which specifies policies, objectives, the results required and the resources available . . . Ministers and civil servants must then stand back from operational details and demonstrate their confidence in the competence of their managers and the robustness of their framework by leaving managers free to manage.

The report also pointed out that while these changes were particularly important for the service delivery areas, the same concepts applied to policy and programme areas: 'precision about the results required and the resources involved is crucial when large programme resources are at stake.'

POLITICALLY SENSITIVE ISSUES

One area of repeated discussion was the handling of 'politically sensitive issues'. There are many occasions when a Minister, or a senior official might judge that a proposed course of action would not be supported by the government party, or by expert views, or that the proposal did not reflect what the government intended. There can be other less dignified pressures – from noisy pressure groups, from the media or personal interest; and there can be the instinctive reaction of a Minister who feels that he or she could not defend a proposal or its consequences in the House of Commons, or that the Government Whips are worried that they might not carry a vote. After much debate the report said that the framework: 'must also specify how politically sensitive issues are to be dealt with and the extent of the delegated authority of management'. It went on to say: 'a crucial element in the relationship (between the Minister, the Permanent Secretary and the agency) would be a formal understanding with Ministers about the handling of sensitive issues and the lines of accountability in a crisis'.

Few grasped the significance of this statement. Government business, unlike much of the private sector, is properly and inevitably bound up with politics, accountability and publicity. A minor issue can be blown up out of all proportion because it is linked to a political issue, a weak or strong minister, or simply a bit of bad administration. Carefully laid plans can be wrecked because the Minister is too preoccupied with something else to take the decision in time, or has misunderstood the argument and refuses to agree, or even when a minister entirely agrees that the sensible solution is the one put forward but refuses to accept it for political reasons.

To an operational organisation an unforeseen decision, however understandable, can be disastrous. Investment decisions are delayed and escalate in cost, staff are outraged when they hear of a major change affecting them on the radio going home, costs are cut without consultation or the appointment of the boss is so delayed that the press announcement is out before the deputy is told. Potential trouble spots – clashes of policy, difficult political decisions and the consequences of sudden budget reductions – are better handled if discussed before the trouble starts. The framework document provided an opportunity for spelling out a basis for dealing with difficult issues before they arise: the role of the Minister, the role of the chief executive, the way decisions might be taken, the impact of external factors on the achievement of targets and the availability of resources.

ACCOUNTABILITY

This part of the debate led into the issue of accountability. At this stage the team aimed at setting out the practical issues of the accountability of Ministers and senior officials to Parliament: how to balance genuine personal responsibility for an agency with the traditional route of ministerial accountability to Parliament. In much of the centrally managed Civil Service lip service was paid to full ministerial accountability to Parliament. Technically the Minister was and was properly responsible to Parliament for everything that happened. The classic illustration of the scope of ministerial accountability, quoted repeatedly, was taken from 1948 when the National Health Service was established. Aneurin Bevan, the Minister of Health had illustrated the scale of his new responsibilities by claiming to hear in Whitehall every dropped bedpan in the new NHS. The Secretary of

State for Health was in theory as responsible for the bedpan in the 1980s as Bevan had been in the 1940s.

The reality was different and those involved knew it. No Secretary of State accepted that kind of detailed responsibility. The limits of Ministers' grasp over what happened in their Departments always depended on their own interest in the Department and on information from civil servants to explain what was happening. Accountability in practice meant facing the House of Commons with an explanation. It seldom meant that a Minister resigned. But the debate about accountability assumed that the Ministers knew or should know what was happening anywhere in their area of responsibility. Because this was so unreal an assumption, the debate was conducted on a basis completely divorced from what happened in practice. It was so important to open up this issue that an annex on the question of accountability was added to the report. With contributions from the Cabinet Office to make sure the position was reflected accurately, the annex was designed as an unambiguous statement of the technical position on accountability for agencies. It is unexciting but perfectly comprehensive as a statement of the present position.

Barry Winetrobe discussed the annex in *Parliament and Executive Agencies* (1995). He argued that the Report: 'appeared to suggest that the Efficiency Unit considered parliamentary accountability a disbenefit in the administrative process'. There is no evidence for this assertion in the wording of the report. The proposals we put forward, which extended rather than diminished accountability to Parliament, followed existing patterns of delegated authority with which there was by then considerable experience. Both officials and academics have been concerned about the accountability of agencies. The annex to the report did discuss the argument that agencies represented a new departure. In 1987 there were both government bodies with delegated powers and Departments who had delegated much of their casework. While Ministers would answer to the Commons on major issues, the relevant select committee would have access to more information about the work of the agency and to the senior executives for cross examination.

Any debate about the Constitution position in the United Kingdom is complicated, especially for those used to a more structured constitution. One could argue that the Constitution can be whatever the government of the day wants it to be within reason. The crucial determinant of the outcome is how the House of Commons exercises its rights and keeps the principle of parliamentary accountability alive. How Parliament uses its powers is almost as important as what those powers are, in the swirling waters of British constitutional practice. Even though the report was designed without detailed prescriptions for implementation, careful and specific recommendations were included on the areas likely to be tricky. Accountability was the first; paragraph 23 of the report said:

> We believe that it is possible for Parliament, through Ministers, to regard managers as directly responsible for operational matters and that there are precedents for this and precisely defined ways in which it can be handled. If the management in the Civil Service is truly to be improved this aspect cannot be ignored.

Annex A explained the details; there were already (in 1987) examples of officials and bodies with independent or delegated authority within major Departments answering directly to Parliament through the select committees. This form of accountability worked well, and continues to do so. It ensures that the committees of the House of Commons can hear from and cross-examine the people directly responsible and not only those who have to rely heavily on detailed briefing. No one who has been in the committee corridor before a Public Accounts Committee (PAC) hearing can doubt that most of the Permanent Secretaries waiting to be questioned by the Committee feel extremely accountable. Even the most formidable will be standing, clutching his or her red folder, inches thick with detailed briefing, wondering whether the Private Office have covered everything which might be raised. In the mid-1980s not knowing the answer was an admission of defeat. Most of them did not know the answer. Their success or failure would depend on the quality of their briefing, not on their personal knowledge of the area for which they were constitutionally responsible. Paragraph 2 of the annex argues that: 'if the concept of agencies . . . is to succeed, some extension of this pattern of accountability is likely to be necessary . . . acceptance of individual responsibility for performance cannot be expected if repeated Ministerial intervention is there as a ready-made excuse'.

The annex continues 'there is nothing new in the suggestion that Ministers should not be held answerable for many day-to-day decisions involving the public and public services'. The examples are well known: individual cases where there is a risk of political interference, management functions in Customs and Excise, quasi judicial or regulatory functions, the Office of Fair Trading, the nationalised industries. The annex pointed out there were already a range of structures to cover these functions: non ministerial boards, non departmental public bodies, internal services bodies, existing agencies within departments, statutory tribunals. The annex explained the way in which statutes specified the accountability and suggested that legislation might be necessary: 'Where it is necessary to change the arrangements for formal accountability for operations currently carried out within departments, legislation (normally primary legislation) would generally be required.' It went on to say: 'Provided that the objective of better management is clearly explained and understood, and that an appropriate form of accountability is retained, the government should be able to present such proposals in a positive light.'

The question of the Accounting Officer, a perennial issue, was tackled. The 'accounting officer' was the official cornerstone of the system of financial accountability. He or she was responsible to Parliament for the legality and propriety of expenditure within a defined area. Traditionally the Accounting Officer is the Permanent Secretary of a Department of State; he or she and not the Minister is technically responsible to Parliament for all expenditure within that Department. Over the years that responsibility had been extended from Permanent Secretaries to include the heads of large organisations carrying responsibility for large blocks of expenditure. The Treasury was responsible for nominating accounting officers. Before the introduction of agencies there were already 76 accounting officers of whom 18 were the most senior permanent secretaries. The report suggested that chief executives should become accounting officers, but 'the modification of accountability we propose should not immediately affect accountability to the PAC'.

It was suggested, as now happens, that the presence of the agency manager would widen the range of questions that could be answered in a PAC hearing and thus improve, not reduce effective public accountability.

The annex on accountability looked at one of the important issues of the report – ministerial overload. It had been abundantly clear in our discussions that most Ministers were grossly overloaded. Their time was badly allocated, delegation was poorly organised within some Ministerial teams. Many of them felt the use of their time was out of control. Ministers said far too many detailed and absurd issues were going to them for discussion and decision, driven either by inadequate delegation or over-sensitivity to local political pressures. Most Ministers appeared to feel they were unable to do anything to control the pressure of work on them.

The annex suggested that the current practice that tax issues went to local tax offices and social security issues went to local social security offices should be extended to other agencies. In both these cases the system had been established by the Minister responsible and included safeguards for reference of any politically sensitive issue to Ministers. The annex pointed out that targets for replying to letters could be set in the framework document and that replies should be received more rapidly than under the current system.

The normal system in most Departments involved sending the papers from the Ministerial office to the local manager for the substance of a reply, the review of the draft reply by 'head office' and then a further review and redrafting by a junior official in the 'policy branch'. The letter would then proceed through a more senior official to the Minister's office where it was retyped. It would be signed by an exhausted junior minister on a train or in the middle of the night or during a debate in the Commons as one among a pile of perhaps thirty or forty letters to be signed before he or she reached the office the following day. The function of the Minister and head office was primarily as a retyping post box, rather than any serious check other than for minor administrative or political inconveniences.

The issue of accountability has proved to be recurrent. The point of the Annex to the report was to explore the implications of the report for the current arrangements for accountability. The annex demonstrated there was little revolutionary in the proposals. The team was using existing experience in the Civil Service in operating practical arrangements for accountability and applying it to the wider canvas of the Civil Service as a whole. Part of the problem may well have been that 'existing experience in the civil service' was little known outside it, so that what were relatively straightforward proposals appeared far more dramatic than they really were.

THE SKILLS OF THE SENIOR CIVIL SERVICE

The other recommendations of the report were consequential on the main recommendation. It had been seen over and over again that the rhetoric and the practice of developing skills did not match. Although lip service had been paid to training and management experience, senior officials were not equipped for the tasks they had to perform.

The real difficulty lay with the 'golden layer' at the top. They were highly intelligent, and they could survive on their wits and their experience with little detailed technical grasp of what the management of a major area of policy or operations might involve. The penultimate job to being a Permanent Secretary was to be a Deputy Secretary, in most cases the principal specialised adviser to a senior minister in his or her field. There would be some personnel responsibilities, and normally a large proportion of the Department's budget to sign off. The better Deputy Secretaries would cope with their resource management functions, but the important fact of life was the absolute principle that further promotion would depend on how they got on with the Minister and the other Permanent Secretaries. Management skills did not matter; they were not part of the test to be applied in deciding promotion. If someone was going to be a Permanent Secretary, it was highly unlikely they would be in a Deputy Secretary's job with much management content in it. At Deputy Secretary level being given serious management responsibilities was the Whitehall equivalent of the Black Spot.

The second recommendation emphasised that the establishment of agencies would depend 'critically on the people working in Departments and the skills they bring to the task'. Training and experience were essential: 'the staff will then be in a position to develop and interpret government policy and manage the agencies in a way that can maximise results'. This section contained an important discussion of the two functions the report identified – policy and management. After discussing the necessary training for management roles the report went on to say:

> It is most important that there should not be two classes of people in Departments – those in agencies and those at the centre. The aim must be to have senior managers who at more junior levels have had substantial experience of the skills and practical reality of management . . . one of the benefits that will come as senior managers in Departments obtain greater experience of management is that the policy areas of Departments will also become better managed.

This is another point that has been largely ignored in the debate about policy and management. Senior managers, we argued, had to understand both management and policy to carry out their functions. There was not an absolute division between those doing policy and those engaged in operations. They were different functions and senior managers needed the skills and experience of both if the implementation of policy was to be effective. The discussion of framework documents reiterates this point in paragraph 28: 'to do it (setting a framework) successfully requires a balanced expertise in policy, the political environment and service delivery which too few civil servants possess at present'. It went on to say: 'operational effectiveness and clarity need to be given a higher priority in the interpretation of policy objectives and the thinking of Ministers'.

IMPLEMENTATION

The final recommendation was about implementation – the need for a constant and sustained pressure for improvement. The responsibility, said the report:

> inevitably rests with the Prime Minister and the Head of the Civil Service. They need the commitment of Ministers and of Permanent Secretaries to ensure that the changes are pursued with urgency and are not sacrificed to other priorities. The pressure for change from within the Government must also be sustained by understanding and support from Parliament for the long term benefits which are being sought. (Paragraph 38)

The role of the Civil Service was fundamental:

> the Civil Service must own the changes; it must not feel that ill-considered change is being thrust upon it. Ministers must feel confident that they can influence political aspect of the changes and that one of the benefits will be their being able to concentrate more on their main political task. (Paragraph 39)

The role of the official in charge of the changes was crucial: 'our recommendations are fundamental and radical. They will only be introduced successfully if there is an extremely senior official who has unequivocal personal responsibility for achieving the change.' We recommended that a Permanent Secretary as 'project manager' should be appointed and be responsible to the Head of the Civil Service and the Prime Minister.

The final section of the report dealt with what the team then called 'the Next Steps'. In this section the path to full implementation was set out. The aim should be: 'to establish a quite different way of conducting the business of government . . . both departments and their agencies should have a more open and simplified structure'. As a target for the benefits of the changes we suggested five per cent of running costs and 'an immense opportunity to go for substantial improvement in outputs, with better delivery of services and reduced delays as an alternative to savings.'

For Ministers the gain should be both resolution about their role in management and that while: 'inevitably and rightly it is open to a Minister to get involved in any part of his or her Department's business . . . In a well managed Department this should normally only be necessary by exception'.

COMPLETING THE STRUCTURE OF THE REPORT

The report itself was deliberately designed to be short and simple. The Unit was influenced by the Northcote Trevelyan Report whose double columns covered only 12 pages and was sensibly as concerned with the effectiveness of the writing rooms as with the principles of public administration.

We were conscious that what we were proposing was that the era of faint acceptance of reform should come to an end; the Government should be far more overtly committed to the reform of government. There should be no ambiguity about the strength of the Government's support; the lack of an overt drive for reform was allowing even the existing systems to idle rather than work effectively.

We had four areas which had to be covered in detail: an explanation of what we had found, the conclusions we had drawn, our recommendations about the next stage and finally, and most importantly, what we considered the results should be. The need to cover accountability was the outcome of much debate which resulted in the separate Annex A. This subject caused much head shaking and even more muddled thinking and emotional reaction. A fuller statement of what we all considered the position to be seemed more effective than cramming the issues into a truncated paragraph in the main report.

The other main annex, Annex B, which set out the detailed findings of the scrutiny, was more of a curiosity. We had received a great deal of evidence from many people, and while that had to be reduced down to two or three pages in the final report we were anxious to record the main themes and views we had come across. Many were deeply critical of the Civil Service and Ministers. What is interesting from a position twenty years on is how mild many of the criticisms now seem. At the time we were genuinely concerned about publishing them and were surprised that no attempt was made to remove the annex from the published report. It was interesting to see subsequently that attention concentrated on the detail of what might happen – the recommendations – rather than on the criticism of what had happened. At no stage was there any serious argument with our findings nor was there any attempt to prevent them becoming public, an indication of the sense of personal responsibility of the senior Civil Service: no one felt at risk from the criticism.

The report itself was completed and presented to the Prime Minister in March 1987 shortly before the April General Election. We would not have been surprised to have seen no more of it. A pre-election week is no time to contemplate unsettling proposals to shake up the Civil Service or indeed to feel enthusiastic about an analysis which is blunt about failures. The timing of the report meant that any further action had to wait until the outcome of the election.

6. The report: discussion and decisions

The 1987 election was over and the Conservative Government was returned to power. The Unit had taken precautionary measures in case a Labour Government was elected. Unofficial discussions with the Labour Party had 'indicated' that Labour would want to continue the line on public service management taken by the previous administration. I had had a discussion with someone from the Leader of the Opposition's office. I described what we were thinking about and what the Efficiency Unit was doing, without going into the details of the report. His view was that the Labour Party knew 'something had to be done about the way the Government was run', but had no clear policy. They felt the changes were broadly right but could say little because of the closeness of their relations with the Civil Service Unions. However, careful insurance proved unnecessary. The new administration returned to its old in-trays, the Civil Service returned to work after the relaxing interlude provided by a general election. Unused briefing material put together for an 'incoming administration' was put aside and familiar issues reappeared.

DISCUSSIONS: THE SENIOR OFFICIALS

One of these issues was the report of the Efficiency Unit Scrutiny. Now titled *Improving Management in Government: the Next Steps*, it came surprisingly rapidly to the top of the Prime Minister's pile. The discussion to persuade senior officials and ministers had to start. The Prime Minister was clear she would only move forward with her colleagues; they were clear they could move only with the support of Permanent Secretaries. The evidence we had gathered on the way things worked in the Government suggested they were right.

The most important figure was the Cabinet Secretary, Robert Armstrong, who had been involved throughout the preparation of the report and discussion of the outcome. He was not only an ally and an adviser but made clear to his colleagues that the recommendations of the report had his full support. He had a reputation as the most mandarin of mandarins and appeared to enjoy playing up to the role in manner as well as appearance. To meet him strolling across the park in formal dress to a garden party at Buckingham Palace was to feel that the familiar urbane Establishment was comfortably in control.

The Unit now had to persuade the crucial groups that what the report said was serious and practical. The first move was a discussion at the 'Wednesday morning meeting' – the regular weekly meetings of all Permanent Secretaries in the main committee room of the Cabinet Office. Most Ministers were convinced that this meeting was where government business was fixed; if so, it was all done by nod and wink and in the corridor. It was normally a rapid business meeting, over in an hour, and its principal purpose was to see that everyone there was informed of what was going on.

Before the Cabinet Office building had to take in so many Ministers in the 1990s, the Wednesday morning meeting was held in the old Conference Room C on the first floor of the Cabinet Office. The long table was surrounded by up to 25 Permanent Secretaries. The Cabinet Secretary sat with his back to the window in the centre of the table – much more difficult to read his expression in that position – and his colleagues ranged round him. They sat in the same seats each week, as though chair and position were part of their hard-won eminence. At least they were all on first name terms; they did not adopt the depressing custom of Ministers who, although they had known each other for decades, solemnly used their official titles at cabinet committee meetings.

The Next Steps Report took a little more time than usual, but was introduced by the Cabinet Secretary simply as a piece of business which Permanent Secretaries would want to know about. The issue for the meeting was how the report should be handled rather than the substance of it. Even a 'handling' discussion needed careful planning. The presentation of the report was not built up into a major event but was a record of the work of the team and of its report. Everyone involved in those meetings needed time to digest the report, to come to a decision about their personal views on the recommendations and the implications for their organisations. If they agreed with the report they had to give some thought to the tactics of implementation. Each meeting of Permanent Secretaries that discussed the issues – the report went to several meetings – had to be planned before hand and as many people as possible talked to face to face or on the telephone to make sure that misunderstandings were minimised. I spent a lot of time explaining and discussing our recommendations.

The time spent on preparation was essential. The Unit had been working on the propositions in the report for months and discussing and refining the ideas with their advisers for almost as long. As Robert Armstrong remarked, we had all had some time to become used to the ideas and their implications; we could not expect the people who had to take the final decisions to take less time in coming to conclusions.

DISCUSSIONS: MINISTERS

Once the Permanent Secretaries had had time to look at the report, the next step was for Ministers to have an opportunity to discuss what was proposed. The Permanent Secretaries did not take a decision – they advised their Ministers on how they might respond. The normal and correct Permanent Secretary response was: 'I can (or cannot) in all honesty advise my Minister to adopt this proposition'. The negative form meant: 'I am utterly opposed to what has been suggested and will do all I can to stop it'. Many an innocent outsider to Whitehall has been misled by the code. There was a considerable amount of explanation and discussion, a few people were opposed to the report from the beginning of the discussions but the majority were in favour of continuing the debate, although with varying degrees of enthusiasm. This outcome was the most positive we could have hoped for. It meant the issues had been recognised as important and had not been either brushed aside or rejected.

The next move was to put the arguments and the recommendations to a meeting of Ministers which would be arranged by the Prime Minister's Office. An informal meeting of Ministers was convened; it was planned as an opportunity for discussion rather than for taking decisions. Ministers should have as long as Permanent Secretaries to consider the proposals. The preparations for the meeting, the circulation of the papers and briefing of the Minister by their officials would give each Permanent Secretary an opportunity to talk through the implications of the report and its recommendations. Robin Ibbs and I were ushered into the Cabinet Room with the Ministers and unobtrusively moved, like good officials, to the outer ring of chairs against the wall. We were firmly waved by the Prime Minister to the chairs opposite her at the cabinet table; this position could have been either for a public grilling or as a sign of support. I was far from clear at that stage which it was to be.

The rest of the cabinet gathered round. We explained what we had done and outlined the proposals in the report. Robin Ibbs made a short presentation of the main findings, our conclusions and recommendations. Each person at the meeting gave their views, varying from enthusiastic to outright opposition. Although he was not a minister with a big department even the Lord President, Willie Whitelaw joined in. I had had a discussion with him the day before and explained what it was all about. He produced some magisterial words of support: 'valuable way forward, good time to make some real progress'. At the end of his remarks he said in a mutter quite audible to most of the room: 'I hope that was what that young woman told me to say'.

The outcome was for 'possible pilot agencies' to be 'worked up' during the summer months so that Ministers and their officials could see how the proposition might work in practice. This approach was sensible; I have no doubt it was designed by some as a delaying tactic but for us it meant continued legitimacy – the report had not been rejected out of hand. The detailed work on what an agency might look like, and what a framework document might include would give us an opportunity to take our ideas forward into some concrete proposals, now with authorised help from our colleagues in Whitehall.

THE PILOT AGENCIES

Permanent Secretaries were asked for suggestions for pilot agencies. After considerable skirmishing, with some proposals rejected by the Treasury on constitutional grounds and others by us on the grounds they were too small, we eventually agreed on twelve, ranging from the big Employment Services department with some 35,000 staff to the Teachers Pension office with 400 staff, and the Queen Elizabeth II (QEII) Conference Centre as an obvious example of a Civil Service organisation operating in a commercial environment. These 'pilots' were eventually to form the nucleus of the 'first wave' agencies a year later.

The plan was for the Efficiency Unit, the Treasury and a team from the potential agency to produce an outline as close as possible to a draft framework document. It was to conform to the proposals of the report, detailing the structure of the agency and the flexibility to be given to management. We plunged into a relentless tide of meetings, explaining, discussing and arguing, first about the principles of agencies and then the details of what a framework document might look like. The detailed work we had done before April 1987 stood the Efficiency Unit in good stead. The concept of the 'executive unit' proved a robust one; it was possible to identify a function that was executive rather than policy. The teachers' pension organisation and the Queen Elizabeth II Conference Centre were straightforward but in other cases, of which the Employment Service was the prime example, the dividing line was not simple.

The vast bulk of Employment Service activity was executive. It was a large organisation carrying out the policy for which objectives and targets could be set; there needed to be close working between the Department of Employment and the senior levels of the potential agency. The larger and more complex an organisation and its services were, the more difficult it was to achieve clarity about the operational implications of policy and all the more important to get it right. A theoretical analysis which is tidy, explicable and can be modelled is often of little use as a practical basis for managing an organisation.

We observed with concern that people became obsessed by the search for a clear dividing line in specific jobs and organisations. Functions might be distinct but not who did them or where. Thus the Employment Service was responsible for providing an employment service, and for at least 90% of the organisation and its staff this was their principal activity. At the more senior levels the development of policy and the implications for operational issues had to be handled jointly while recognising that there needed to be different skills and responsibilities.

A decision about the policy for the Employment Service had to take into account the operational consequences of that decision, and to involve both the officials of the Department of Employment and the officials of the Employment Service. The lack of clarity about who was responsible for taking the decision had led to much confusion in the past. An artificial distinction based on 'the division between policy and management' is not helpful in establishing clear lines of responsibility and accountability. What is needed is normally a sensible practical solution based on each case.

The dangers of specifying an organisational solution were already evident. Our recommendation that what was important was to find the best organisation for the job to be done could be quickly lost when nervous officials became anxious about doing what was expected of them. At this preliminary stage the signals about what was expected of officials were often ambiguous. The meetings were trying to establish, within each organisation, a level at which someone could be held to be responsible for a set of executive objectives to be achieved by a definable part of that institution. If there was a genuine intermingling of policy and management, the institution might well need another solution, not an executive agency. These issues had in theory already been considered in selecting the agencies to be pilots, although the grasp of those directly concerned on this point was often shaky at the start.

As the process of testing the ideas in the report continued, there were debates about the principles of reform as well as the specific 'pilot' examples. The Treasury slowly realised that the proposals they had regarded fairly lightheartedly earlier in the year were gaining both substance and supporters as the process of developing pilot agencies gathered momentum. We had sensible and constructive discussions around the big table in the Efficiency Unit's offices, looking at the changes for each organisation if it were to become an agency. We were sometimes able to iron out long standing differences of opinions between the departments and the Treasury; we could in some cases demonstrate that long term difficulties were based on assumptions of what Treasury thinking would be if they were asked, rather than a result of a specific Treasury rule or intervention. This problem was a constant in the uneasy relationship between the

Treasury and the 'spending' or operational ministries. Relationships could be tetchy and distant and ideas and assumptions developed about 'what the Treasury wants', which did not recognise where the Treasury had changed policy or developed their thinking. The Treasury was moving, in some cases quite swiftly, to dismantle the more absurd restraints but they were singularly poor at understanding how they were seen in departments. It was, and to some extent remains, a recipe for misunderstanding and unease.

In one case, after a difficult and uncomfortable two hour meeting, it was agreed that nothing, at the present time, stood in the way of setting up a small, single operation as an agency – the QEII Conference Centre. As far as the Department and the Treasury were concerned, it could be an 'agency' immediately. It was almost comic to see defences crumbling as a senior manager who had claimed he faced huge obstacles to effective management and making good financial returns suddenly realised he had been given complete freedom to go ahead and negotiate a deal to remove his perceived problems. The reality was not always as comfortable as it had seemed when the flexibility he needed had appeared impossible.

It was not easy for anyone. To be faced with a request to imagine an organisation operating with a different set of rules was difficult, even when for years the organisation had complained about the damaging effect of the pressure on them. However, not many achieved the level of response of one official whose sole request for greater flexibility for his organisation was the ability to pay consultants up to £35 000 before going to the Treasury for approval. He was dumbfounded when he was asked by the Treasury why he should go to the Treasury at all on such a trivial issue – and what about freedom to devise his own pay scales for his staff? As the work continued the effect of thinking through the details of how agencies might work helped to develop and refine the possibilities of greater managerial flexibility.

However, overnight in mid-August, the Treasury suddenly withdrew co-operation, the first serious sign of the battles that were to follow. It was also an indication that our proposals were beginning to be taken more seriously. The relaxed discussions, resolving difficulties and sorting out the outstanding issues were at an end. The Treasury had apparently decided that the direction our work was taking was too dangerous to the Treasury. We had to continue with the Treasury 'represented' but not contributing other than informally to the discussions.

Despite the negative stance of the Treasury, the work on pilot agencies was completed in the autumn and a meeting of ministers approved the concept of the report. There was more than one agenda around. Acceptance of the report on Improving Government did not mean a sudden conversion by Permanent Secretaries, or their Ministers, to the principles of better management. Some were genuinely convinced what we were proposing was a sensible way forward. But underlying formal agreement was a realisation by many Permanent Secretaries that this change would alter the Treasury's increasingly detailed control of everything done inside the 'spending Departments'.

The Treasury were right to defend their point of view, although their withdrawal of co-operation in August weakened their bargaining position. The battle was about the way in which spending was controlled. Neither the Treasury nor most Departments were interested in the finer points of better delegation or clarity of management responsibility or indeed the quality of service provided by the Government. Most Departments simply wanted to reduce interference from the Treasury and considered that accepting agencies would be a way of achieving a diminution in detailed Treasury control. The Treasury did not want to give up any of their hard won power. In this war we knew that we were simply catalysts. We had provided for a change in management which was regarded as an opportunity to alter the way in which Treasury control was exercised. For us, this second agenda – the battle between the Treasury and the spending Departments – strengthened our own position. We were, and remained, convinced that the control of public expenditure would be strengthened not weakened by our proposals; in the longer term the Treasury as well as the rest of Whitehall and the tax-payer would benefit.

DECISIONS: THE LONG WRANGLE

For the Government as a whole the position was very difficult. No one, least of all the Prime Minister, would embark on a major reform without the support, however grudging, of the Treasury; this was not an issue where rank was relevant. The Treasury, in the shape of its Permanent Secretary had to be prepared to accept what was finally agreed. The main decision to accept the report was taken by a meeting of Ministers in the autumn and the debate shifted to the difficult area of the detail. The Ministerial meeting reviewed the twelve 'pilot agencies' and agreed that work should then move on to how the report should be implemented. This decision initiated four months of continual negotiation on the details of what an agency would look like, the staffing, the formal agreements, the funding and the process of implementation.

We had to be alert to every shift and nuance of what was suggested. There were lengthy debates about the role of the chief executive, their terms and conditions of employment, or the role of accounting officers – could chief executives be accounting officers, what exactly should the words say in the framework document, what areas should it cover? Everything was hammered out at Permanent and Deputy Secretary level in long, stormy and sometimes acrimonious meetings and then reported at the Wednesday morning meetings.

We had spent a great deal of time with Permanent Secretaries but relatively less time with the Deputy Secretaries. Our main channel of communication was through the Directors of Establishment meetings – the next level down in the Whitehall hierarchy from the Wednesday morning meeting – to which a representative of the Efficiency Unit went regularly to discuss progress. In theory this group of personnel and finance managers from the whole of central Government acted as a communication channel to their Departments on major issues. Our reception was invariably sceptical, if not openly hostile. Our information sources remained effective; we knew that people returned from these meetings and briefed their staff that the Efficiency Unit was bound to fail, the Treasury was opposed and no one should expect any changes. This approach continued in several big Departments right up to the announcements in February 1988 of the first pilot agencies. All we could do was continue to work on the substance of the proposals and listen to our many supporters as well as our detractors.

During the autumn and winter of 1987 the process gathered momentum. The outcome of the work on the pilot agencies was encouraging; we had established that one of the twelve, the Conference Centre, could be an agency immediately. There were no further flexibilities necessary for it to function as a fully fledged agency – all it needed was a good framework document. The opposition of the Treasury grew as the process of final decision grew closer. It developed into a classic old style battle. First, there had been the refusal to co-operate during the first phase of work in August 1987 aimed at destroying the planning for the autumn Ministerial meeting. Then there was opposition, in all the meetings at every level, to work on the detail throughout the last quarter of 1987. There were battles at each stage of drafting the final documents; half sentences were fought over as if the Cabinet Office conference rooms were the Western Desert. As we had expected, one final attack was to try to downgrade the Permanent Secretary status of the project manager. We had been right to regard that as of crucial importance. A Deputy Secretary could have been marginalised with ease; a Permanent Secretary would be far more difficult to ignore.

We were in unusual territory. The Head of the Civil Service was openly supporting the report's recommendations as were most of his senior colleagues. The Prime Minister, while cautiously waiting for the outcome, had agreed to the discussions continuing, although her private office were known to be opposed to the report. Ministers were divided and many of them simply not interested. The Treasury were fighting a determined battle against the report and its recommendations. It was an indication of how powerful they were that they came so close to winning. It would have been difficult for the Prime Minister to take a decision on such a sensitive issue to which the Treasury appeared to attach so much importance against their strong advice.

Another change affected the situation. Sir Robert Armstrong was due to retire at the end of 1987. He had defended the report since its first appearance and cheerfully out manoeuvred the Treasury. His successor was to be Robin Butler, who had been Second Permanent Secretary in the Treasury. The timing was crucial. Could the report be accepted before Robert Armstrong retired leaving his successor with the decisions taken and the responsibility of implementation or would it be left over to the new year and the tender mercies of a solidly Treasury team? Robin Butler had already left the Treasury and was preparing for his new role in the Cabinet Office. He was in a difficult position. Robert Armstrong's message to the Prime Minister on New Year's Eve 1987 was advice that the changes in the report were essential if the Civil Service was to modernise.

Although even the Whitehall antennae failed to pick up the detail, a deal was done. The report would be accepted, a project manager appointed but, said the gossip, the Treasury would still sabotage the detail. When the decision had moved against the Treasury, the attack moved to personal attacks on the Efficiency Unit through the press. I was banned from speaking to journalists but the Treasury continued their assault through the media on our professional competence, intelligence, and in one article, our mental stability.

Eventually, only the Prime Minister's formal statement to the House of Commons accepting the recommendations of the report was left to argue over. It had to be negotiated phrase by phrase. Even the announcement was presented to appear as a Treasury 'victory'; the press were told that the Treasury had 'won'. It was at this stage that the false story that the report had been radically re-written and 'watered down', was circulated among the journalists: it can only have come from the Treasury. That story has lasted through the decades – I am still being asked what it felt like to have 'my report' so altered. With all this childish manoeuvring, they missed the big picture – the main point. Agencies were to be set up, the government was committed to the programme and a Permanent Secretary was in charge of implementing the recommendations of the report. Much of the precise wording of a press statement didn't matter in the longer term, although, as ever, the detail could be important.

If I had been intent on sabotaging the idea of agencies, I would have adopted an approach of broad support; the report could have been lost so easily by being swamped with faint kindness and then ignored. Turning the whole thing into a major and public war with fictitious secret documents and rumours of huge battles and smoke pouring from the windows of Whitehall made it all much more interesting than, at that stage, it really was.

The position of the Treasury was bizarre. At the 'working levels' – under secretaries or assistant secretaries – there were plenty of people who understood what the report was about and supported its recommendations. The opposition was entirely from the top and was about a reduction in power, together with concern about the overall control of public expenditure. But instead of a sensible, balanced discussion of pros and cons it became an emotional crusade to stop what was presented as 'wrecking the system' rather than a balanced argument. It reflected the defensive mentality which can affect Ministries of Finance anywhere. The essence of the argument was a conviction that tight input control was the only certain way to control public expenditure. That is a true, but far too limited, view of public expenditure. If controlling public expenditure were what government was about there would be no disagreement, but as the point of public expenditure is to spend money on something, how the money is spent and on what and with what results is an essential part of the total task.

The extended and emotional opposition had its advantages. We tested our facts and our ideas to destruction. We made sure they could stand up to the irrational onslaughts as well as the rational ones. One memorable meeting nearly floored me when a senior and distinguished official for whom I had considerable respect sternly announced that these proposals called into question the system established by the 1667 Treasury Commission. I could not find one rational argument to support this proposition.

A footnote to the curious and idiosyncratic nature of the Treasury opposition to Next Steps was that, although the two most senior officials appointed to implement the report were from the Treasury, within a very short time they became its most public and enthusiastic proponents. And by 1994, at the most senior levels in the Treasury, the view was that the entire NHS, the jewel in the crown, could and should be an executive agency. By 2006, even the Labour Chancellor of the Exchequer was in favour of such a move.

THE PRIME MINISTER'S ANNOUNCEMENT

On 18 February 1988 the much debated announcement was made. The public build-up had been modest. I was still banned from talking to the press so all the information that went to the newspapers went from the Treasury or the Cabinet Office Press Office. The House of Commons was moderately crowded, the Officials' Box at one side of the Speaker's Chair was crammed. The Efficiency Unit had to sit at the back of the Chamber under the galleries, no room for us in the box – the heavies had taken over. A Prime Ministerial statement on the future of the Civil Service was still worth some attention but it was not a rip-roaring Commons occasion.

The Prime Minister referred to the Efficiency Unit's report and its recommendations and endorsed the view of the team that a new form of organisation was necessary. The recommendations 'will set the direction for further development of management reform in the Civil Service . . . The Government will develop a continuing programme for establishing agencies, applying progressively the lessons of experience gained' (Hansard, 18 February 1988). The much debated words were used, the establishment of agencies would be the responsibility of Mr Peter Kemp as project manager in the Cabinet Office, the staff of agencies would continue to be civil servants and the arrangements for accountability would remain unchanged.

For the Unit it represented a major achievement. We had won the battle on every count. The report published the next day was virtually unchanged from the draft I had sent to the Prime Minister nearly a year before, apart from an informal timetable which had been added to show her how implementation might work, and had been overtaken by events. The statement, for all the arguments, reflected what we wanted. The Prime Minister's announcement of a unit – The Next Steps Unit – to implement the proposals in our report was a far more significant move than most gave it credit for at the time. The Treasury had confused careful wording with strategic direction. Their briefing of the press emphasised that they had 'won'; it was a bizarre interpretation of a Prime Ministerial announcement of a major change to which the senior Treasury officials had been deeply and noisily opposed for the best part of a year.

When the report was published, at the Press Conference and in the press beforehand, rumours of slashing the report abounded. It was, *The Times* said, 'emasculated beyond recognition' on the basis of no evidence at all. The other papers followed suit. The remarks in the press and by the commentators were outrageous. No-one had any evidence of the dilution of the report. They produced nothing that supported their assertion. It looked as if they had fallen into a well-laid trap.

What was important, leaving the semantic joustings aside, was that the Government had formally accepted a specific direction for reform. The substantive point that mattered was that the Government was committed to act. If what had been accepted was a 'test' or 'pilot' to see if agencies could work, we would have been faced with an ancient device which almost invariably killed initiatives off with delay and relative obscurity. We had argued, with the same tenacity as about the Permanent Secretary's post, that this announcement was committing the Government to the changes and the pilots were to find out not if but how to do it. Once the point was in the statement all we then had to do, in best Whitehall style, was simply refer to what the Prime Minister had said.

IMPLEMENTATION: THE PROJECT MANAGER AND THE NEXT STEPS UNIT

A significant appointment was that of the Permanent Secretary whose job was to make the new development successful. He was not, in immemorial Whitehall terminology to 'be responsible' for the change, he was to make it work; his appointment depended on his success. We had deliberately kept the profile high. The Head of the Unit was to report to the Head of the Civil Service and to the Prime Minister, no other part of the system would be in a position to intervene. In particular, the Treasury was not able to insert itself into that group directly. The irony was that the Head of the Civil Service and the Head of the Next Steps Unit had both come from the Treasury. It was interesting to watch how their views changed with a change of role. A year before one of them had said 'Mad – you can't hope to get that through'. The other, more diplomatically, had said 'Don't be too radical, they'll never let you get away with it.' Within a year both had espoused mad radicalism with enthusiasm.

The new unit was set up within the Cabinet Office and the Efficiency Unit handed over all responsibility for the project to them, and returned to its normal work. The deputy head of the Unit, Charlotte Dixon (an Assistant Secretary from the then Department of Transport who had taken over from Karen Caines at the end of 1987) acted as liaison between the two groups, handing over our background policy papers and helping to discuss issues and make contacts as the work with the new pilot units gathered pace.

Peter Kemp made it clear that radical change was going to extend to the way he worked as much as to the proposals he was working on. He embraced the suggested openness with a determination which to Whitehall eyes looked almost manic. He spoke trenchantly to the Treasury and Civil Service Select Committee of the House of Commons about targets, still a word little used in the upper echelons of Whitehall. He projected his ideas forward, he cheerfully gave hostages to the future in predicting the numbers of agencies to be set up. He made even the dangerous radicals of the Efficiency Unit feel a little staid.

Above all he took his responsibility to make what he called 'this thing' happen deeply seriously. He befriended the press and talked openly and indiscreetly to them on the principle that the more that was open the more difficult it would be to sabotage. The possibility of sabotage was real. The rest of Whitehall was extremely wary, Peter Kemp made it clear in our regular conversations that he needed some quick success to win over the Whitehall barons who had a vested interest on seeing him fail. The Next Steps Unit committed their small but determined energies to proving them wrong. I was impressed by the speed with which the first agencies, set up in late summer 1988, were followed in swift succession by a wave of new organisations. By the end of 1989 there was a respectable group of agency Chief Executives to attend a meeting in Downing Street to celebrate their existence and discuss common subjects of interest and difficulty.

MOVING ON: THE RADICALS AND THE SYSTEM

Ironically, although the first Project Manager, Peter Kemp, was spectacularly successful at this job, he left the Civil Service after four years in the job. He could be argued to have been the most successful Permanent Secretary for a very long time – to have succeeded, under constant public scrutiny, in driving though a very significant reform. It is on his success that so many of his erstwhile colleagues congratulate themselves. The expert Whitehall watcher, Peter Hennessy, has a theory that overt success is death to a successful Whitehall career; Peter Kemp exemplified the validity of the maxim.

Equally significantly for the Hennessy theory, by 1989 most of the Efficiency Unit Next Steps team had left Whitehall. I had left the Civil Service, as had my predecessors as Heads of the Efficiency Unit. Karen Caines who had carried much of the burden of the scrutiny with skill and rare determination and had been a major and significant contributor to the substance of the Report, returned to the Department of Health to work on the reform of the Health Service, to leave finally for Guy's Hospital in 1991. Andrew Jackson, who had worked with great commitment throughout the scrutiny and the difficult follow through to the announcement, left to join one of the major consultancy firms.

These changes are not surprising. The effectiveness of the Whitehall machine lies in two things. First, ensuring that the nuts and bolts activities of policy formulation happen, decisions are taken, recorded and acted upon. Second, in persuading people of considerable intelligence that the smooth facade of government business, complex and difficult as it is, requires experience and deep thought, and that overseeing this process is a satisfactory way of spending their careers. As a result the parts of the system which receive this high level attention work remarkably smoothly.

Radical thinking does not fit into this world picture. As we found in working on scrutinies and on Next Steps, many civil servants either lacked the psychological and intellectual bent for radical thought or had learnt to disguise it in the interest of their careers. People found it difficult to think openly and laterally from within the system unless they could be certain that the system itself would protect them. The Efficiency Unit deliberately encouraged radicalism where it could be shown to be necessary. The work on scrutinies had shown how much capacity for innovative thinking there was within the Civil Service.

In the Efficiency Unit we had managed to supply protection for people who had done scrutinies once their reviews were completed. The same protection was not available for the Civil Service members of the Efficiency Unit in the Next Steps Report team. The team all left the Civil Service, as had my two predecessors as Head of the Unit. Radical thinking about how the system worked was regarded as dangerous to the status quo within the Civil Service.

Anyone identified with radical change was likely to be seen as guilty of the ultimate sin of what was called 'unreliability', no matter how strong or how powerful the support for them had been at the time, or whether radicalism had been part of their job. It was made subtly clear to all the authors of the report that while they could continue to have a career in the Civil Service, it was unlikely to be an interesting or successful one. All left for interesting and rewarding careers; the world 'outside' was more welcoming than Whitehall.

7. Next Steps: implementation

The Efficiency Unit's job was done. Producing the report and getting it accepted had been hard but past experience demonstrated that implementation was the weak point in changing the Civil Service. The new project manager was faced with a Herculean task. The Prime Minister had announced that his job was to implement the report's recommendations 'successfully'; the atmosphere was hardly encouraging. The Treasury remained suspicious and unhelpful. He was expected to produce fast results and had to start from scratch. He needed staff, an office and a programme. The Efficiency Unit could give him the results of the work on the twelve pilot agencies, the background work done the previous year and the working papers produced in the early months of 1987. The Efficiency Unit team had departed. Sir Robin Ibbs was leaving his role as Adviser to the Prime Minister. Karen Caines and Andrew Jackson had left the Efficiency Unit and I was coming to the end of my term there.

There has been much discussion of what happened, but the simple outlines demonstrate how valuable a moderate amount of forward planning, determined management and a clear sense of overall direction are. Academic work has been done on the development of particular agencies as they have adapted to the changes imposed on them by the new agency structure (for example, Greer, 1994). The Child Support Agency, the first organisation to be set up from its start as an agency, faced exactly the problems foreseen: politically difficult policies and inadequate forethought given to both how sensitive issues were to be handled and to the effectiveness of the organisation. Agency status could help improve management, but it could not turn weak or difficult policy into good policy nor, most importantly, could it provide a barrier behind which a Minister could hide when the policy or the operations turned out to be flawed.

This chapter discusses the main issues that faced the Next Steps Unit in the early years of implementation. The changes in individual agencies and the development of the agencies over the past fifteen years has been the subject of much analysis and comment elsewhere, but the questions which the project manager and the Unit found had to be resolved demonstrate some of the common themes in introducing a change on this scale. While most of the issues were those originally envisaged as likely to be difficult, some unexpected ones emerged. The role of the chief executive took considerable efforts to sort out – and in some cases was ill thought through and caused problems. The crucial importance strongly emphasised in the report of resolving 'politically sensitive issues' emerged when the later and most difficult cases of the CSA and the Prison Service were established.

Between 1988 and 1992 regular six monthly reports were made to the Prime Minister; it was possible for both Mrs Thatcher and Mr Major, who replaced her in 1990, to keep in touch with progress. The important pressure came from Robin Butler and Peter Kemp to maintain the momentum through to the end of the process. Peter Kemp was appointed to the job of project manager in February 1988 with a challenging job description and the need to demonstrate progress urgently. Next Steps had the overt support of the Prime Minister and the Head of the Civil Service; it had to be successful. He was one of the very few people at a sufficiently senior level in Whitehall with some of the practical experience needed. It was ironically a vindication of the Next Steps thesis that there were very few officials in a senior position who were qualified to implement a difficult managerial task. It was an indictment of the Civil Service's investment in Fulton and of the management of the 1970s and early 1980s.

The difficulty was to find someone whose authority the Civil Service would accept, who had the determination to keep going under the expected pressure, who could gain the respect of the Prime Minister and who could deal with opposition from the Treasury on its own terms. Peter Kemp had been dealing with public sector pay in the Treasury, a difficult and contentious job, and had developed new payment systems for the public sector. He was well known to the senior departmental managers around the system. He was not always an easy person to work with, but he was determined, radical and known to the Prime Minister. Whitehall might not find him easy to deal with but he was not a nonentity. He was also not a Whitehall grandee on the smooth route from Oxbridge but had entered the Civil Service as a 'direct entry' principal, a relatively new recruitment route for 'older' fast stream civil servants with experience. Unusually for a civil servant, Peter Kemp had a rare and valuable training as an accountant. He had a Treasury background and he wanted the job, despite its unusual requirement in Whitehall terms to make Next Steps successful.

THE ROLE OF THE TREASURY

The view of the Treasury remained ambivalent. The Treasury's public stance was that the process had been sanitised by them, its wilder aspects removed and it was now in safe hands. The traditional conspiracy theory, much beloved by journalists, claimed a Treasury takeover: Robin Butler in the

Cabinet Office, Peter Kemp in Next Steps and the normal galaxy of senior treasury knights around Whitehall. A popular view was that the placing of Treasury supporters was all carefully plotted and planned beforehand. It wasn't; the Prime Minister had chosen Robin Butler to succeed Robert Armstrong in the summer of 1987, long before Next Steps was anything more than a set of proposals. Peter Kemp was identified as a possible choice when it seemed likely that something would emerge from the discussions, before the end of 1987. At that stage open discussions with the Treasury on the working assumption that Next Steps would need a Permanent Secretary project manager would have produced yet another explosion.

The Next Steps team were responsible for implementing the report. The Treasury could make or break it. The important first step was to find a way of working with the Treasury so that the new agencies could become a legitimate and effective part of the Whitehall system. It is difficult to answer the question who or what is 'the Treasury'? It is a habit of many governments to personify ministries, and particularly Ministries of Finance as though they were a single organisation, with a collective leadership driving forward their personal policy objectives. The public expenditure 'side' of the Treasury in the 1980s was a collection of intelligent, independent people, working with a relatively straightforward objective – the control of public expenditure – in a complex and unfriendly world. They were grossly understaffed for what they tried to do. Senior staff, often supported by less competent junior people, controlled huge areas of public expenditure with little experience of the subject for which they were responsible. Their lack of detailed knowledge of the field they were dealing with was stunning to an outsider; it led to absurd arguments about minutiae while the big issues were ignored.

There appeared to be little systematic gathering of information about the purposes of the big expenditure programmes. Attention still focused on the lack of control on spending, not on how the money was spent. The Treasury had to change its approach radically or be out manoeuvred, as departments became more managerially competent. In one instance, the Treasury quite rightly urged the use of unit costs to measure performance on departments. Unfortunately, some of those negotiating had failed to find out precisely what this exciting new phrase meant. A senior departmental official emerged chuckling from the expenditure discussions: 'we have done our homework on unit costs, they had no idea what we were talking about. We could have had anything we wanted!'.

There had been changes in the Treasury, one of the most significant was probably the impact of the labour market of the mid-1980s. The City and the financial services sector was booming and in need of staff. It turned its attention to the pool of highly intelligent, experienced and under-used staff in the middle ranks of the senior Civil Service. The subsequent recruitment drives hit the Treasury particularly hard. In one year in the early 1980s the Treasury lost a very high proportion of its 'starred' principals – the group selected and managed to form the future group of senior officials. The losses continued in most departments in Whitehall throughout the 1980s and left substantial gaps in the senior administrative grades.

The consequence of high turnover was not all bad. The Civil Service had become accustomed and even complacent about its ability to cream off the best brains from universities and to add to that group a few people with experience and ability recruited as 'direct entry principals'. The Civil Service was awash with extremely able people, who were in general underused and under-valued. The departures of the 1980s forced departmental managers to recognise the need to move to effective personnel management and away from their traditional approach; some departments still treated their hand picked high flyers as if they were junior officers in the army. In the Treasury the gaps had to be filled, and they were increasingly filled from the most immediately available source – the spending departments. The Treasury became a much healthier mix of people with experience in the big operational departments – DHSS, Energy, DTI and Employment – who could bring practical experience to the processes of expenditure control.

Implementing the Next Steps Report successfully involved a quantum leap in the relationship between the Treasury and other Departments. Some Permanent Secretaries ignored the necessary changes to their management of large areas of their departments implicit in the requirement to develop a framework document and to plan effectively, but many saw the Next Steps structure as a way of removing some of the grinding frustrations of the public expenditure round. Psychology was important; as the Treasury's opposition grew more virulent and well known, the supporters of Next Steps became more determined. The debate about the terms of appointment of a chief executive in the last months of 1987 showed the Whitehall philosophers at their most inventive – angels were dancing on pins all over Whitehall. The argument was no longer solely about improving management, it was a fight between the Treasury and the rest of Whitehall about the control of public expenditure.

The argument was complicated by the refusal of many parts of Whitehall to accept that the Treasury had modified the rules. The belief that 'they (i.e. the Treasury) would not allow us' was so strong, that any challenge to accepted orthodoxy was regarded as a waste of time. I had considerable sympathy for the officials in the Treasury who were trying to adapt the system while working in it. They had to deal with an intensely complicated system which was, by the late 1980s, in a state of constant revision. They also had to deal with the effects of rumour and misunderstanding, much of it the consequence of past difficulties: too much meddling in detail, the impact of gladiatorial contests about public expenditure and problems of communication. We were none of us good at communication but the Treasury was in a class of its own. Some of their instructions for the public expenditure round were classics of saying what you wanted to say, without thinking about what your readers might understand.

While I was Head of the Efficiency Unit we had had a number of discussions with the Treasury about how to improve their communications – it would have simplified many difficult arguments if the relationship between the Treasury and Departments had been better. But nothing could persuade the Treasury that a change would produce benefits. The only change they tried was a circular letter to Departments saying that if there were difficulties, then Departments should specify any changes that might improve matters and 'the Treasury would consider their suggestions sympathetically'. Not entirely to our surprise this warm invitation produced no response at all. When I challenged one of the most vociferous complainants in the Home Office on why they had not responded, his reaction was a shrug, rolled eyes and a firm response that 'there would be no point at all'. This reaction was from a department with a relatively helpful expenditure division in the Treasury and one of the most widely experienced and sensible Under Secretaries in charge.

A postscript to the Treasury's views on Next Steps appeared in 1994 when I was reviewing the management of the NHS. The Chancellor the Exchequer wrote to the Secretary of State for Health suggesting that the best solution to the management problems of the Health Service, the largest government organisation of all, was that it should become an executive agency; ironically the Department of Health, whose previous Permanent Secretary, Sir Kenneth Stowe, six years before had been one of Next Step's strongest supporters, did not want that degree of 'loss of control' within its own empire.

THE FIRST PHASE

Into this maelstrom of difficulties, Peter Kemp was pitched in February 1988. The Prime Minister's announcement was deliberately drafted to push action forward quickly. There were twelve pilot agencies, ready to start work, a great deal of press speculation, and a bubbling cauldron of Civil Service organisations to be dealt with. By July Peter Kemp was able to report to the Prime Minister that progress was being made. The first agency would be ready in August and the development of the processes to establish agencies was already underway. Recruiting staff and building a team was not easy. Next Steps was new and untried. No one could be sure it would succeed; the staff were taking career risks in working in the Unit.

The process of implementation, especially in the early stages, was never going to be easy. The Next Steps team had to devise their policy as they went along together with the pilot agencies and the Treasury. It is to all their credit that the first ones were robust and have survived and developed well. What the project manager needed above all in these first months was strong and public support from the Prime Minister for the principles of Next Steps and encouragement of the maximum of devolution and the minimum of central control. By the third quarter of 1988 the first agency, the Vehicle Inspectorate, had been launched, and the project manager could report to the Prime Minister that he could feel he was making progress.

By January 1989, less than a year after the Prime Minister's announcement the project manager reported there were three executive agencies – in the autumn, Companies House and The Stationery Office – and, by May, 32 potential ones: a coverage when established, of 185 000 central government civil servants, about one-third of the total. Three units of the Northern Ireland Civil Service were also in the list. This was astonishing progress. Within a year the 'Next Steps' idea had taken sufficient root for the senior officials responsible for large areas of the public service, who had been waiting on the sidelines, to become converted to establishing agencies.

This first year was encouraging for the Next Steps team. The first six months of operation had involved the familiar Thatcher government process of stick and carrot which we had used in the Efficiency Unit: 'this initiative is important, you can choose what you want to do – it is entirely voluntary but we expect you to produce two candidates'. It gave scope to the enthusiasts and embarrassed the unconvinced or laggards into some kind of action. Many big Departments put forward, as in the pilot round, fairly modest candidates – their research stations, pensions organisations or clearly out-housed operations like laboratories or licensing activities. There was nothing unwise or foolish about that. Learning how to set up an agency properly was a necessary and sensible first move before restructuring a huge organisation. In several instances what was proposed was simply a delaying tactic, but fortunately in most cases it proved to have been sensible as well.

As the process of development progressed, the difficult issues began to emerge. The question of accountability to Parliament was the subject of early debate. The theoretical question was who was ultimately accountable for policy and operational outcomes – the Minister or the chief executive. The answer was clearly the Minister: he or she made the appointment and must be answerable for the actions of that appointee. But, if Parliament wanted answers on questions of organisation and management then it made sense for the chief executive to answer because he or she would be taking the decisions and knew the detail within the agreed delegations of the framework document. The argument then ran: but who was responsible if the customers were dissatisfied? The final responsibility was still the Minister's; he or she had the power to dismiss a chief executive if what had been done was unsatisfactory. What the Minister should not be able to do, as some have tried in notable cases, is shrug off responsibility.

Ministers could not have it both ways even though many would have liked to do so. What the appointment of chief executives had done was to bring into the open the weaknesses in the fiction of ministerial accountability. This weakness had been there when the management was internal to the Ministry and protected by the Official Secrets Act; now when objectives and performance were clear and open it became a more obvious problem. Parliament had access to much more information than before; it had to learn to use it.

One underlying difficulty was the reluctance of many officials to be blunt with Ministers about their personal responsibility. Even the *Notes for Guidance for Ministers* were coy about Ministerial responsibility. The published 1997 version did not contain a clear statement of the responsibilities of a minister. They are 'expected to behave according to the highest standards of constitutional and personal conduct'. In particular they must observe certain principles. Those quoted are about relations with Parliament and conflicts of interest, both personal and political. There is a suggestion of function in principle ii: 'Ministers have a duty to Parliament to account and be held to account for the policies, decisions and actions of their Departments and Next Steps Agencies.'

But the reader might still mutter 'yes, but what are they supposed to do?' on reading the pages of the *Code*. There is a section on 'Ministers and Their Departments' which sounds hopeful, until one reads elaborate arrangements for the notification of the Prime Minister when a change in Ministerial responsibilities is contemplated, with a glancing reference to the Head of the Civil Service and the Permanent Secretary. The code is about Ministerial relationships at the apex of Whitehall. It says nothing about the responsibilities of Ministers for taking decisions about the policy and the operations of their Departments. This question of the role of Ministers was to surface repeatedly and was not solely a complication of the Next Steps process. It demonstrated the fundamental weakness in accountability in British government which the spectacular cases during the 1990s of the Prisons Agency, the Guns for Iraq scandal and the subsequent Scott Report had brought into the open.

Other issues were worrying the Next Steps Unit early in 1989. The way in which agency funds could be treated was in need of attention. If a process could be devised which could give them a trading fund – an internal business account – instead of the remittance of all receipts to the Treasury, their ability to improve services in response to demand would be greatly enhanced. It was an essential part of being an agency that there should be enough flexibility to respond to demand. The case of the Passport Agency was an example of the effect of using a system which was not suitable for the task it had to perform. For some years there had been serious delays in providing passports. These delays always grew far worse at peak holiday times as holidays abroad became more popular and the demand for passports peaked in the summer. Under the old system the Passport Office was not permitted to increase its staffing to cover the known times of pressure, even though its income rose with the number of applications. Because of the budget rules – expenditure was fixed at the start of the year, all variations had to be approved and very seldom were – the citizen needing a passport received a deplorable service at some times of the year at the same cost whether the passport took three days or three months to arrive.

The development of the 'agency trading fund' was the route out of this mess. As with many other Next Steps changes the idea of a different structure for handling receipts was not new; the 'trading fund' had been in existence for several years and had been used in a few cases. The agency trading fund was an existing mechanism applied on a wider canvas. The short Bill giving effect to it, introduced in 1990, was the only legislation necessary to introduce the whole agency structure into government.

The Next Steps Unit worked with the new agencies on the detail of the framework documents; they had to be specific about flexibilities in pay and financial matters. The changes had to be defined and negotiated. Most potential agencies, as the Efficiency Unit had found during 1987, would complain about constraints but found it more difficult to be specific about the changes they needed. Personnel rules would need attention. Both the Treasury and the Management and Personnel Office constantly emphasised that there was more flexibility in the system than people used. The existence of unused flexibility was one of the arguments used by the opponents of Next Steps, particularly those in the central departments. Their point was that little change was necessary; most of the changes asked for by Departments were already available. It was a matter of negotiation and the development of adequate systems.

This argument for the status quo ante left two significant factors out of account. First, most officials in other departments did not believe the protestations of the central departments. Junior and often inexperienced staff were given the task of day-to-day relations with departments but they could not take risks. It was easier to say no, especially if sympathetic consideration of a request for a change will mean more work and probably intervention from a more senior official. A decade later in Mexico City I observed the same phenomenon. No matter how hard the reformers tried to persuade junior officials to use the new simplified systems, especially for procurement, they did not believe that the changes were solid. In Mexico public servants were subject to rigorous checks from the auditors and personal liability if they were found to have flouted the rules. They did not believe that changes agreed in the central departments would be recognised by the auditors, and they did not believe that they would be protected by their senior management if that happened, so the new systems atrophied.

The second factor was the internal dynamics of agencies. The establishment of an agency legitimised requests for flexibility which had hitherto received little support; it made it possible to clarify the confusing rules on financial flexibility which gave greater freedom to agencies, often in the teeth of opposition from their departments, who had been sheltering their own control systems behind the Treasury for years. The initial reaction of an agency was to ask for modest incremental changes, as the pilot agencies had demonstrated during the work for ministers in 1987, but it did not take long in the hands of innovative chief executives for a more radical course to be planned out and negotiated.

People working in the new agencies needed specialised training. The staff of an agency would need to understand what the change in status was designed to achieve, what their role would be and how they could use and develop the new approach. There were the technical questions of running finance and personnel systems as well as specific issues of management and development for each agency. This territory was potentially dangerous – the use of training can be a weak part of a programme of change. The temptation to indulge in great swathes of formalised chatter about the theory of the changes could have wasted expensive time as well as money. Working with the Civil Service College, Kemp's team realised that at this stage there was no off the shelf package that they could use to help prepare people for their new roles. They had to devise the new courses and give time to them in the midst of everything else.

Communications were important from an early stage. The development of the Report had been shrouded in the traditional secrecy of the British Civil Service and the Efficiency Unit had been banned from any public explanation of what it was about – probably as part of the deal between the Cabinet Office and the Treasury, and no doubt to save the Treasury's face. A limp press conference after the parliamentary announcement had been the only formal public statement. The new communications programme devised by the Next Steps Unit was lively and, for the public service, innovative. Glossy booklets, public reports and a video about the report narrated by a well-known journalist all built up the impression of an innovation that was going to succeed. During 1988 and 1989 Peter Kemp also developed his remarkable relationship with the Treasury and Civil Service Select Committee (TCSC). He quite rightly used this forum deliberately as a platform to discuss the changes openly and honestly with none of the careful wording normal for Permanent Secretaries making a public statement. He made guesses at outcomes, set what appeared to be hopelessly optimistic targets and defended himself robustly against attack. The Select Committee was both genuinely interested and well informed. With Giles Radice's balanced and rational chairmanship these discussions provided a valuable example of how well Select Committees can work. The Committee's reports were an important source of information and support for the work of the Next Steps Unit, and were instrumental in publicising their activities both within Parliament and more widely.

Their reports are crisp and to the point. The conclusions of the Fifth Report for 1988–1989 set out eighteen points ranging from the need to speed up the pace of establishing agencies, to the content of Framework Documents and the structure of the Civil Service. Quality is not ignored: 'We expect the success of the Next Steps programme to be judged in large measure by the extent to which it improves service to customers'. The report reiterates the need for management experience in the senior Civil Service; three of its eighteen conclusions are about senior management. Conclusion xvii asserts the need for 'those reaching the highest ranks of the Civil Service in the core departments to have experience of both policy and management work' (TCSC, HC 348).

By early 1989 the experience of beginning work with the pilot agencies was demonstrating the need to think about wider issues in a more consistent manner. While it was essential to 'tailor make' the agency in each case, a principle Peter Kemp rightly maintained, experience from organisations which were, at this stage, still very similar could be shared with newcomers to the process. Training was one of the first examples of joint working. There were obvious gains from providing short introductions to the theory and practice to groups from a number of agencies. The agencies were beginning to learn from each other – a valuable lesson in sharing experience. Another development was less easy to resolve. Targets for objectives and evaluation had been part of the paraphernalia of management discussions for several years. Targets for improved performance had been one of the more testing of the Efficiency Unit's innovations which met with incomprehension and bewilderment on all sides in the mid 1980s. But they were part of the central premise of Next Steps. Effective targets and objectives with clear accountability were the substitute for rigid input controls, so their development was crucially important, and they had to be right. Badly constructed targets became actively damaging in succeeding years. The ultimate absurdity was reached in 2007 when the Government solemnly announced a target to reduce the number of targets.

The team had two other topics to watch. First was the link with the Government's privatisation strategy: the statement in 1988 had said that 'generally' agencies would be established within the Civil Service and in October of that year there was a further statement on the links between privatisation and agencies. Few of the commentators were prepared to accept the proposition that establishing agencies was simply designed to improve the management of public services; but while it was neither rational nor possible to isolate agencies from the challenge of whether it would be more effective to run an organisation by privatising it, the test should always be how best to run the organisation.

There were few areas regarded as untouchable in the discussions on contracting out as the subsequent market testing experiment introduced in 1992 showed. For the Next Steps team as well as for the original Efficiency Unit team the question that was relevant was: 'how can this organisation be run most effectively?' The answer to that question was not necessarily an agency. The agency was one possible answer, privatisation was another. The October statement said carefully that agency status 'could' lead to privatisation – where that was the best solution. This debate became far more difficult to sustain once the 'best solution' as the basis for setting up an agency was lost. Once the Government started to set up agencies because it wanted to set up 'Agencies', not because an agency was the most effective solution, the flexibility in the original proposition atrophied and a more dogmatic approach to 'agency or privatise' inevitably developed.

The second topic to watch was the type of activity suitable as an agency. The service organisations, Social Security or Employment, which had to provide a similar service across the country to national standards were good candidates. It was one of the reasons Employment, as the smaller of the two organisations, with about 35000 staff, was encouraged to be in the pilot phase, although it took two years to establish as an agency. The organisations that were paid fees to provide a service, the 'quasi traders', were another group providing licenses or passports, where a simplified funding regime and internal flexibility to respond to demand were important elements in their quality of service. Companies House, one of the first agencies, was an example of this type; its early reports record a steady improvement in service standards, with clear objectives and a straightforward function.

The Land Registry was another example. Its performance was a source of constant complaint and its management were anxious for greater flexibility to allow them to improve their deplorable service standards which affected almost anyone who bought or sold property. The old system gave them little spare capacity to respond to peaks in demand so that service standards would regularly decline when house sales rose in the spring and early summer. The licensing and regulatory organisations were another group suitable to consider as agencies. They had a clear task, could be set straightforward targets and needed flexibility to deal with specialised markets. The Vehicle Inspectorate – responsible for HGV testing – was an early candidate. The tricky balance for regulators of providing a good service while being tough on standards needed constant attention; staff had to adjust from the old style of control to using a clear set of standards, properly understood, while being efficient and courteous.

It was important for Peter Kemp and his team to develop as many straightforward agencies as quickly as possible. The less obvious agencies, where the changes in status might produce problems as well as solutions, were for later once experience had built up. Pure administration, in Civil Service terms, the provision of support and policy advice to ministers, was not likely to be an agency: there was no function to devolve. The more difficult issue remained how to ensure that the 'pure administrators', who were both policy and resource managers, gave enough priority to their management functions. They would need the right experience to develop framework agreements to define what their agencies should do.

By July 1989 the project manager reported that 7000 civil servants were now working in fully fledged agencies. Eight agencies had been established, each one with a formal launch and a public statement from the relevant Minister. The launch was an important feature of the early agencies; becoming an agency gave many of them a status they had seldom achieved before. Peter Kemp knew that a Ministerial appearance would emphasise the importance of a new agency and demonstrate it was a serious part of the government. Kemp and his team were using every available means to raise the public profile of the new agencies. Announcements in Parliament, press coverage and well designed documents all helped to register with Parliament, journalists, the public, and internally in the public service that agencies were new and interesting.

The Next Steps team provided more information about their activities than any other public sector organisation would have considered necessary or desirable. They produced quarterly reports, in a simple photocopied format which recorded developments, new agencies, new policy changes, a reference section of all the existing agencies and a 'Next Steps reading list' of government publications. In 1990 the reading list took one page, it had grown to four pages by 1998. A formal annual report was produced from 1990. The main source of information about the approach and priorities of the Next Steps team was the regular appearances of the project manager before the Treasury and Civil Service Select Committee. The published record of these discussions gives more information about the issues which the process of implementation raised as the number of agencies grew. In one early discussion, in May 1989, the debate ranged from Peter Kemp's job description, the role of the Treasury, the scale of obstacles to making progress, the need to avoid false distinctions between policy and adminis- tration, privatisation, the process for setting up agencies and the content of the video made for the Next Steps team of work in the new agencies. The reports of the Committee and in particular the record of the discussions with witnesses brought together the views and experiences of many of the people involved in the implementation of the Next Steps Report.

AGENCIES AND DEPARTMENTS

At the start of the Next Steps programme Departments tended to deal with Next Steps agencies as a one off – a response to an initiative, rather than as part of a strategic approach to the overall management of a department. The most effective way for a Department to benefit from managing through agencies would be to look at its entire operation and decide which activities should be agencies and what the consequences were for the rest of the department. This should have led to better balanced and informed policy departments with practical working links with the Departmental agencies. Peter Kemp found that the reaction from most Departments was piece- meal, most pushed sacrificial lambs towards the Next Steps Unit to slake their demand for agencies and retreated.

Although after a year some Departments were taking a more construc- tive approach, the real need – to look at the structure of the Department as a whole and find the most effective way of managing it as an entity – was seldom attempted. The exception was the two revenue departments. Already by early 1989 Customs and Excise and Inland Revenue were being considered for 'agency status'. Senior officials in both departments had been involved in the work on the Next Steps Report. The Deputy Chairman of Customs and Excise, Sandy Russell, had played an important part in advising the Efficiency Unit throughout the development of the report and Angus Fraser and, later, Valerie Strachan, as successive Chairmen, were interested in the issues and the potential of the new organisations.

For both institutions the question was were they a single revenue col- lecting agency or should they build on their existing organisation by estab- lishing local offices as agencies within a network working to the Boards of Customs and Excise and Inland Revenue. Both organisations were large with 35 000 and 60 000 staff respectively and going through considerable changes already as computerisation was introduced against a background of a downward pressure on costs. The changes had to be right – there could be no damage to the operational activity of either organisation. They settled on the network solution. The Ministry of Defence was another organisation which had at first been wary about agencies. By 1989 it was working on a management strategy which was to include a range of agencies to manage the mass of organisations which had grown up around the Defence function. Each year the new agencies list contained at least two from MOD.

DEVELOPMENT OF THE THEORY

The increased numbers of agencies by 1990 provided enough subject matter to identify areas for new thinking. The management of contracts between agencies and suppliers had been identified as a problem in the development of 'contracting out' and had proved to be its weakest link. The procurement element in public sector contracting had always been poor. Peter Levene, with extensive private sector experience, had been brought into the Defence Procurement department to try to improve the quality of defence contracting, an area in which Derek Rayner had worked fifteen years earlier. It had been a hard task, much public sector purchasing was slovenly, naïve and ineffective. Few people in Government understood the work that was necessary in preparing and negotiating a contract; even fewer understood what was necessary to manage the operation of a contract once it had been agreed.

The significance of the role of contract manager emerged again in the management initiatives of the 1990s – market testing demonstrated the need for contracting skills. The Public Finance Initiative demonstrated beyond question that most of the Civil Service did not understand what contracting meant. It was to be a constant theme. Until Departments learned to recognise the need to manage what they did – to be clear about objectives and resources and how to manage the outcome, they would demonstrate how weak the processes of managing public services were.

As the first agencies began to operate in their new form, the role of the chief executive was thrown into higher relief. Hitherto, running an executive organisation had been regarded as a task for someone in their fifties with nowhere else to go or for a potential 'high flier', for a short time 'to learn how to manage'. One of the toughest discussions before the Government's announcement on Next Steps had been about the role of the chief executive. The Efficiency Unit's view had been that the agencies would be serious organisations controlling large amounts of public resources, and important public services and therefore senior people should run them with high level skills and qualifications. There was a strong case for the appointments to be treated openly and on merit, which argued for public advertising of appointments, an open selection process and personal contracts tied to performance. None of this was either revolutionary or difficult but it did reverse the cosy system of patronage which operated within the Civil Service and the use of these appointments as part of the patronage of a Department.

There was extensive debate about what was called 'the role of the Chief Executive'. Ironically, this expression did not mean what job he or she did. It meant whether they would be public people able to criticise the government's policy or resource allocation priorities. This terror haunted the Treasury for reasons which were neither logical nor comprehensible. The chances of a maverick chief executive risking his contract or her future over such a public stance were remote. They were to be civil servants and therefore subject to the rules governing the conduct of senior civil servants. The Treasury had more than enough power to deal with any chief executive who stepped publicly out of the well-trodden path of conformity. But the fear of public disagreement remained, unjustifiably as it turned out; even in the most celebrated cases chief executives seldom rounded on the hands that fed them, or at least not until the feeding stopped.

Finding the right people was, and remains, a difficult task. There was a view within the Civil Service that running an agency was just management and as easy as running anything, large or small. Anyone who has run any organisation can run an agency, so the theory went, and if they have been in the private sector, so much the better. Failure to understand what the job entailed meant that there were failures as well as successes. In the early stages people responsible for selection were flying blind. The appointments to the first agencies were confirmations of the officials already in the job. The appointments to the 1989 agencies were the first that were publicly advertised with a formal selection process.

The main difficulty for a newcomer to the Civil Service lay in understanding what was going on. The appointment of a chief executive could be made even though there was a lack of clarity about the boundaries of the role, the relationship with the Department and in many cases the Department's minister. If the chief executive was new to the public service much of what happened was incomprehensible, unspoken, or in code; it was only if the new appointee was able to deal with the difficulties of working in an alien environment with colleagues who had known each other for decades as well as the normal pressures of a new role and a new organisation that he or she had any chance of understanding the expectations of the job. Some of the most successful appointments were surprising. There were civil servants who might well have been appointed under the old system but who found the new role more interesting, and a few who had been in both public and private sectors and could grasp what was happening quickly.

Implicit in the structure of the new agencies was the need for greater delegated powers. Any organisation trying to delegate knows the familiar obstacle: you should delegate to me, but I can't delegate any further. The Efficiency Unit had met this reaction frequently. On one visit an experienced Director for the Inland Revenue in central England explained at length why he should have more delegated powers; he and not headquarters had the right skills to take local decisions. His arguments were logical and convincing. The Unit representative scribbled notes earnestly and eagerly and then asked what would be delegated from that office to local branch offices. 'That lot?' was the explosive reply 'I wouldn't trust them with chocolate buttons!' Not only were people reluctant to delegate but they were also reluctant to recognise delegated powers when they already existed, or indeed to encourage their use. The potential advantages of greater responsibility and the ability to delegate took time to be recognised. Careful delegation should open up new ideas and new directions as organisations began to think more creatively about what they could do and how they did it.

Effective evaluation was always going to be an important part of implementation. The first reports in the Next Steps briefing notes gave examples of improvement which were an indication of how much had to be done to introduce the use of measurements that could really demonstrate progress. The Next Steps Unit was beginning work on performance targets and the measurement of outcomes. The process of evaluation was in its infancy. It tended to be whatever could be measured rather than what needed to be measured. It was difficult, in a culture where evaluation was still either activity or anecdote based, to try to implant ideas of measuring either absolute or added value. In many cases it could not be done at the start, because of the absence of information; evaluation in the early years of Next Steps agencies tended to be weak and not very convincing. The evaluation reported in the early Next Steps briefing provided little that was of real value; better ways were needed.

THE SECOND PHASE 1990–1992

By 1990, two years into the changes, the number of established agencies was still modest but the planning of new agencies was building up to a rush. Ten agencies had been established with 7700 staff. What was more significant was that by January 1990 forty-four candidates had been formally announced and were working on their plans. Next Steps was no longer a pilot project for the very committed or those under pressure; it was the way a large part of central government was to be managed. With the passage of the Government Trading Act in 1990 the institutional framework was in place.

The change of Prime Minister had not affected the scale of the work of the Next Steps Unit. While John Major might lack the commitment of Mrs Thatcher in dealing with management problems which had been so significant in the development of the ideas behind Next Steps, he understood the arguments and had been part of the original debate – although he had then been in the Treasury arguing the opposite case. Not only did he continue the support which Mrs Thatcher had given to the Project Manager and his team, he also contributed to the development of the Citizen's Charter, a new process to put pressure on public services for better performance.

The Next Steps Unit's methodology had developed and was able to deal systematically with the new candidates. The momentum was considerable, 190 000 civil servants – one-third of the total – were working in the potential agency sector and the task of keeping common themes across the fifty agencies was increasingly difficult. The Efficiency Unit had argued that in many cases there would not be common themes. Many of these organisations were now proving that they were indeed different.

Evaluation continued to be an issue, particularly how to evaluate what the agency itself did and what performance indicators would be effective. Performance indicators were still what could be measured or even what was currently counted rather than what should be measured to demonstrate that the agency was meeting its objectives. The Vehicle Inspectorate measured the average number of tests conducted by an employee and the training days they had. The Ordnance Survey counted the number of maps available in digital form. Second, however, was the evaluation of the success or otherwise of being an agency – a more difficult concept. Was it possible to demonstrate that being an agency had produced improvement, rather than simply that, since an organisation had become an agency, some of its performance had improved? The first analysis could be done, the second, involving judgement as well was regarded as much more difficult, as indeed it was. The Next Steps Unit had a vested interest in demonstrating that being an agency was clearly better. What was going to be necessary for the Unit was to be able to demonstrate the success of agencies in clear and independently verifiable terms.

The formal requirements on agencies were now becoming more systematised. The 1990 White Paper required them to produce and publish accounts, performance targets and reports. The development of a more formal record was a follow up to the original suggestion that all framework documents should be public. So far 'laying in the library of the House of Commons' had been regarded as sufficient, a Whitehall fiction which provided only the semblance of openness. The papers were effectively inaccessible to anyone other than MPs. The new requirement to publish was a significant step forward in the process of opening up government agencies to public scrutiny.

As larger agencies were established and the first wave agencies developed, more competent management increased delegation and greater management flexibility needed renewed attention. The Next Steps Unit was determined to increase delegated responsibilities and the Treasury too were increasingly enthusiastic, especially about the delegation of personnel and recruitment functions. Some of the old tight central control of 'establishments' still firmly in place in the early and mid-1980s, had been delegated already under pressure from the Management and Personnel Office and the Treasury. Several of the big Departments handled their own junior level recruiting and most central personnel work was concentrated on 'Service wide issues' – common reporting standards, equal opportunities and the professional groups. The more difficult question was what departments were prepared to delegate to their agencies.

Smaller agencies were daunted by the prospect of taking on the full range of human resource responsibilities, where technical and legal accuracy was important. Staff with the relevant expertise had to be recruited and trained, and the agency would need to develop its own policies and human resource priorities. In the early agencies, attention focused on the process of developing the framework document, the identity, the flexibilities and the tasks of the agency. Managing a new and continuing relationship was complicated and difficult especially where there was no experience to draw on.

The reports on evaluation continued. Outcomes still tended to be anecdotal rather than specific and managerial – all sides were still learning about how to measure and test what was happening. By August 1990 there were thirty-three agencies employing 80 000 staff. In addition twenty eight candidates were going though the process of establishment covering 200 000 staff, including the 'agency basis' established within Customs and Excise. The Government had set itself a target of covering half the Civil Service by the end of 1991 – three years from the start. The Revenue departments were now committed to 'operating fully on Next Steps lines'. It was difficult to decide whether the position of the Revenue Departments, accountable through a Board and a Chairman to the Treasury, could have a realistic form of delegation to agencies within their structure when legal rules bound large areas and nationwide equality of treatment was important. The debate demonstrated the flexibility of the agency structure at this stage in its development; the search was for the most effective arrangements for the functions of the Revenue Departments, not whether their systems conformed to a central model.

By mid-1990 the established agencies were receiving new powers. The first agencies would be operating with Trading Funds under the Government Trading Act from April 1991. The first annual reports, and for the early agencies, the first three year reviews of framework documents were being published. The Next Steps Unit reported that they had now established a procedure for the review of framework documents.

The Unit had hoped that a programme of evaluation would be in place by the end of 1991, but even in 1990 Peter Kemp was arguing that Departments needed to sharpen their work on targets and evaluation. The crucial need was to link the outcome measures closely to government policy. The real prize towards which the process was directed was the development of a systematic approach to the management of resources and outcomes. The implementation of government policy had seldom been monitored effectively and there was little evaluation of the outcomes of policies. Research was predominantly academic in its bias, the emphasis in policy making was on new policy rather than the effectiveness of the old. Audit was slow and pedestrian – primarily concerned with where the money went and not with the effectiveness with which expenditure met its objectives.

In 1990 the inclusion of outcome measurement, linked to specific performance indicators in the agencies' annual planning and reporting round for the first time, was designed to produce the evidence of whether policy and resources were achieving the expected results. The Next Steps Unit began to record all the principal performance targets set for the agencies; some are pitifully weak as examples of the best these large and influential organisations could do. They demonstrated both how much had to be done and how inadequately the Civil Service was still equipped for its job. The 1990 review which listed targets for the new agencies did demonstrate that the longer established agencies were becoming more adept at using them. Companies House, one of the first group of agencies, records targets which reflect performance: a reduction in non-filed accounts, as a contribution to a wider objective of increasing compliance; newer agencies tended to record simple activity rates.

By mid-1990 20 chief executives had been appointed following open competitions. The standard Civil Service advertisement did not necessarily find good people – only those with the time and the inclination to read and answer advertisements. Into this vacuum moved the private sector head hunters for whom the public sector was a valuable potential market, as the private sector was moving sharply into recession. The head hunters provided a means of measuring civil servants against a broader peer group outside the public service and brought a new range of skills into the field. However more open recruitment demonstrated how naïve public servants could be about people of whose skills and background they knew little. The strong culture of selecting people on the basis of their intellect and their personality rather than their achievements could result in poor decisions.

I had a telling discussion at about this time with the then first Civil Service Commissioner responsible for overseeing the system for senior appointments. I suggested that the Commission was in a commanding position to become a serious resource for senior appointments. They could set up the necessary data banks, cover public and private sectors and ensure that the new appointments covered the widest possible field. 'Good Heavens, no' was the response: 'We couldn't do that kind of thing properly from here. We simply don't have the skills.' Lack of confidence, lack of vision and an unwillingness to try a new venture were summed up in that simple exchange; they had been overseeing old style appointments for years and had seen nothing wrong with the outcome.

In October 1990 the first major review of the process to establish agencies was published by the Cabinet Office – *Improving Management in Government: The Next Steps Agencies* (Cm. 1261). It was a glossy and expensive document (£8.30) of 44 pages and a sign that the Next Steps Agencies were a serious part of central government. By 1995 the annual report had 357 pages and cost £44.00. In 1997 it had been cut back to 310 pages but cost £45.00.

It is tempting to ask if anyone in government thinks about these prices. The reports seemed to be aimed at Departments, libraries and institutions. It might have been useful to explain to the taxpayer what was going on. The admirable custom of producing short, accessible and cheap government publications had vanished; large, glossy expensive publications give the impression of massaging the ego of the producer rather than a serious attempt at communication with a defined audience. The impression they give is of a communication for those with a professional interest in the structure of government and not the concern of the user of public services or the taxpayer. Quality of service was in danger of being captured by the supplier.

However, within the first report were some important points. It emphasised the continued need for firm budgets and good targets: '. . . what Next Steps is about: progressive and durable improvements in the way government services are delivered'. In Peter Kemp's view many agencies and Departments were still learning how to handle numerical detail. They were reluctant to negotiate and use increased flexibilities; there was a danger of the process ossifying at this point unless there was continued pressure for greater flexibility. Most Departments were far too close to their agencies – although one or two went to the other extreme and behaved as if they had no responsibility at all. The balance had to be carefully struck in sensible and realistic relationships between the two parties.

The number of agencies continued to rise – early in 1991 there were thirty-four agencies covering 80 000 people, with thirty-two candidates and a further 280 000 people in the new rubric as 'agencies or managed on Next Steps lines'. The definition was important. If it was becoming politically necessary in Whitehall to have agencies, it was important to see that what was significant about being an agency was in place. In Kemp's view the emphasis on obtaining specified results, the most effective organisation and as much management flexibility to obtain improvement as possible was at the heart of the Next Steps process. If there was any danger of 'Agency' simply becoming a label it should be challenged: a significant part of the original purpose for developing agencies was to improve the quality of public services.

The requirement that all agencies should produce annual reports was now in place and they show the range and scale of the new agencies. For the first time information was openly available about what happened in all these organisations – what they were doing, how much it cost and what direction they were going in. Almost imperceptibly another significant change was happening. Public servants were coming into the public gaze. Logos and photographs of people at work in Agencies in 1990 had become line drawings and people at work in 1991. In 1992, drawings and coloured photographs had vanished but been replaced by small portrait photographs of the chief executives; the cheerful pictures of agency staff at work had all but disappeared. It was another sign of the bureaucratisation of the system – the boss was more significant than the staff and the function.

Traditionally the Civil Service had been almost obsessively secretive not only about the work they were doing but even who they were. Some reference books gave snippets of information. *Whitaker's Almanac, Who's Who* and *Vachers' Parliamentary Companion* listed names and job titles. The *Civil Service Yearbook* provided some information but only with magnificently obscure job titles and telephone numbers hidden behind enquiry points. The annual reports gave names, pictures, recognisable job titles, functions, expected outcomes and occasionally pay. Pay was not an issue of significance in the old Civil Service; pay ranges were publicly available, with the aid of *Whitaker's* or even one of the Civil Service union diaries, if you knew the grade, you could find out the occasionally pay range. But the new system, particularly for chief executives, meant personal pay ranges and performance bonuses.

Whitehall had never been comfortable with performance pay; the cultural norm of a centrally negotiated pay rate, annual increments and a fixed pension was too deeply entrenched. There was, in theory, a link between pay progression and performance as part of the performance review system but the link depended on the rigour of the assessments made and transmitted in individual annual performance reviews, a process which assumed a management capacity and good interpersonal skills which many of the senior Civil Service lacked. As a result the connection between pay and performance, provided for in the rules, was seldom if ever made. The norm was for everyone to be paid according to grade and seniority. There had been a serious attempt to break the link between promotion and seniority with the introduction of selection boards and the erosion of 'age bars' – a system which prevented the young from being promoted 'too early' but these changes did not provide a direct link between the measurement of successful performance and pay. Publishing pay and performance information for the senior staff of the agencies gave politicians and public commentators an opportunity to challenge performance.

In July 1991 the service element in public organisations was revived. The Prime Minister, John Major, announced the introduction of a 'citizens' charter' to guarantee specified levels of service from public organisations (The Citizen's Charter, 1991). The charter initiative had political pressure behind it and succeeded in pushing many public institutions into taking their quality of service more seriously. It had taken surprisingly long for politicians to realise that improved service quality was or could be a political bonus; it took more time for people to realise that setting targets did not guarantee quality. The task of organising management so that it could provide a specific level of service was still, in many cases, a long way off. Ironically the charter was one of the few public service innovations which the private sector copied.

The charter was a useful step towards service quality – but it was service quality set by the supplier, not by demand. Standards were set by the organisation and were what the management of the organisation thought it could do – or ought to be able to do, and in some cases what it was able to count. The standards did not reflect research into what customers, users or clients might want – many public service providers were convinced their users, if asked, would demand a level of service which would be difficult or more expensive to provide. The service or customer driven organisation was still some way off and had substantial barriers to overcome. Most public services considered that their role was to decide what services to provide, not to provide what their customers might want or need. Balancing service levels required by users, public policy decided by politicians, public financing set by available resources and the capacity of public service management to deliver what was expected was the essence of the public management demanded from senior officials and agency chief executives, but the user requirement remained a low priority.

The pressure to improve standards in practice often took the form of payment of modest compensation for service failure – which was regarded as an adequate response. This was carried to its extreme form by British Rail which was discovered to have been paying out millions of pounds for service failures such as late or cancelled trains for some time before they realised that they should be dealing with the cause rather than simply the effect, and put as much effort into improving punctuality. The charter did strike a chord with users and could have become much more effective if it had been supported by sustained implementation. I walked through a small hospital north east of London one weekend and heard the two women in front of me discussing their reception in the hospital: 'I waited well over 30 minutes; it's not good enough, that charter said no more than 15 minutes'. Not many government initiatives get such recognition so quickly.

Familiar themes in managing the process of setting up agencies were recurring in 1991 and 1992: the processes and controls within Departments, the need to improve financial regimes and the capacity to set targets and performance measures. There was also a more difficult issue – the longer term implications of these changes for the Civil Service. The role of the new chief executives needed to be clear not only in their agency but also within their departments. In many cases their distinctive functions were far from obvious. In the case of the Prison Service, in the 1993 Framework Document, the Chief Executive was described as being both the Chief Executive of the Prison Service and the Home Secretary's 'principal policy adviser on matters relating to the Prison Service' an almost impossible balancing act. In other words he was to be both agent and principal. In the 1994 Highways Agency Framework Document, the role is more specific and less ambiguous: 'the Chief Executive advises the Secretary of State on operational policy affecting the Agency's work'. In the 1992 Framework Document for the Public Record Office, a short note under 'reporting and monitoring' spells out where the work will be done: 'As necessary, the Keeper will also meet the Grade 2 in the Law and Policy Group . . . to enable him to advise the Lord Chancellor.'

The early enthusiasms were beginning to come up against the reality of performance. The results of 1991–1992 were mixed. Unrealistic expectations of constant improvement, in many cases with little or no investment, showed up in reduced performance outcomes. Some enthusiasts expected that a change of name would be as effective as a magic wave of a wand; there was a reluctance to recognise that improvements would need hard work and probably some failures along the way. One important link was forged in 1991 – the Citizen's Charter and the agencies were pushed together. All agencies were instructed to 'seek charter accreditation' for their services; but the quality of the accreditation process appeared to be far from rigorous and fairly bureaucratic. Nevertheless agencies were reminded of the importance of service quality: they were required to have consultations with customers, to set explicit service standards, to be open in their dealings with their customers and to provide full and accurate information about the services they provided. These steps emphasised yet again that service was important and that an organisation should face outwards to its clients and not inwards to itself.

By January 1992, the expansion of the programme had progressed reasonably smoothly; there were fifty-seven agencies; thirty executive units (in Customs and Excise), thirty further candidates and thirty-four Inland Revenue Executive offices. The second annual review was published – giving a clear signal that action was continuing, performance was improving and Agencies were fully part of the system. The Citizen's Charter was in place in Agencies, and the first Agency 'Charter Marks' – awards for specific service excellence – were being awarded. The Government's other new scheme, market testing, a requirement to 'test' the cost of supplying services with costs in the private sector, was beginning and plans for market testing services were already underway in several agencies.

A report in 1991, by Sir Angus Fraser the Prime Minister's Adviser on management and recently retired Chairman of Customs and Excise, on the organisation of central Departments made some recommendations for their new role. The report, *Making the most of Next Steps: The management of Ministers' Departments and their Agencies* (HMSO, 1991), focused on the consequences of the development of agencies. It did not consider the causes of the original Efficiency Unit findings about the managerial competence of the senior Civil Service and the confusion of roles between permanent secretaries and ministers. It made some useful comments on what was needed to improve the way departments worked with their agencies but it did not observe that the emphasis on agencies had allowed implementation of the recommendation on the training and selection of people within Departments to fall.

The other gap within departments – the development of an approach to policy making which took account of the existence of Agencies and the need for a new specificity in programme design and measurement was not considered. The recommendations included a statement of a Department's strategic role and a 'relatively modest target' reduction in the size of finance and personnel departments of 25%. It recommended enlargement of the delegated powers of agencies, and clarity in the distinction between the accounting officer roles of Chief Executive and Permanent Secretary, properly customised pay and personnel regimes for Departments and Agencies and urged Departments to keep up with the need for a constant process of change. It was sensible and balanced and reinforced many of the points made by the project manager in his discussions with the Treasury and Civil Service Select Committee. It was a report which gave Whitehall few difficulties.

By 1992 it was five fast changing years since the Next Steps Report had been written. The government was quite right to draw a line under the process of setting up agencies, and target completion by 1993. In the 1992 Annual Report the new project manager said 'I expect to see all agency candidates announced before the end of 1993'. The process was becoming institutionalised. Half the Civil Service was working in developed executive units: the 'principles' of Next Steps had been applied in a range of different ways through 'executive agencies' and 'executive offices'. There were still a further twenty-six candidate agencies working on their proposals but by 1992 the main organisational task was completed – the structure of the Civil Service had changed radically. It had taken only four years to achieve the critical mass which was eventually to put most of the public service – by 1995 70% – into distinct management units.

The processes were improving; there were simpler procedures for small agencies and the Citizen's Charter principles were now part of the standard package, giving a service and customer focus to a large part of the public sector. The financial arrangements were improving and the possibility of greater delegation in pay bargaining was now more realistic. There was still a strong reluctance by many agencies to accept the responsibility of delegation but the Treasury were now committed to it. They had accepted the arguments for delegation of the pay systems to departments and agencies and were finding it frustratingly difficult to persuade organisations to accept responsibilities for which they had been clamouring five years before.

THE END OF THE BEGINNING

In the middle of 1992, there was a substantial change in the management of Next Steps. Peter Kemp left the Government, to be replaced by a senior career civil servant, Richard Mottram. His job was to complete the Next Steps initiative but he represented an inevitable break with the commitment shown by Peter Kemp to the ideas and the philosophy of Next Steps. By 1992 the revolution was over, the changes were in place and accepted as part of the machine. The glamour was transferred to the Citizen's Charter and market testing while the Next Steps Unit continued to implement the remaining agency candidates and to 'administer' the process of review and assessment which was the essence of the more centralised and formalised management process.

There were two serious failures out of the 105 agencies and they failed for precisely the reasons described in the original Efficiency Unit report. In the case of the Prison Service there was a flawed relationship with the responsible Department, a misunderstanding of the roles of Home Secretary and Chief Executive, culminating in an unpleasant and public row and the dismissal of the Chief Executive. In the case of the Child Support Agency, highly sensitive functions were badly planned, political rows were poorly handled and the agency proved to be seriously under-resourced for its tasks and subject to frequent changes of policy. Most of the other Agencies flourished; the success of the changes was recognised and reflected in much of what the Civil Service did.

'Next Steps' did fall victim to its popularity. The Civil Service system embraced the structural changes. A radical programme for devising new approaches to management and service quality became a process which gave more attention to its procedures than to its outcomes. The Civil Service's glossy booklet on *The Origins of Next Steps* presented the programme as warmly embraced by the Civil Service – but it was about setting up agencies. The criticism of the senior Civil Service and the confusion of roles between permanent secretaries and ministers were airbrushed out. The arguments and disagreements were ignored. It even went so far as to say of the report: 'like the best tunes the idea seemed familiar on first hearing', an extremely odd description of the long drawn out and bitter process of reaching agreement on the Efficiency Unit Report. What this disingenuous record does demonstrate was how eager the senior civil servants, whose cheerful pictures illustrate the booklet, were to show that they were taking the challenge seriously (Goldsworthy, 1991).

Like so many people at the top of organisations, the senior Civil Service were requiring change from those below them in the hierarchy but failing to change themselves. The need for more management experience was ignored; the focus of organisations on the job they had to do was ignored and the need for systematic improvements in public service was lost. Instead Whitehall became mired in greater bureaucracy while dangerously believing that it had modernised because it had 'Next Steps' Agencies. The reports, recorded earlier in this chapter demonstrate the number counting approach to the changes – so many agencies, so many civil servants. It began to feel uncomfortably like 'implementing Fulton' all over again.

At the beginning of the twenty-first century the Civil Service was to find again that a radical government was not content with the same excuses. The Civil Service was falling behind, not leading, in the management of the public sector. Public services were failing to provide the quality and scale of services demanded by the public and promised by the politicians. Lord Fulton and his Commission's warnings thirty-five years earlier were still relevant: the leaders of the public service should adapt and evolve to deal with continuous changes. They should focus, not on systems and procedures, but on the job to be done. The ideas in the Next Steps Report may, in retrospect, have seemed 'familiar on first hearing' but they seem to have had the same response as before.

Not only were they familiar in 1989 they would continue to be so. The senior Civil Service had reorganised its empire. It still failed to recognise the need to modernise itself. In the next chapter we consider the reaction to the introduction of the proposals in the Next Steps Report from commentators, academics and politicians and draw some lessons from the events surrounding it.

8.   Views and comments: a success or a staging post?

By the mid-1990s agencies were no longer a 'reform'; they were regarded as a part of the government. The management structure of nearly three quarters of the Civil Service had been altered, in many cases irrevocably. Most agencies worked to specific, published targets with published performance indicators. The function, objectives and results achieved by each organisation were all available. The chief executives of the agencies had a recognised public responsibility and published personal objectives against which their achievements could be tested; their pay was influenced by performance, and failure could be the subject of public debate. The establishment of organisations designed to focus on Fulton's basic, guiding principle: 'look at the job first' had been achieved. But the concern expressed by both the Fulton Commission and the Efficiency Unit report about the management skills and competence of the senior Civil Service remained largely unmet.

The agency changes have not only been radical in organisational terms. If that were all it really would be just a change for the writing paper and organisational theorists; the changes have forced forward improvements in service levels and the culture of the public service. Offices are open at more convenient times, staff are generally more helpful and courteous. There does appear – to the member of the public at the end of the telephone – some improvement in the attitude of the staff and the services available. These changes are not all or only attributable to 'Next Steps' as it had become generally known. What Next Steps did was make it possible and legitimate to think about and introduce new approaches. The flexible structure, the speed of the changes and the principle of focusing on the job to be done meant that ways of introducing improvements were a mainstream activity and expected, not something that had to be fought for. As Foster and Plowden noted a decade after the Next Steps Report was accepted by the Government: 'the Prime Minister's statement (in 1988) was momentous' (Foster and Plowden, 1996).

There are some negatives. Once Next Steps was accepted as part of the Civil Service structure, it began to conform to Civil Service habits. Agencies and the central Unit developed their own bureaucracy and processes. It would have been more encouraging to see a constant revision of rules and regulations reducing them to a minimum rather than increasing them. The development of agencies should have seen a reduction in bureaucracy as part of focusing on the job. The tendency in all public sector organisations to do more, even when they are supposed to be doing less, needs constant vigilance. There is enough for the public sector to do without indulging in unnecessary regulation. Any bureaucracy costs money. The priority for action should be compelling if it is to take precedence. Government action frequently imposes a cost elsewhere in addition to the inevitable unintended consequences. The value of that cost needs to be taken into account in deciding whether to act. Next Steps should not have imposed more than marginal costs. I suspect that it did; some of those costs might have been incurred without Next Steps but the 'systems' and the rules that have grown up around UK agencies have imposed more. Ironically, the pressure for privatisation in the early 1990s increased the complexity: the three year reviews of framework documents (a fixed requirement, not at a time best for the agency concerned) had added to them 'a prior options exercise' and a market testing process to be completed before the framework review.

Previous chapters have traced the background to Next Steps, its origins in the management changes of the 1980s, the process of discussing and establishing what was impeding improvement, the production of the report and the process of implementation. I have deliberately recorded what happened as it happened without intruding hindsight into the record. There have been many questions about the work of the Efficiency Unit and the approach to developing the ideas that emerged as the Next Steps Report. In its origins, the work was an internal review of progress based within the Efficiency Unit – using the Unit's resources of team members and advisers from within and outside the Civil Service. This was not an occasion when outside consultants could bring more fresh thinking. We had an exceptional range of senior advisers from the Civil Service and the private sector and Efficiency Unit members from the private sector working with the team. We drew on practical experience of the Civil Service and major private sector enterprises at all levels.

The reaction of the Civil Service to the Next Steps Report and the introduction of agencies was mixed. As we had demonstrated there were significant differences between parts of the 'unified civil service'. For those who worked in a local office or a small operation, the advantages of the potential changes were at least as great as the disadvantages. Greater flexibility, more freedom in taking decisions, the ability to improve quality of service were all advantages to those struggling with the day to day restrictions in government offices. There should have been other advantages; reductions in rules and regulations, less heavy handed head offices, and clarity about what was expected or required from the organisation.

These changes, properly handled make management easier, together with the advantage that people responsible for achieving good results could receive recognition and responsibility, instead of the numbing and discouraging effect of being part of an anonymous machine.

For senior civil servants the picture looked different. Their established patterns of working were being disrupted, their way of managing had been heavily criticised. It was significant that no-one, at any time, challenged the diagnosis in the Next Steps Report. Even the Treasury argued only about the solution. It was the conclusion that as the system did not work it should be changed and the solution proposed that aroused opposition. In a bitter and emotional outburst one senior civil servant accused the unit of deliberately destroying all that was precious about the Civil Service. He would not accept the argument that it could be strengthened, not destroyed, by becoming more professional and effective.

Many of those at Deputy and Permanent Secretary level carried a heavy burden of responsibility and public accountability. The existing system, for all its defects, appeared to those involved in it to work. There was accountability to Parliament, answerability to the Public Accounts Committee (PAC), scrutiny by the National Audit Office and a decent veil of secrecy over all the rest. The proposals in the report, while offering benefits and challenges to executive agencies, implied more substantial changes to the senior Civil Service. The new relationship with the agencies altered the role of senior management by introducing chief executives, and implied a shift in power to senior officials with management responsibilities.

The wariness of Ministers reflected these concerns. They had few collective discussions of the Efficiency Unit report; for many Ministers the arcane debates about accounting officers and framework documents were for the civil servants, not for them. Much of the support in the Ministerial discussions in 1997 reflected the Prime Minister's obvious interest rather then any widespread conviction or indeed interest in management or the quality of public services. The management of the Civil Service was not an issue which raised tempers unless there were problems in individual cases within a particular Department. Most ministers concentrated their attention on their own policy areas and did not stray outside.

Implementation began to change these reactions. The caution of the first year or two, while the Next Steps team were exploring the implications of their task and winning over converts, had altered by the third and fourth years to widespread acceptance. The support of the Head of the Civil Service and the Prime Minister were important factors in the first couple of years and by the third year of implementation it was possible to assess the scale of the change, to see how far the impact was substantial or minimal and what the real benefits were. Some mistakes were inevitable, but the majority of the agencies worked smoothly from the start.

The official record of the processes of implementing Next Steps has been fully documented by the agencies themselves and the Next Steps Unit in their annual reports, in the Next Steps 'briefing notes' published quarterly by the Cabinet Office and in evidence to the House of Commons Treasury and Civil Service Select Committee. Some organisations, notably Social Security, the Child Support Agency and the Prisons Agency have had close external scrutiny and have demonstrated the difficulties in establishing agencies which had a high level of political scrutiny or difficult policy issues. The test of whether it was all worth it should be set against the three aims in the original report and the tasks set for the team by Peter Kemp. Assessing the outcome is difficult; government is difficult to assess and evaluate, the issues are complex, the outputs far from clear and affected by circumstances beyond direct control.

ASSESSING THE OUTCOME

The difficulty of assessing the outcome has not deterred the commentators who, as Peter Kemp once remarked, have had a field day. Articles, chapters in books on modern government, whole books, seminars and conferences have fed an apparent thirst for information. The speed of academic reaction was unusual. Within two years MSc students were studying the report and holding seminars to discuss it. Modest dissertations began to appear, deferential students asked for interviews, the Government's Economic and Social Research Council funded academic researchers who arrived with questionnaires. There were few sources to draw on about the origins of the Efficiency Unit report.

Those who have tried to disentangle what happened have had a difficult time. The facts are hard to come by, and in some cases, genuinely confusing. The government's own publication, *The Origins of Next Steps*, smoothed out the difficulties and gives the impression of a trouble-free piece of sensible administrative change. It ignored the criticisms of the dominance of policy making over management and the weak skill base of the senior Civil Service (Goldsworthy, 1991). The reasons for this kind of presentation are obvious. Most people are only interested in what finally happened rather than in how it happened. The Government is interested in presenting the outcome, once the proposition has been accepted, as successfully as possible.

Other commentators watching the genesis of the report unfold tended to latch on to one part of the story and emphasise that. The gossip about rows with the Treasury was too good to be ignored and there was no alternative version available. Peter Hennessy in his epic 'Whitehall' reflected the outsider's view. He was doubtful of any chance of success in his first edition written as the report was published: 'All in all, it seemed to be the revolution that never was' (Hennessy, 1989). Even so experienced an observer appeared to accept the stories doing the rounds of Whitehall: 'the report was sat upon for months and then diluted liberally'. He was caught by timing. By the time his second edition appeared he was more enthusiastic; his analysis of the structural changes caused by Next Steps by 2000 is masterly.

Clive Priestley, Lord Rayner's Head of the Efficiency Unit, reflected accurately in an article in *The Independent* that 'ministers lack of interest in management is echoed by many Parliamentarians, much of the media, and, alas much of the public' (*The Independent*, 26 February 1988). Clive Priestley raised a fundamental issue: the politicians, who are responsible for the results achieved by the government machine, hold it to account and use its services, are in most cases not interested in how it works, and nor is anyone else until something goes wrong. And if how an organisation is managed is ignored, sooner or later it goes seriously wrong. In Britain, the government of the 1960s and 1970s, about which politician after politician complained, was badly managed. Few people took management at all seriously. Even Mr Heath's administration, which tried to improve the workings of government, concentrated on the comfortable topics, more training, more thinking. They did not take on the more difficult areas: facing up to the difficult choices linking priorities, outcomes and resources.

The Efficiency Unit scrutiny identified a wide range of Ministerial involvement from indifference to what Mrs Thatcher had described as 'meddling'. The solution proposed in the report had been to place on the policy makers the obligation to be clear and specific about how the policy for which they were responsible should be carried out in practice and to agree what was to be done with those responsible for implementation. Senior management should be responsible for how the policy should be implemented. In government the line was never going to be an easy one to draw; but there were many new agencies that performed the same function from year to year for whom this structure was ideal. But while politically sensitive areas were marked out as needing special attention, they seldom received it.

The case of the Home Office, where Agency status for the Prison Service appeared to be a way of avoiding political trouble, contrasts with the several ministers responsible for the Child Support Agency where operational and political problems were dealt with by a stream of detailed intervention in the operation of the Agency. It is possible, given the tendency in the government to ignore the importance of managing resources effectively to achieve objectives, that without the changes in the 1980s the system of government would have spiralled downwards out of control. Accountability would be poorer than it is now, and the inability to control outcomes and resource use would have led to costly and clumsy cutting of services and more expensive and poorer government.

THE POLITICAL REACTION

In the political memoirs of ministers who took the final decisions on the Next Steps Report, there is an indication of interest they took in the Civil Service. The politician most involved, Mrs Thatcher, demonstrates the Priestley theory to the full. She barely mentions Next Steps – in a footnote on page 49 of *The Downing Street Years*, a realistic reflection of the significance of management issues in a busy politician's life, but under-valuing her role in a significant change in the structure of central govern-ment. She provided support and encouragement, she knew that her policies depended on the competence of the supporting management systems but she understood that this was an area for others to give real priority to. She never let go of the importance of sustaining interest in how matters were progressing but she knew it had little political priority. Next Steps was argued out by officials not by ministers.

Prime Ministers with experience as officials – the most recent examples were Harold Wilson and Edward Heath – spent their time in the classic mandarin roles as advisers on policy and were nowhere near a management task. In Wilson's *The Governance of Britain* (Wilson, 1976) which one might expect to contain some substance on the Civil Service, the references amount to two topics and half a dozen passing comments. George Brown took the issue more seriously and discussed both the Crichel Down and the Sachsenhausen cases ending with the unexpected remark: 'I was not going to have a civil servant pilloried for what was a ministerial decision' (Brown, 1971). Ministers with departmental experience view the senior Civil Service role more seriously. Mrs Castle found the attentions of the mandarins, even at the more plebeian Ministry of Labour, something to regard warily and respond to with caution (Castle, 1993). But even Mrs Castle wrote of the people immediately around her, not of the thousands who worked in her Departments.

Most politicians' views of changes in structure and management in the UK government demonstrate how little most of them know about how the organisation works. The only preparatory route to ministerial office is the dogsbody life of a junior minister where a minister learns on the job, not as in some other countries, by running big departments or agencies.

Those roles are all regarded in the United Kingdom as the preserve of officials for constitutional reasons; the barriers between official and politician are substantial and difficult to overcome. In the mid-1980s the central departments ran a series of seminars for new junior Ministers to explain what happened in the Cabinet Office and the Treasury and how the Civil Service was organised centrally. Most of those who attended the seminars appeared to be surprisingly grateful for explanations of an organisation about which they clearly had little or no knowledge.

As politicians become younger and more specialised the chance of them having any experience outside politics recedes and the opportunity to understand how large organisations are run, other than the political parties, is rare. Trade Unions, the Bar, academic life, the press and the party organisations which provide the background for most politicians are none of them organisations where a wise person would look for experience in how to manage things well. Politicians bring what they have experienced personally with them to the House of Commons, as a journalist, a barrister, an academic, a political researcher or a back-bench MP. Some have an instinctive idea about how to take decisions and what is necessary to make a large organisation work effectively. The rarer politician also understands his or her own limitations and stands well back from 'meddling' in Mrs Thatcher's phase. But most are confused and uneasy. One constitutional expert at the London School of Economics (LSE) said when there was a reshuffle or a new government his phone rang constantly as scared new Ministers begged for advice on what to do when faced with a Department and officials.

The few comments on Next Steps in the main political autobiographies of the 1980s confirm politicians' lack of interest in the workings of the machine. A change to the organisation of government, described by their colleagues on the House of Commons Select Committee as 'the most important change this century' is effectively brushed aside. Nigel Lawson's autobiography does discuss Next Steps in some detail but it appears to be written, understandably enough, to justify the Treasury's position. Although Next Steps was said to threaten the public expenditure control of the Treasury fundamentally, it is covered in three pages out of 450. He was concerned about accountability, but perhaps he had never read the note on accountability annexed to the Next Steps Report. He had had no trouble with the same model of accountability for Social Security and the Inland Revenue, where it had been operating for some time.

His description illustrates admirably the difficulties of dealing with the Treasury. It consists of setting up imaginary horrors and then explaining how the Treasury successfully defeated these non-existent giants. He claimed that Robin Ibbs had no interest in controlling public expenditure – an absurdity since one of the main purposes of the debate was about how to control expenditure effectively. What Nigel Lawson was arguing was that there was only one way to control public expenditure – the way the Treasury did in 1988. Anyone who did not accept the current form of Treasury control as the only possible route had to be against the whole process. Controlling public expenditure meant Treasury control of public expenditure; no one else had a valid interest or competence in the matter. The Treasury solution, Nigel Lawson argued, was that the management issues could be solved by setting targets and getting the Treasury to monitor them. Indeed, and that was part of what had been suggested all along – but the Treasury seemed too busy fighting imaginary battles to listen to what was being said. Lawson implies that Peter Kemp's appointment was part of fixing the Next Steps row so that the Treasury had control. That may be what he was told but that appointment was considered long before the Treasury were prepared to admit that there would ever be agencies of any kind.

The basis of Lawson's argument was that, in his view, it was not possible to achieve a better use of resources by the way government was managed. He posed a simple alternative. The only choices which would provide effective control over expenditure were market forces or the current system of Treasury control: 'Treasury control was essential. The alternative was no financial discipline at all'. He used, as a clincher to his argument, the example of what happened in Russia where he claimed without a free market the removal of communist control inevitably led to anarchy. The modest progress to greater flexibility suggested in the Next Steps Report hardly added up to anarchy. 'Towards the end of 1987, out of the blue a new Ibbs initiative' is how he describes the discussions on Next Steps. He must have forgotten the informal cabinet meeting in the summer of 1987 to discuss the proposals. Admittedly he sent John Major, then his ministerial deputy as Chief Secretary to the Treasury, to the first meeting with a stiff Treasury brief to oppose everything. He may well not have known that work on pilot agencies had gone on from July to October 1987 and that I had discussed the origins, the findings and the conclusions and recommendations of the report with his permanent secretaries from late 1986 and throughout 1987. But, it is surprising that he was not told about a row that has raged for many months and to which Treasury officials attached so much importance.

Both Nigel Lawson and Margaret Thatcher demonstrate in their record of their time in office how small a part the management of the Civil Service plays in a United Kingdom politician's world view. For both of them, the appointment of Lord Rayner, the Top Salaries Review Board pay review award in 1986 which created a political storm, and a reference to Next Steps is the totality of any substantial comment of the huge machine which made their policies work. In the central departments there is no close contact with the main body of the Civil Service. But although Ministers are completely dependent on the Civil Service for the implementation of their domestic policy the system for achieving their policy objectives appears to have been out of sight and taken for granted. For most senior Ministers the 'Civil Service' is the small group working closely with them at the apex of the hierarchy, with whom they often develop good working relationships – the vast organisation beyond head office is out of sight.

PUBLIC SECTOR THEORY

The group which has expended most effort on Next Steps is the political theorists and those still interested in that 1950s topic, public administration. The interest and attention given to agencies has been unusual, as has the development of a vocabulary, jargon and a typology to discuss it. Using the tag line 'the Next Steps' as the title has led to confusion about which part of the process is being discussed. The original main title of the Efficiency Unit report, *Improving Management in Government*, disappeared at an early stage; it was dropped from the Cabinet Office annual reports in 1992.

The literature on public sector reform is tricky to interpret. The traditional political theorist approach of setting up theoretical models is clearly part of academic debate and may assist in exploring what happens. In the case of Next Steps it seems to have been neither very helpful nor particularly illuminating. Patricia Greer in her study of Next Steps in Social Security has perhaps gone as far as any commentator in using theoretical models to explain events (Greer, 1994). Her discussion of the 'origins' of Next Steps is hampered by her search for a theoretical basis for the ideas in the report. No one would disagree with the proposition that the Next Steps Report is built on what has gone before but there were few people in Whitehall in 1986 who would use public choice or agency theory as justification for the direction of the debate about management.

What is missing from much of the analysis is a recognition of what was distinctive in the Next Steps Report. The report was based, not on theory or academic research but on what the people involved said was needed: a severely practical basis for recommending changes. The sources for the conclusions of the report are set out in both the main text and the annexes but Ms Greer, while delving deep into agency theory, public choice theory and the issues of transactional costs, ignores the data at her fingertips in the report. Our collective sub-conscious is drawn on: 'The ideas behind Next Steps, albeit unconsciously, clearly draw on micro economics' agency and public choice theories'; 'history and theory have played a large part in shaping the development of Next Steps.'

The crucial recommendation in the Next Steps Report: finding the right organisation for the job to be done, explicitly rejects establishing a model. The significance of implementation receives little mention in the literature. These gaps make any discussion of agency theory or the development of 'contract government' misleading: 'Next Steps has learnt from these earlier experiences and has sought solutions to the dilemmas by, albeit unconsciously, drawing on theory. Next Steps has . . . looked to administrative theory in its attempt to avoid the ambiguity, uncertainty and distortion which resulted from earlier arm's length relationships.' (Greer, 1994) This assertion ignores what is written in the report. I suppose one could be accused of doing almost anything 'albeit unconsciously' but when the alternative evidence of what we did consciously is readily accessible it seems odd to read so much that was not there into a relatively simple document.

The confusion which is easy to slip into between 'Next Steps' as shorthand for the report, or for the work of the Next Steps team, or for the whole process from 1986 onwards, makes the task of understanding some of the discussion more difficult. There is an implication in much of the literature that there is a concept called 'Next Steps' which appears to encompass the whole of what is often described as 'new public management'. This assumption, too, is inaccurate. The Next Steps Report was about clarifying responsibilities, objectives and relationships in a way that made it possible to give greater flexibility to one specific constrained and centralised institution. It was not a theory and it was not a model. Financial management information, budgeting, encouraging greater efficiency, contracting out and a range of other activities began before and would have continued without the Next Steps work. What the work of the Next Steps Unit and especially the first agencies did was to provide and develop an approach to organisational structures within which these developments could be used more effectively, and to demonstrate how to do it.

Ms Greer is not alone. Other commentators have had even more difficulty understanding what was going on. Goldsmith and Page in 1997 wrote a forlorn essay 'Farewell to the British State'. They made the fair point that there is some danger in talking up the existence of a serious revolution in the public service under the Thatcher and Major Governments. They argue, reasonably, that there are few periods of 18 years in the past 100 in which there were not substantial changes to be seen. They go on to say that: 'There were many experiments, as well as false starts, before the Next Steps were developed.' Many different ideas were canvassed and, in some cases, tried out. In a huge organisation like the Civil Service it would be worrying if that were not so. But the implied criticism of the 'earlier experiments' is simply not justified. A good outcome often depends on experiment and it is frequently from false starts that better ideas emerge (Goldsmith and Page, 1997).

A less accurate proposition that: 'the Next Steps initiative was in large part a reaction to the failure of FMI' was based on a misunderstanding of what the FMI was designed to do and did (Goldsmith and Page, 1997). It was shared by another academic, Spencer Zifcak, who was one of several commentators drawing out common themes between the UK and other commonwealth countries (Zifcak, 1994). The FMI was designed to provide management and financial information and a basis for management systems for an organisation which had very little of either. By the time the FMI Unit was disbanded most departments had reasonably competent systems and most understood what had to be done to improve them and continued to do so. But the public service management systems could not provide the greater flexibility that people with the information and the systems available through the FMI wanted to make progress. Peter Hennessy identified the problem, quoting Tom Stratford, a manager at the Sheffield testing station of the Vehicle Inspectorate, one of the first agencies: 'we are getting to a point where they are actually putting brakes on us. I think we're moving a little bit . . . faster than they might want us to at this stage'. Mr Stratford was demonstrating why the flexibility of agencies were so needed (LWT *Whitehall*, May/June 1988, in Hennessy, 2001).

The underlying point about the origins of Next Steps and our worry about the failure of management reforms to produce substantial results by the mid-1980s was not 'the failure' of the FMI, it was a recognition that the FMI on its own could not produce the improvements that were needed. The FMI was generally well organised, well managed and an essential building block in the process of improving the way the public sector is managed. The FMI could never have provided a complete solution to the issues of public management, and no one directly involved thought it would. It provided more and better information. The Civil Service had to decide what to do with that information. The Next Steps recommendations were the next necessary part of the process, not a reaction to failure.

The problem in 1986 was the absence of the results which had been hoped for. It could be argued that the Civil Service had 'failed' to analyse what would be needed to achieve those results. The interest in the outcome of Next Steps suggests they were not alone. At that stage in management development there was a popular culture of introducing 'projects' which dealt with one topic or problem. There was pressure to define a project properly and implement what had been defined, a reaction to badly managed projects in the past. The difficulty was that this approach ignored the impact of a project on the rest of the organisation. A 'project' tended to be cut off from its surroundings and could fail to produce what was hoped for. 'Project culture', a feature of development aid as well as organisational change, sounds good, but in a complicated setting projects can fail, not because they are bad projects, but because they do not take into account the world around them. The FMI 'project' did need someone to take the changes to management which the FMI had put in place on to the next and wider stage. It would be perfectly reasonable to argue that the Next Steps Report performed that function among its outcomes.

The Civil Service before Mrs Thatcher had successes as well as its dark corners but it is important to be careful about how they are described. Critics of many government reforms are fond of glossing over the mess the reforms were designed to clear up. In Britain, the National Health Services changes of the past quarter of a century are almost invariably criticised as though what went before was adequate, just as the defects of the nationalised rail company, British Rail, are forgotten in the chaos of the privatised industry. Goldsmith and Page (1997) consider that the impact of the new approach to customers as a result of the changes of the 1980s has been overemphasised: 'a long-standing public sector ethos has *probably* (my italics) encompassed those interests (the customers) in any case'.

The 'public service ethos' is a curious construct. It is seldom defined precisely and can be used to describe both working conditions and dedication to providing a service. In many public employees it reflects a genuine pride in performing a useful task: the policeman settling a rowdy argument without violence, the postman delivering letters through appalling weather, the nurse caring for patients in pain and fear. But it is also used to describe life in the cosy institutions of the state where the struggle to find an answer to a difficult problem is modified by what is 'practical' and by personal advancement. It used to be sanctimoniously advanced as a reason for admiring the professional public servant over his better paid contemporaries in 'business' in the days when business was not for gentlemen. Goldsmith and Page's assertion is wishful thinking. Individual public servants were indeed kind, courteous and helpful to individual members of the public; but the system they worked in was directed to process and not to people who were entitled to a service. The predominant ethos for both civil servant and user was that the public were fortunate to receive help or a service. The users were expected to thank the provider politely, forgetting that they had paid for it. It is not possible to assert that 'probably' customers interests were considered because the government provided a public service – the ethos was closer to that of a nineteenth-century charity than a modern public service.

Goldsmith and Page conclude: '[a] customer orientation among officials at all levels was, *as far as one can tell* (my italics) present amongst public employees before 1979'. No-one who used public services then could possibly write these words with any eye to reality. There is an important distinction, which is fundamental to any discussion of culture change, between people answering a question with: 'Yes I am customer conscious' and what their organisations do in practice. Most civil servants had no idea who their customer was. One of the difficulties faced by teams doing efficiency scrutinies in the early 1980s was the inability of many civil servants to understand that they might have someone who could be described as a customer. The organisations dealing with transfer payments regarded the public as 'clients' and more usually 'claimants', that is, in a suppliant role, rather than as customers. The systems showed no sign of being 'customer conscious'. Office hours were, at best, 9.00am to 5.00pm regardless of whether the customer, user or client could be there during the working day. Staff worked office hours and had no flexibility to increase numbers to meet demand over lunch hours or before holidays. If a customer was lucky they might be dealt with by someone who was courteous or anxious to be helpful but that was no substitute for an organisation run to meet the needs of its customers.

Brian Hogwood's essay on Next Steps, 'Restructuring central government', describes Next Steps as 'a major development in British Public Administration' and then asks reasonably enough – is it a completely fresh start? (Hogwood, 1993). He picks out the point that the Rayner scrutinies dealt with efficiency rather than new policies. He was quite right; it was the 'how' of policy implementation which was traditionally ignored by the policy makers, the 'what' received all the attention, which was why the efficiency strategy was instituted by Rayner. There was a marked lack of information about what worked or could work passing from operators to policy makers. The scrutinies were a serious attempt to improve the information flow by forcing senior people to confront the operational stupidities of badly made or ill thought out policies. On the surface, as in the first scrutiny of the Treasury typists, the scope looked modest, and scrutinies were described as dealing with candle ends, but over the years, the evidence they provided forced attention onto policies as well.

Hogwood asserts that, though dramatic in a British context, the establishment of agencies brings Britain closer to the Swedish and United States models. This is to be confused by names instead of looking at the substance. Almost all the commentators, including Hogwood, ignored the detail. United Kingdom executive agencies are distinctive above all because of the structure of the framework documents. The requirement for specificity in outcomes, linked to resource allocation and performance indictors was a significant development because it was a formal requirement for each agency. Both sides had to agree to what was expected.

Describing what policy outcomes were wanted and how they should be achieved was the responsibility of senior civil servants, and ultimately of Ministers. It is an exceedingly difficult task. One very senior official reflected that there were probably at most a handful of people in Whitehall in the 1980s who would be capable of making the intellectual link between policy, implementation and outcome. Most political policies are broad general statements of intent; sometimes publicity is given to statements of planned expenditure and occasionally when a specific outcome is wanted – a hospital, a road or a new examination system – there is a clear outcome in mind but more often the detail is left unspecified. If there is legislation the legal position has to be specific, but not the administrative arrangements. An executive agency could not operate effectively unless the policy makers, working with the agency, could interpret their policy in terms which could be implemented. It is difficult for an outside observer to identify the gap between policy statements and implementation, or perhaps to realise how serious that gap could be.

In theory the elegance of the United Kingdom administrative system pre-supposed the smooth movement of policy to guidance to instructions to operational action. In practice this process was fractured and inadequate. Inarticulate and vague policy generalisations had to be interpreted and transmitted to the people responsible for delivery. Success in delivery of policies, where it occurred, owed a great deal to the common sense and competence of relatively junior but experienced staff. As a very junior principal in my late 20s I was handed a single sheet of paper with seven headings on it by a newly elected Minister and told that that was the legislation the government wanted for the next session. There was no more 'policy' to guide me and my colleagues. It took a year and over 250 clauses to translate that sheet of paper into legislation even before the task of implementation could begin.

The search for a methodology for Next Steps has been extensive. The original point of agencies, as both the report and the Project Manager made clear, is that they were not designed in categories, they were designed because categories were unhelpful, and in some cases positively harmful. An agency should be designed to fit its tasks, not a system: once that basic point was forgotten, or, in the case of many of the commentators – and possibly the Civil Service – overlooked, the survival of the fundamental purpose of the Next Steps agency was at risk. It was in part a reflection of the serious problem rightly identified by Greer: what was wrong was a heavyweight, over centralised bureaucracy. The solution was to free up the institutions to make them work better. If you forgot that the point was to provide a better service, not to set up a particular kind of organisation, the distortion of the analysis and the outcome becomes inevitable.

Hogwood's comment that there is no typical Next Steps agency risks missing one of the cardinal points, repeatedly emphasised by Peter Kemp. His analysis by size, status or chief executive, funding origins, staffing or monopoly status tells us straightforward things about the structure of a range of agencies, and could possibly tell us something about similarity of functions if the 'tailor made' structure proposed by Peter Kemp was always followed (Hogwood, 1993). This kind of analysis can compound the confusion. It implies that the size, status or the role of the chief executive tells us something significant about all the agencies in a similar group, although there is no real reason why any of these factors should be relevant other than at a simplistic level. The significant factor should be diversity, especially if the proposition in the original report holds good. What would be really interesting would be to know whether the concept of the importance of diversity proved to be valid. Hogwood appears to suggest that it might be valid, although for his analysis it is a 'problem': 'one of the problems in presenting a brief overview of Next Steps agencies . . . is the huge variation in size and characteristics of agencies. There is no such thing as a typical Next Steps agency.' Nor should there be.

Were we right to conclude that organisations needed different approaches to escape from the stifling controls of a centralised system? My own view was that we were, it was only by establishing the principle of individual organisations that flexibility could develop. By the early 1990s when the Treasury was pushing agencies to use greater flexibility in their internal personnel management, it was evident that part of our argument had been accepted.

Campbell and Wilson in an exhaustively researched work on the changes in the 1980s, *The End of Whitehall*, range from the Weberian model to the more homely but significant issues of the training of senior civil servants (Campbell and Wilson, 1995). The problem here is not the subject matter but the imposition of the intellectually seductive model – 'the Whitehall model' – on a shifting and, for all its inertia, dynamic institution. The 'Whitehall model' is a phrase used to cover a range of characteristics, some of which continue to exist – and many of which do not. It is seldom an accurate description of a real world with all its features crisp, clear and unchanging. Even as a theoretical model it is confused. It appears to cover a range of disparate ideas from Ministers and civil servants to probity, centralisation, crown status, accountability and recruitment on merit. As a theoretical model it may be clear and unambiguous to some; as a description of reality it is, as most models are, inadequate.

The inaccuracy of a model would not matter if people did not believe that models reflect reality. Campbell and Wilson struggle to cope with the glaring discrepancies between their model and the reality they confront in their research. It was almost inevitable given their starting point that they should have been led to the conclusion that 'this (Next Steps) is the end of the model' but they might have questioned whether the model was ever there. They did put their finger on two crucial points: 'British central government . . . has a fondness for delegating practical tasks to others', and '[m]any senior civil servants had chosen the Service for a career almost to avoid management'.

But the analysis goes wrong as soon as Campbell and Wilson come to the Next Steps Report – it is as though the ideas of flexibility and openness were almost incomprehensible. The Efficiency Unit, Campbell and Wilson say, 'took stock of FMI and concluded that organisations would function more managerially if they operated *once removed* from ministers'. The point in the report was that they would function more effectively at *one remove* from Ministers, after both Ministers and officials had been involved in constructing a framework. Anyone dealing with the Civil Service needs to watch drafting carefully.

What is also surprising is the 'golden past' approach to the senior Civil Service pre-Next Steps. Campbell and Wilson imply that Next Steps agencies made it possible for senior officials to 'sequester themselves from the most mundane divisions of their departments'. The point was that this was precisely what they had done before agencies, and as a result nothing was done with the mundane divisions. After the Next Steps Report was accepted, those divisions could at least become someone's personal responsibility. When Campbell and Wilson say 'Next Steps has again enshrined the principle that true mandarins need not get their hands dirty', they misunderstand both what the report says and what happened. The Next Steps Report challenges that principle and demonstrates what had happened when senior officials shied away from management. Writing and agreeing a framework document should involve a great deal of hard thinking and understanding of the agencies work in order to provide policy objectives that would be realistic and practical and that was the job of senior officials.

OPERATIONS AND POLICY

One of the long standing accusations about the Executive agencies has been that they divide operations and policy. This is a misreading of the whole basis of the recommendations of the report and the establishment of agencies. The report was clear:

> Although setting a framework is not a new task for government departments, it is one which has not generally attracted the attention it deserves. To do it successfully requires a balanced expertise in policy, the political environment and service delivery which too few civil servants possess at present. Operational effectiveness and clarity need to be given a higher priority in the interpretation of policy objectives and the thinking of Ministers.
>
> (Next Steps Report, paragraph 28)

Everyone involved in the process of running a government organisation has to have an understanding of the implications of what they are doing. The defects the Efficiency Unit team identified were not defects only within the Civil Service but also in the approach of Ministers. Everyone had to work together, with understanding and experience, to achieve the sensible statement of policy and operations which was important both for effective management and for meeting political objectives.

Underlying this misunderstanding is an important point. Traditionally in the Civil Service the distinction between managing operations and making policy, for all its apparent closeness, has been reinforced by a class system more pernicious than any organisational division devised by a system of agencies. It was based on the principle that only eccentrics or the fairly simple-minded could be interested in management. Operation experts were addressed as 'Mr Jones', policy makers were called 'Christopher' or 'Simon'. A policy maker was one of 'us', an executive was one of 'them' – a well worn distinction long before Mrs Thatcher employed it. So when Campbell and Wilson imply that a Permanent Secretary was likely not to have run an executive agency after Next Steps, they ignore the important fact that to have run an executive operation before Next Steps would have ensured that an official would not become a Permanent Secretary.

All researchers have a problem with their inside sources. They quote interviews, which read to an insider like indiscreet and sometimes biased gossip, as if they were considered and factually accurate research evidence. Most civil servants talk to 'outside' research workers as light relief from work, with a slight – or strong – sense of wasting time which could be better spent on serious work. Material gathered in this way has to be treated with care: it can supply useful background and local colour but seldom more than that. Many senior officials genuinely do not recognise the enclosed and selective nature of the world they live in.

Senior officials at the top of Departments have always been responsible for the management of the functions of their organisation, they have always been answerable to Parliament for the expenditure; they should have had no option but to 'get their hands dirty'. Permanent Secretaries are accounting officers, and they and their colleagues have now to construct a framework document and approve annual plans for their agencies. To do this they must understand the reality as well as the language of financial management, performance measurement and unit costs and they have to produce a public statement of the role and functions of their agencies. Some people may never spend any part of their career directly managing an agency but, and this is another significant omission from much of the academic analysis, they now have the same disciplines applied to themselves. The pre-1980 position where it was possible to spend a career in blissful ignorance of basic management techniques has gone forever.

Campbell and Wilson admit that: 'the Next Steps system did create a new dynamic within the Whitehall model precisely because it created new institutions', although both they and Hogwood consider that the transfer of the concept of agencies to other governments is unlikely (Campbell and Wilson, 1995; Hogwood, 1993). The international agencies did not share this view, notably the World Bank, which, not surprisingly, could understand agencies, if not the 'Next Steps' agency, and during the 1990s was urging them on their client governments. Executive agencies crop up all round the world. In 2004 the BBC reported on the evening news the activities of the 'Imperial Household Agency' in Tokyo – a far cry indeed from the mundane divisions of the British Civil Service.

Many of the comments on the Next Steps changes demonstrate interesting ideas about the way Whitehall is run, but a lack of understanding of what the changes were about. In the absence of data, and in some cases in spite of it, commentators have tended to look at Next Steps as though it were another piece of the administrative jigsaw to fit in and describe using traditional approaches. But, just as the Civil Service had to learn what was important and different about the new institutions, so did the commentators, many of whom, like the senior Civil Service, had little experience of management.

The analysis in the report demonstrated that the old organisational structures were unhelpful and recommended a new approach to organisation based not on theory but on what would work best in any particular situation. Most of the commentators missed the significance of the 'tailor made agency'. They ignored the emphasis on focusing on the job to be done, they ignored the detail of the framework document and they missed the importance of the emphasis on implementation. These were the pressures that were designed to produce new results, which may be why organisational theory so often failed to describe adequately what was going on.

If a model had to be drawn for Next Steps it would be a simple one. It would be a model of outcomes rather than processes. The crucial factor in it would be the importance to be attached to a practical solution that would enable management to carry out their functions successfully, provide improved services and better use of resources. The solution could be anything which achieved those results within the structure of public sector rules, the resource base available and the requirements of being a good employer. In many cases the changes were relatively modest, especially at the start and the simplicity of the initial changes may well have confused observers. The 'flexibilities' given to agencies were precisely to give them the capacity to change and develop in their own way, not according to a predetermined model, to meet the needs of their objectives.

The analysis demonstrates how difficult it is to understand what happens, even in recent history with memories relatively fresh. Michael Oakeshott once commented that government can be understood only by using 'the pattern of practice, talk and considered writing' (Oakeshott and Fuller, 1996). Perhaps that helpful list needs amplifying. He was right: practice was the most reliable guide to what actually happened, if we can find it out. Talk is the most revealing but has, like all good talk, to be taken with a pinch of salt. Considered writing which, as he remarks, is most difficult to interpret, may be just wrong, because the prism of the first two sources, unless used with great care, can be very confusing.

WHAT WAS THE OUTCOME?

Looking back over the twenty years since the Next Steps Report was first conceived there are some lessons to be considered. The report had its detractors and some of the experiences with implementation, especially in the later stages were less than satisfactory. Nevertheless, exceptionally for public sector changes in the United Kingdom, it has been generally regarded as a success. From the reasons for that success lessons can usefully be drawn.

The first lesson is in the form the analysis took. It combined the practical experience of people working within the system day-by-day with the longer term experience of senior management. The analysis of that material led the team responsible to develop serious and radical ideas and turn them into practical propositions for changes, without being deterred by opposition which was by turns emotional, defensive and dismissive.

The second lesson is in the simplicity of the recommendations. They were constructed so that they could be accomplished only by undertaking a range of changes, each necessary in itself, which in total would achieve the end result: detailed prescription was avoided to give as much flexibility as possible in how the result could be achieved.

The third lesson lay in the quality and the attention given to implementation. Chapter 7 has described the process. The skill with which the implementation was planned and the care given to its swift and measured roll out accompanied by tailored training and good internal, as well as external, communications all contributed to its success.

The fourth lesson is that managing government needs constant attention and simple objectives. The Next Steps Report was aiming at better services as its ultimate objective but very few people at the time or subsequently remembered that. It became a reform about structure, organisation and control. Whitehall became comfortable with it; there were many better run organisations among the 105 agencies, most of them seldom mentioned in public. There were the well publicised disasters – but they only represented a small percentage of the total. Many public services improved and the public benefited from the change. But the real drive for better service has got mired in initiatives which have come and gone. The return to public service issues by the Labour Government since 2002 has demonstrated the importance of public services but not how to achieve results. Policy and management are both important but one cannot succeed without the other.

The fifth lesson is more worrying. While the senior Civil Service and Ministers contributed to the criticisms of themselves which were a feature of the Next Steps Report, and the Fulton Report before it, little was done to implement the recommendations of either report to enhance the skills of people at the critical senior level. While more managers were introduced, it was by appointing chief executives from outside and inside the Civil Service not by changing the people who were in line to be made Permanent Secretaries. The skills of senior civil servants and Ministers remain much the same; the way they work has changed little, the obsession with the short term, the political and the media are as strong if not stronger. As one senior official said privately of the centre of government in 2004, when serious failures in the public service during the Blair administration were becoming evident, 'it hasn't changed at all; underneath it is just the same'.

9. The spread of public sector reform

The last chapter considered the results of the British Government's introduction of executive agencies and drew some general lessons from the experience of implementation. There had been considerable interest in the developments following the Next Steps Report, Ministers and officials from many countries visited London to discuss the changes being made to the organisation of central government. This was partly a reflection of the international standing of Mrs Thatcher and her government but was also because the United Kingdom was not alone in the 1980s facing the need to modernise and increase efficiency in government.

THE FISCAL CRISIS

Many governments were under pressure to reduce costs and improve the efficiency of their public sector. Growth in public expenditure, rising costs in public services, the growth of transfer payment costs driven by demographic changes all forced governments to investigate ways of reducing or holding costs steady while facing demands from their voters for better services and fewer taxes.

Improvements in management were part of the solution. Ministries of Finance in many countries brought pressure to bear on their colleagues to find ways to deal with uncontrolled public finances. The international financial institutions demanded government reform in countries needing external support. They were less helpful in the recommendations they made for reform. Structural adjustment programmes, under the auspices of the IMF, demonstrated the weakness of their analysis: managing a public sector effectively could not be done by simple economic modelling. Stiglitz commented that 'once a country was in crisis IMF funds and programs not only failed to stabilize the situation but in many cases actually made things worse, especially for the poor' (Stiglitz, 2002). The World Bank too subsequently discovered that management theories of reform were not adequate to deal with the interrelated and far reaching problems of poverty, infrastructure failure, corrupt governments and damaged economies.

The need for reform faced the member countries of the wealthy OECD as well as the developing world. By the 1990s the size of the 'government sector' (for OECD countries) ranged from 8% to 32% of total employment; public expenditure ranged from 30% to 60% of GDP. There was clearly no rule about a 'right' size or cost, although most countries fell somewhere between 15 and 30% of employment and 30 and 50% of expenditure. The outliers – the Nordic countries, Japan and Switzerland – were explicable for specific historic or policy reasons. Public employment at about 30% and public expenditure at about 50% of total public expenditure appeared to be at the upper level of what might be regarded as 'normal' (OECD, 1993).

Governments looking for ideas to help with burgeoning public sectors could link in to the work of the international organisations. OECD had a public management office, PUMA, which brought together members of the new 'expert' groups who were beginning to emerge in several countries, to share their efforts at reform. New Zealand raced ahead, leading the world in restructuring, contracting out, slashing numbers, cutting costs. But, as commentators pointed out, it could afford to be more radical with a small and dispersed population. Nevertheless the New Zealand government not only attacked unwieldy and expensive public services, they demonstrated that even a left wing Labour government could take on the politics of public employment, which inhibited many governments from facing the need to modernise. The grip of the public sector unions was demonstrated in the United Kingdom throughout the 1970s where constant industrial disputes brought two governments to political disaster and an IMF rescue package. The atmosphere of continual industrial unrest strengthened the political power of the revived right wing led by Mrs Thatcher.

Employment protection designed to provide secure jobs for public service workers had become a stranglehold as public service unions prevented the development of better services or redistribution of resources that might damage their members' interests. This was the case even though it was the poor, many of them public service workers themselves, who suffered most from inadequate education, social welfare and infrastructure development. Soaring public sector costs, exemplified in governments as diverse as Sweden, Mexico and Brazil demonstrated the seriousness of the problem and, in the case of Brazil and Mexico, the political difficulties of making radical changes in the face of employee vested interests.

These changes were not simply driven by fashion. Most states faced serious financial problems. The costs of running many public services were spiralling with rising standards, growing populations and the predominance of directly employed labour. Public sector unions became an important part of the equation. The taxation and revenue base of many countries was inadequate for the demands on government and in many cases the financial management of government activities was unequal to the task. The development of ideas of financial management and the accurate costing of activities, familiar to the private sector, were, in many government systems, completely unknown. The relationship between cost and value, or between inputs and outputs, were not reflected in the management tools in use in most publicly funded organisations (Foster and Plowden, 1996).

Rising costs and poor productivity, driven by weak management and powerful trade unions posed problems for governments across the world. In Sweden a Ministry of Finance expert group identified a plunge in public sector productivity starting in 1960 and continuing up to 1980. The aggregated productivity change 1970–1980 was minus 1.4% per year (Sweden, 1997). In Brazil, leading the long list of necessary reforms, was, and remains, the need to reform the public sector pension system which consumed a large and increasing proportion of GDP. The targets for reform varied widely. In some countries, the first serious move was to change the structure of the budget to achieve a more effective grip on expenditure. In Mexico in 1998 a new budgeting system was designed to allocate resources more effectively and delegate decisions to individual departments. In Sweden the budget reforms focused on the Swedish Agency annual reports with a new emphasis on productivity improvements against a background of a rise in public spending from 31% of GDP in 1960 to a peak of 70% in 1994 (Sweden, 1997).

DEVELOPING COUNTRIES

Developing countries faced a different set of problems. National governments were not the only sources of ideas and expertise. After the Second World War the Allied nations agreed to set up a World Bank, an International Monetary Fund and subsequently the United Nations Development Fund were all designed to help countries which needed financial and other expertise to rebuild or build for the first time institutions which could form the basis of a modern state. The condition of under developed countries was a cause for much concern as the economies of Europe and America grew while less developed countries stagnated. From the early 1950s onwards the export of experience and skill from developed countries grew to a flood funded by bilateral and international aid budgets. Big international organisations, the Red Cross, Oxfam and Save the Children in the United Kingdom, grew rapidly as the information flows about disease, malnutrition, lack of education and dire poverty poured into the developed world.

The main aid agencies took an early and significant decision to pass all money through governments on the assumption that governments would then handle the specified needs. Money was needed to support programmes aimed at alleviating desperate poverty in countries with poor communications, few roads and little commercial or public sector infrastructure. The government was the only visible organisation with whom aid donors could have working relations, and to whom they could pay money. But the donors did not take enough account of the kind of governments that were in power; relatively few governments had the capacity or the desire to manage large social welfare programmes and those most in need of international help were inevitably those with the least capable government machines.

Slowly and expensively the donor agencies discovered that they could not rely on governments to spend their money on the programmes it was designed for. They discovered that the capacity to manage and run big welfare programmes did not exist in communities with weak, corrupt or underdeveloped governments. Private sector development did not occur simply because public sector activity was shut down. Running public services was difficult and complicated. The simplistic agreements for loans conditional on structural adjustment programmes were doomed. Unfortunately structural adjustment was enhanced by even more simplistic 'public sector reform programmes' which compounded the problem (Jenkins and Plowden, 2006).

The expression 'governance' coupled with 'good government' entered the vocabulary. The countries of the Commonwealth, with the support of the Commonwealth Secretariat and the aid agencies of the wealthier members of the Commonwealth extended their activities from industrial, agrarian and social support to systems of government. It was not until the late 1980s that the United Kingdom Government, which had been struggling with its own internal reforms, admitted that improvements in public services in developing countries did depend on the way in which they were administered and the decisions taken politically by central and local government. The international agencies embraced governance and good government with enthusiasm but they failed fully to understand the difficulties they faced. Even the United Kingdom, with an advanced and complex government structure, after twenty five years of trying, had made at best modest progress in public sector management reform.

Public services could deteriorate with shocking rapidity. In Jamaica, a sharp decline in government revenues, aggravated by rising international debt and structural adjustment rules created conditions where basic public services degenerated from tolerable to appalling. Levels of poverty rose abruptly and hardship and economic decline followed (Oxfam, 1992). The same pattern could be observed in many countries where, with weak domestic economic infrastructure, a reduction in expenditure on public services, enforced under structural adjustment programmes, had an immediate impact on the poorest economic groups. In some countries the abrupt reduction in public employment when large extended families depended on a single wage earner had a far more serious social impact than those in Washington setting the rules had understood.

REFORM AND THE PUBLIC SECTOR

Many countries were struggling to find adequate solutions. While the acute rift between policy and management in the United Kingdom was not mirrored in many other countries there was no shortage of difficulties. One of the more damaging divides was that between fiscal pressures and the solutions of the economists on the one hand and hard pressed officials and management experts on the other. A creative tension between the two groups could have produced effective results; but in many governments the division ran deeply through both political and official roles. Political pressures on both meant that what appeared to be sensible fiscal or managerial changes were not pursued. In Brazil, the long running fiscal damage to the economy caused by an absurdly generous system of public sector pensions drained money from Federal budgets but the political power of public sector workers was such that governments of both left and right were not prepared to contemplate changes to their labour legislation.

In Jamaica, in the 1990s, poorly conceived public sector reform programmes were forced on the government in exchange for IMF credits even though it was accepted by the aid donors that similar reforms had failed in the past and would no doubt fail again. For the Ministry of Finance, short term necessity outweighed long term indebtedness, while naïve and inexperienced donor staff forced wasteful and irrelevant reforms on the public sector – a double disadvantage.

Immigration policy in some European countries has demonstrated the damage caused by a failure to consider the link between the economic advantages of inward migration and the short and long term social costs. In France, the Netherlands and the United Kingdom new pressures from the social and cultural consequences of long term migration have been ignored until the pressures of unemployment, social deprivation and cultural incomprehension have become explosive. The liberal assumptions of the old right and left wing political groupings proved wholly inadequate to deal with so complex a series of social and economic issues.

The complexity of public sector reform has been consistently underestimated. OECD countries, with a reservoir of skill and experience to draw on, still underestimate how difficult changes can be and how far even their own members are from achieving their objectives. Some OECD reports recommend reforms to developing countries which OECD members themselves find it difficult to implement, even with the benefits of stable economies and established government institutions.

There is always a genuine interest in improvements in service quality; better services sound seductive. Better schools, better hospitals and better roads are easy to talk about and relatively easy to build. Managing and maintaining them can be more difficult. The conundrum for most governments with complex economies was how to get better services at less cost. Without more competent management, improved services meant more cost and were unaffordable. Some governments welcomed the fashions in new management ideas as a way of shedding costs with politically difficult expectations. At one extreme, in Columbia in the mid-1990s, the World Bank urged delegation to local levels of government, without fully comprehending what was involved. An official responsible for education policy announced with pride that the process of devolving all primary and secondary education to regional and municipal tiers of government was well in hand. It would be completed in a matter of months. 'How impressive,' I remarked, 'it must have been a massive task to set the standards and budgets for such a change.' 'Oh, no', came the airy reply, 'we are not worrying with any of that, we are just giving them the responsibility, how they do it and how they pay for it is up to them.' 'No money?' I asked, concerned for the future of public education. 'Oh, no. Why should we give them any money? It's their responsibility now.'

While 'management' was becoming a recognised and necessary skill for the public service in many parts of the world, the urgent necessity for a constructive link with cost and value was no less evident. Ministries of Finance clashed with social welfare ministries as costs and demand rose. Hacienda, the finance ministry in Mexico City, tightened its controls and its detailed audit but failed to deal with rising costs and rampant corruption. Inefficiency, poor financial management, and damaging expenditure cuts reduced the capacity of many governments to provide the services expected from them. The downward spiral of public provision, exemplified in many countries in Sub-Saharan Africa, demonstrated the poverty of the solutions that were being urged on struggling communities with weak, corrupt or incompetent governments by international donor organisations.

The complexity of the problems defied the simplistic solutions put forward: covering school costs by charging fees ignored the desperate poverty of many of the families concerned and denied the poor access to the one service that had been demonstrated to lift them out of poverty. Local hospitals could only survive as long as their running costs could be met – ignoring the budgetary consequences of a new hospital meant that the capital costs were wasted. Providing computers when the electricity supply was intermittent or non existent meant they were junked in a shed. These errors were not only a function of developing countries: cutting maintenance on the London Underground led to dangerous services and enormous long term repair costs. Gross under-investment in the water industry in the United Kingdom has still not been made good twenty years after privatisation.

Governments are often their own worst enemies; the visible priorities set by politicians damage the case for care in the use of public resources. Expensive travel, lavish entertaining and absurd Ministerial housing can damage the struggle for better resource use just as effectively as slovenly local management. Television news can demonstrate that political leaders have lush cars while hospitals lack drugs and bandages; it does them no service with their electors or with their employees. This too is not a feature only of corrupt or 'failed' states. The lavish and much publicised entertaining indulged in by the leaders of the European Union during their rotating presidencies only emphasises their wasteful use of public resources. They are not alone; a regional chairman of a health authority in the United Kingdom in the 1990s drove an official Mercedes as part of the perks of his non-executive, part time office, while complaining about the shortage of funds. Although the relative costs of each individual extravagance may be small, the taxpayer feels it directly and the public employee's enthusiasm for economy in the use of public money wanes in the face of lavish expenditure by their political boss.

ADVICE AND SOLUTIONS

There was no shortage of advice or solutions. Many governments had access to the information resources of the international organisations. OECD disseminated best practice for the developed nations through the work done by its public management office and its specialist advisory group for Eastern Europe. European Union countries were subject both to the pressures from Brussels for reform in economic and social areas and to the impact of the Human Rights legislation and the European Court on the content of domestic legislation and administrative action. The World Bank and the IMF operated throughout the developing world.

The flourishing consultancy industry made expert advice available to anyone prepared to pay for it, linked into the burgeoning training industry supplying both trainers and full courses to governments struggling with the pace and scale of the changes. The new public sector consultancy industry developed to meet the need for expertise in management and reform. As governments discovered the need for improvements in administration and the advantages of the 'science' of management, they recognised that they would have to pay for the expertise they feared they lacked in-house. Management consultants had been working in the private sector for decades and governments turned to them and to academics for assistance, even though much of the experience and ideas stemmed from private sector practice. Management 'gurus' appeared, lecturing and writing about ways in which business and industry should be structured for maximum effect. *In Search of Excellence* an American analysis of the elements of private sector company success sold worldwide and generated a new set of management slogans (Peters and Waterman, 1982). '*Reinventing Government*', a public sector successor urged governments to greater efforts at reform: 'We believe there *are* solutions' (Osborne and Gaebler, 1992).

Academic interest in the detail of public sector management was demonstrated in analyses of individual cases and projects. In the USA, at state and local level, there were developments in the type of services introduced and in the way in which they were provided. Among others, Pressman and Wildavsky investigated the internal workings of public bureaucracies to see what lessons could be learnt. They made the case of the Oakland Economic Development project – which should have worked and did not – a classic case study of how public sector management can go wrong. Their long title summed up the reactions of many to public sector management: *How great expectations in Washington are dashed in Oakland, or, why its amazing that Federal Programs work at all* . . . (Pressman and Wildavsky, 1973).

Michael Barzelay, more positively but less dramatically, argued that: 'specific organisational strategies that go against the grain of the bureaucratic paradigm offer workable solutions'. His solution was 'breaking through bureaucracy'. In a study of reforms in Minnesota he argued that people could be persuaded to accept radically different ways of working provided that the value of the achievements of the bureaucratic systems was recognised (Barzelay, 1992). James Wilson, after considering a range of public services, argued that it was a 'mistake to suppose that the frustrations arise out of management problems; they do not, they arise out of governance problems' (Wilson, 1989).

An older and even more experienced voice joined the debate. In 1994, Peter Drucker, taking a wider canvass, thought the condition of government was not susceptible to simple solutions: 'the "mega state" in which this century has indulged has not performed, neither in its totalitarian nor in its democratic version. It has not delivered on a single one of its promises' (Drucker, 1995).

THE NEW PUBLIC MANAGEMENT

The phrase that encapsulated much of the urge for reform was the 'new public management' (NPM). Much quoted in the 1980s and 1990s, it was used, initially by academic commentators, to describe a more managerial approach to public services by providing greater flexibility, greater freedom for local managers to manage their operations and a structure of budgets and accountability. It was also used to imply the introduction of private sector management techniques into public sector institutions. It became a shorthand term for almost any change in management. The confusion about the precise meaning of NPM was compounded by its use by commentators who had no experience of management and little idea of the implications of the introduction of new approaches. The concepts of NPM may still be new for some observers, but for many public servants NPM has set the structure of their office since they first started work. The change and the novelty has come and gone. Budgets are basic to operations, setting priorities, counting activities, opening at different times, flexible working, training courses and treating the public as 'customer' not 'client' have all been changes long since accepted.

Many of the structures of the 'reforms' have vanished; most have become simply part of the background of management, an accepted way of doing business rather than a trumpeted and identified 'reform'. That does not mean, as so many observers assert that the 'reforms have failed'. Many have not developed, but have left new thinking, new approaches or just a different way of working behind them. The tendency to exaggerate the significance of new approaches in the marketing of public sector reform, of which Peter Drucker complained back in the mid-1990s, distorts both expectations and the significance of events (Drucker, 1995).

Attempts at reform in public services are widespread and the search for the philosopher's stone of the well managed state continues unabated. There is no shortage of suggestions. The newer language of public service reform – decentralisation, leadership, strategy, capability, joined up government and the rest provide a wide range of possible directions; they can also confuse. Simplistic slogans are not always a help in a huge and complicated system where care, sensitivity and lateral thinking as well as sheer hard work are all essentials for any chance of improvement.

Public services anywhere show familiar scenes. Story time in the Rio nursery school with the same rapt faces as in Battersea in London or Honiara in the Solomon Islands; the waiting area of the Municipal Hospital in Mexico City with better seating than in St Bartholomew's Hospital in the City of London but the same strained faces and desperate searching eyes looking for someone with news, reassurance or help. Even the Passport Office in Spanish Town, Jamaica was providing the same service as at Petty France in London with smaller queues, the same forms and much the same end product. The emergency area in Soweto (South Africa) dealt with similar horrors to those in Belfast and the nurses had familiar faces, tired and worn but providing kindly help with swift, deft hands. The farmer up in the hills above Oaxaca (Mexico) had received his grant to irrigate his avocadoes. The role of government in all these activities means that they only occur after the involvement of a hierarchy of activity which transmits instructions and resources from a point where decisions had been taken about priorities, finances, staffing and equipment as well as the quantity of service to be provided.

Once decisions were taken, recruiting the staff, finding the premises, setting the rules, the environment, the service levels and making them happen has to occur before the political decision is translated into reality. The communication in reverse of what has happened tends to come well after the event, and frequently does not happen at all. Any flaw in the system of transmitting information, instructions and resources mean that the activity may not happen. There are very few detailed descriptions of the laborious process of translating a political decision into reality. Surprisingly one of the most graphic occurs in a classic detective story, *Death of a Train*, written in 1942 by Freeman Wills Crofts. He took fourteen pages to describe the process of finding, putting together and delivering a special train to transport a secret cargo from a military depot in southern England to the main port – a journey of some fifty minutes. 'Easy enough' say the Generals taking the decision with no idea of what was actually involved.

The supporting cast of the new public management was supposed to ensure that the process of running public organisations could operate smoothly. Delegated budgets, management information, plans, models were all brought into play to make the systems work. The big bureaucracies of many states were reluctant to face changes. Most public services failed to recognise the speed at which society and economies were changing. While the United Kingdom systems were unnecessarily complicated and frequently poorly administered, other countries had even deeper rooted problems to deal with. In Ecuador legal systems based originally on Spanish law were, until recently, used for personnel management for civil servants. Elaborate regulations were applied and every civil servant had a copy of the relevant code on their desk for frequent reference. In Mexico the task of buying a computer was so complicated by the rules imposed by the Ministry of Finance and the Auditor General that the specific machines ordered were invariably no longer available by the time consent to purchase was obtained.

The search for answers continued throughout the 1990s. The work done by PUMA at OECD demonstrated how widespread the developments in the management of governments were. Round table discussions, research and reporting reflected awareness by OECD governments that questions of management in the public sector were ones they all shared. In the 1990s, as public service reform became fashionable, Ministers were happy to give speeches at conferences explaining how successfully they had dealt with weaknesses in their official systems. Models were developed, earnest conferences took place at which carefully constructed systems were displayed which appeared to answer many of the problems of beleaguered governments.

Public sector management was big business. Private sector consultants moved into the public sector. In the mid-1980s six departments in the British Government were estimated to have spent about £15 million on consultants between them, a figure that was greeted with disbelief at the time. (Jenkins *et al.*, 1984). By 2006 the United Kingdom public sector bill for consultancy was estimated at £7 billion for the previous three years, of which the central government share was £1.8 billion, a reduction, it was argued weakly, of £200 000 over the previous three years (National Audit Office, 2006). By 2000, the World Bank was spending some $7 billion on government reform in many client countries, a substantial proportion of which went on consultancy support and advice.

THE INTERNATIONALISATION OF PUBLIC SECTOR REFORM

Public officials changed their habits. Inward looking officials recognised that interesting experiments were being tried elsewhere; they travelled to see what was happening. The international conference on government reform was born. Informal groupings of countries in Africa and South America met to learn from each other and to discuss what they had been doing to reform their governments. In Swaziland, the Zambian and the Ugandan ministers spoke at a seminar explaining what had been happening within the Zambian and Ugandan governments in 1994, funded by the British Council. All the 'anglophone' countries of Sub Saharan Africa met in Cape Town in 1995 at a huge World Bank and United Kingdom funded conference to discuss what should be done 'to redefine the role of government in meeting the development needs of the country and to raise the efficiency of the public sector.'

In Brazil and Mexico Ministers and officials met in seminars in 1995 and 1996 with officials from the United Kingdom to hear about what was happening in the public sector in the United Kingdom, and to discuss what should be done in their governments. The countries of Latin America met as a group to discuss state reform (in Brasilia in 1998). The Commonwealth Secretariat established a Commonwealth Association for Administration and Management (CAPAM), to research and discuss common issues of public administration. Private conferences in England, funded by the British Council, were attended by Ministers and senior civil servants responsible for their countries' reform programmes to hold private discussions of the issues they faced. The participants came from India, Pakistan, Vietnam, South America, the Caribbean, Africa, Europe, and Australasia (Jenkins and Plowden, 1995). In Brisbane in 1994, the Fulbright Association for Australian-American relations held its annual symposium with an international audience to discuss 'Public Sector Management: emerging world trends' (Weller and Davis, 1995).

The bilateral aid donors were active in supporting reforms of governance. The Swedes and the Danes put carefully planned assistance where they perceived the need, Germany and France concentrated on ex colonies, the USA put money and expertise into the Caribbean, Central and South America and Africa among other places. In the 1990s the international agencies began to build up their divisions of 'governance' experts. Some countries kept their reforms in house but exported their experience – Chilean government experts, proud of their own system, helped the Ecuadorean Government to develop their economic planning system. The United Kingdom set up a central consultancy department specifically to explain their changes in government to other countries. Its Customs and Excise Department developed a substantial business advising other governments on their customs work.

OECD countries were also at work. For several years OECD issued a report of public management reform with separate reports on individual country reform programmes which illustrated how far from following a set pattern most countries were. Evidence from the reports suggests that while problems may be similar, solutions are different; in Italy in 1993 public sector management was concentrated on size, institutional reform, culture and technology, Greece had nineteen 'reform goals, priorities and policies', ranging from establishing general directorates, facilitating citizen access to administrative files and awards to employees for good ideas. In Norway, organisational change, competitive mechanisms, performance measurement and financial resources management were the priorities (OECD, 1993). What the changes showed was that organisational solutions were not a simple cure. The world of 'Reinventing Government' and, indeed, of Executive Agencies did not guarantee that government would be any better. It might not have been rearranging the deck chairs on the Titanic but at times it looked perilously close to it.

THEORIES OF PUBLIC MANAGEMENT

Governments also looked to academic institutions for assistance. Political science, government and their related disciplines provided academics who specialised in advising and assisting governments. Some university departments built close links with government. People from Harvard, Oxford, the London School of Economics, the Getulio Vargas Foundation in Sao Paulo and many other universities all moved smoothly between their academic roles and work for governments. It was not necessarily an easy move. Joseph Stiglitz, who did move between the two, remarked more modestly than many: 'I wanted to see what really goes on . . . as an academic I needed to understand the world better first' (Stiglitz, 2003).

The contribution of academic analysts was however considerable. The analysis of public policy has ranged widely, reviewing structures, organisations, models and implementation and evaluation. As one leading expert remarked 'conceptual models of government reform are themselves constantly in flux' (Minogue *et al.*, 1998). The task of devising an intellectual framework for what was happening in many governments was considerable. Academic commentators were active in trying to understand what was happening and occasionally were involved in steering some of the reform programmes, but, inevitably, analysis followed events rather than preceding them. The time lag between the new policy and the academic review of it might have mattered less when changes were not conducted at so hectic a pace. It is rare for the analysis to be still relevant by the time the lectures are given or the article published.

There might be widespread recognition of the difficulties of running a modern government, but the detail of public services, invisible to the political elite, tended to be ignored or overridden unless something went spectacularly wrong. The world was segmented into the rich countries which handed out money and advice, the less rich countries which took some advice and a little of the money, and the desperately poor, referred to discouragingly as 'failed states' by their richer colleagues who often had little conception of the difficulties they faced. The analyses produced by academics and by experts in the international organisations were sometimes trenchant and blunt. They pointed repeatedly to failures of political leadership, the lack of sustained management and badly designed reform programmes which have littered the path of attempts to improve government over the past thirty years. Learning the lessons of experience has not been a notable feature of these attempts. Willingness to try new approaches, especially when attached to the strings of an international loan or a bilateral grant, is not necessarily an advantage when the reasons for past failures are not fully understood.

Public recognition of the problem of quality and effectiveness can be seen and heard in every country which allows open criticism of government activities. Newspapers and television are crowded with complaints; street corner discussions feed on the latest iniquity. The activities of government, its institutions, its policies and its outcomes, have been subjected to relentless scrutiny by politicians and journalists as well as by the single issue activist. Much of contemporary comment is provided by journalists and politicians whose books feed the work of academics assessing and analysing the political process. Governments are more ready to use the media than ever before – Bob Woodward's descriptions of the Bush administration and its policy planning for war, from the inside and so close to the events described would have been unlikely fifty years ago (Woodward, 2002, 2004, 2006).

MODELLING THE PUBLIC SECTOR

There has been an extensive debate about models of public sector policy making and organisation. Analytical models can be helpful in analysing what has happened and what might happen, but they depend heavily on assumptions about reality which are, sometimes deliberately, divorced from reality. While the assumptions do not invalidate the diagnosis, particularly as a means of considering how an organisation might be analysed, they can make the process seem irrelevant to those directly involved in the practice of public sector policy precisely because the models do not reflect the trials of what actually happens.

The academic analysts have produced theories and models. Both reflect much thought and endeavour to reduce what happens, or is thought to have happened, to a more generally applicable structure which might reflect a larger reality than a single example could do. Some analysis can be helpful in clarifying thinking about possible approaches to a particular problem but there are two obstacles to the relevance of models in practice. The first is that the model will never fit a live issue exactly; at best it may have relevance but it will not provide a complete or even a near complete solution. At worst, it may persuade people that the solution they need is neatly encapsulated in some other experience. I have talked to eager officials in South America who, pens at the ready, were demanding the 'model' which would set out for them what they should do. Nothing could shake their conviction that somewhere there was a solution which could be easily transmitted and implemented in full. The international agencies also fall prey to this simplistic view. One World Bank official in the Caribbean talked with enthusiasm about what he described as his 'tool kit' for government reform, into which he had put, along with other 'tools', something he called 'executive agencies' without any grasp of the basis of the idea or of the limitations on its use.

The second obstacle to the use of models – whether public administration, public policy, public choice or the host of possible structures – is that few of the people who make the operational or political choices about what structure to put in place or which analysis to use have time to make use of complex models. One senior official reflected: 'there's no time for any of that, all we can do is grab what seems possible and get on with it'. The cavalier attitude taken by public officials to public policy theory in the heat of the day to day battle is reflected in the plaint of the experts that 'there is an urgent need for more interaction between policy analysts, practitioners and policy makers' (Lane, 1993).

The reality of most public sector policy making would dismay the serious academic analyst. There is seldom time for careful thought; politics, public demand, money, other priorities push the policy maker into optimistic assumptions and fast decisions. The gulf between analysts and governments is a gap between those responsible for action in a political environment and those whose task is to reflect on what has been done and to produce some explanation of what happens and why. However elegant a construct the model may be, it ceases to be compelling to a practitioner when it does not allow for political horse-trading, the pressures of elections, the timetable for legislation, constitutional complexity or different levels of government.

The existence of models does encourage the belief that they represent a swift and easy path to that other danger – transferability. Not only do models tend not to work in reality, they seldom work outside their original environment. The public sector is different in each country, however similar the names given to its institutions or its processes may appear to be. Public institutions are often a consequence of history, not function. They have grown up in response to the political, social, economic and cultural environment which surrounds them, and on which they have a profound impact. In consequence they differ from each other. Even passport offices issuing very similar documents have different populations to deal with, a different type of investment available to it and different expectations of what a passport represents and what it can do for its user group. Thus, in Britain, the issue of passports is regarded as time critical: the British are annoyed if a new passport takes more than a week, while the German passport holder is apparently content to wait for forty days. Even the simplest task, the issue of a document, puts different pressures on an office and involves different investment and procedures. The transfer of ideas between governments can be useful, but complete models are seldom of more than limited use.

The academic analyst is dealing with theory applied to a series of conditions which it is exceedingly difficult to understand from outside. Organisations constantly change, people change jobs, policy changes often as a result of external, and often unforeseen, events. The gulf between theory and reality increases the difficulty of understanding what is going on. For some, that gulf almost appears an advantage in the construction of a good theoretical model. Christopher Hood's list of the conditions for perfect implementation, however helpful in analysis and however significant as a warning, can reduce a practitioner to despair because it is the unforeseen that creates the serious problem (Hood, 1976).

Lane refers to the need 'to know more about the politics of (revenue) decisions . . . model evaluation has to pay attention to how the models satisfy data – correspondence with fact – as well as to how well the data are organised' (Lane, 1993). That the need for correspondence with fact needs stating emphasises the gulf between theory and reality and hence the difficulty that those dealing with reality have in understanding what the theoreticians are saying; while many theorists are trying to understand and explain what is or may or should be happening, the politicians and officials are searching for practical solutions.

Part of the gulf is about relevance but another equally significant difficulty is language. The technical language of rational choice or public policy creates an area of analysis which is closed to many public officials partly because familiar words used in their technical sense have a very different nuance. For many an official 'rational choice' means the sensible decisions they might make, taking account of all the variables with which they work. Evaluation is something that can be covered swiftly in a paragraph at the end of a paper, carried out as a special exercise, or built into contractual obligations.

The more arcane world of graphs, models or theories does not immediately relate to the fast, politics driven world of practical policy making. The outcome of the academic analysis would arrive long after the political wave had gone by and was moving in another direction. The public official will argue that there is seldom time to learn the language in order to review the material. Doing the work properly needs precision in language and more time for thought the analyst will reply. The consequence is often that while the analysis may be commissioned, the report will seldom be read but join the pile of dust-edged documents behind the doors or on the shelves of so many offices.

In the United Kingdom there was a particular difficulty for the academic analyst. While many social scientists were attempting to explain what was going on, the link between what happened in practice and what was or could become public knowledge was bedevilled by the Official Secrets Act, until it was modified by the Freedom of Information Act in 2001. The legislation made virtually everything a state secret unless it was 'cleared for publication'. The culture of secrecy was far reaching and damaging. British civil servants were trained not to discuss what happened in the office, whether it was a matter of public interest or indeed public knowledge or not. It was made clear to junior officials that any information which they gave to people outside the office which became public could damage their careers. In such a situation people were wary of talking to journalists or friends of journalists and academics were frequently regarded as in the same category.

The degree of caginess with which any information was provided made any analysis difficult without distortion, especially as it was difficult for the analyst to understand how limited the information was. The atmosphere of secrecy, not a feature in other countries, notably the US, made accurate or helpful comparative analysis very difficult to achieve. Grant Jordan (Jordan, 1994), Walter Williams (Williams, 1988) and Colin Campbell and Graham Wilson (Campbell and Wilson, 1995) all tried to get a feel for the changes to government in the UK in the 1980s by recording and analysing what senior officials thought was happening. Most officials when asked what was happening would list the problems, seldom the successes, and would assert solemnly, whenever serious changes were in the air, that 'morale in the civil service is lower than ever'. It was the standard answer.

The division between policy makers and analysts caused many wasted opportunities. Both had much to give the other, however challenging or inconvenient their contributions might be. Effective use of some of the lessons from modelling could prevent absurdities; better understanding of political realities could enrich and deepen the value of much analysis. But the limitations of both activities needed to be comprehended fully if the defects were to be avoided. Many governments have accepted models and transferred experience as part of their reform programmes. The outcomes have not been uniformly successful. The context of each government is different, as is its stage of development and its capacity to deal with change. The programmes of modernisation in the United Kingdom demonstrated that internally constructed changes can fit better and be implemented more effectively than many externally driven reforms.

THEORIES AND CONTEXT

It can be argued that the chorus of complaint has grown rather than diminished. The vocal and entitled citizen, much more a feature of the second half of the twentieth century, has come to expect the standards promised by politicians at elections and to resent failure. The government is no longer an extension of a system of public sector charity doling out benefits to grateful subjects, the approach until the last quarter of the twentieth century, especially in the United Kingdom. It is now regarded as the provider of services paid for by the recipients who consider that they are entitled to, rather than grateful for, what they receive.

It is still difficult to know whether the providers of services have really made a change in their approach to their 'customers'. Michael Barzelay in his book analysing the reform programme in Minnesota (Barzelay, 1992) described the change in culture as suppliers become service providers in an internal system of demand and supply. His definition of public service as a 'transaction between equals' (Barzelay, 1992) may be emerging but is far from universal, even in the most reformed public service.

In parallel with the higher standards that citizens expected, the tasks undertaken by governments became increasingly complex. Within most modern economies few activities have not experienced changes to function, scope and organisation. Journalists have tried to chart what has been happening in the short term and in the more visible areas. Academics have tried to understand and to define the changes to the public sector and to supply an analysis which both explains what has happened and provides bases for future actions. Politicians and the media have a professionally negative view of the public sector; adversarial politics makes it difficult to find a detached view either of what is happening or of the effectiveness of what is achieved. Successful public services disappear from political discourse. Failing services are under the spotlight because that is where the problems lie, but as a result it is easy to assume that there are few successes and to fail to recognise and reward those who have achieved improvements.

Negativism can be accepted as part of the job by many public servants, but it can breed cynicism and inertia. Unjustified praise has a similar effect. But most governments have an extraordinary capacity, once the need is accepted, to develop new ideas and new approaches, in response to changing political imperatives, economic and social pressures. Recognition of the need to change is frequently the point at which the delay occurs. New policy ideas are the easy part; it is in implementation that the problems arise. Unless the process of implementation is part of the development of policy, the results will not occur or will develop in unforeseen ways.

Rapid change is not necessarily good. Many changes made by governments are short term and ephemeral. The security provided by public sector functions has been a significant element in their popularity and a major reason behind the reluctance of the public to accept changes however rational. A policy change which involves a change in priorities requires a sensitivity to what is happening which most governments lack. The fondness for much publicised 'reform programmes' or 'change' rather than sensible and modest adjustments compounds the problems faced by those who want to see improvement.

Two priorities often need more attention than elaborate reform; first, to ensure that the core function of a public service is properly run and that it is provided in a way which meets the expectations of its users. Second, the need to put as much emphasis on prevention as on the consequences. Much of the rapid growth in social welfare needs stems from preventable conditions which are ignored for too long – poor nutrition affecting educational attainment, impoverished services because of corruption and a poor tax base, or poverty and ill health in the elderly because of failures in the pension and health systems.

If changes are to be effective the process of reform has to continue to the end point – an educated child or a built road. In many countries the policy making process comes to an abrupt halt with decisions taken or legislation passed. The process of implementation: instructions, new staff, training, decisions about funding, priorities, management systems, budgets and the unintended consequences on other parts of organisations, all follow the political and analytical process of reaching the original decision but are frequently ignored or neglected in considering what the policy should be (Parsons, 1995).

The context is always significant. As the state has become more powerful it has also become more difficult to manage. Peter Drucker observed that 'the mega state is bankrupt morally and financially but its successor cannot be "small government", there are too many tasks' (Drucker, 1995). Rudolf Klein and Patricia Day described 'the problems of complexity, of remoteness and of specialization in the 20th century' (Day and Klein, 1987). Aaron Wildavsky has written of 'policy evolution, a kind of flux where ends and means replace each other in a consecutive fashion' (Wildavsky, 1980) – a better description of modern reality than the cycle of fanfare and failure so familiar in the past twenty years, heralded by 'reforms'.

Reforms may be necessary, radical reforms may be essential, but the major compulsion is to keep public services going at all costs. Hospitals, schools, air traffic controllers need to be there every day. Construction of a new plan from a blank sheet of paper is a rare event. Small scale improvements are frustrating and can seem slow. In the race to accommodate all the changes, the crucial parts of the system, the local office, and the service to the public get lost, as does what the outcome should be. If one visits almost any public office anywhere and asks to see the rule book, it will be a dog-eared, browning document whose most evident features are crossings out, replacement slips of paper, handwritten changes over the original printing and lists of changes at the front. The changes are too many and too frequent for them to be applied with any consistency.

Slow pace is not inevitable. Policy changes after elections or budgets can be put in place immediately, countries go to war overnight, emergencies have to be dealt with; but changing how policies are carried out, how departments are run without a crisis or external pressure seems to be extraordinarily difficult. The context of reform is critical. The internationalisation of reform ideas and experiments have widened horizons and encouraged new approaches. But in the end changes must fit the circumstances for reform to be effective. Commentators have frequently come to the conclusion, however reluctantly, that institutional change needs crisis in one form or another to be really effective. The crisis may be economic, social or political. It will almost invariably need political support if it is to achieve results. In the next chapter we consider how far the efforts of a series of governments in the United Kingdom have achieved results and the central role of politicians and senior officials in managing the government effectively.

10. The most difficult task: change at the top

In the United Kingdom there has been much discussion of the way the government machine has been handled over the past two decades and what the solutions might be. The Prime Minister for the decade between 1997 and 2007, Tony Blair, was deeply critical of the way the public service worked. Exceptionally, members of the senior Civil Service have been publicly critical of the way Ministers work. There have been 'reforms' both of the Civil Service and of Parliament, political advisers worked closely with Ministers, Select Committees took a more active role in reviewing and criticising government policy and delivery. No one could accuse the public sector of doing nothing; the scale of changes has been remarkable in many ways but there are glaring gaps in the picture and familiar and fundamental criticisms continue to recur.

THE SENIOR CIVIL SERVICE

The British senior Civil Service is a classic example of a self regulating professional group. Despite the platitudes of the Armstrong memorandum of 1985: 'Civil Servants are the servants of the Crown. For all practical purposes the Crown in this context means and is represented by the Government of the day', the senior Civil Service controls itself. Its reaction to proposals for changes to its own way of working is defensive. As a profession it has been involved in sustained changes to almost all the public sector, much of the economy and the personal lives of most of the population but there appears to have been little grasp by the senior Civil Service of the changes they themselves should make.

I have already discussed the need for both officials and politicians to have a professional working knowledge of how the entire government machine works and an understanding of the basic processes of management. Good management cannot be a replica of military discipline or the state control of the old socialism – handing out orders and demanding obedience nor can it be a simple aping of private sector management. It is the skill of getting the best out of an organisation – its staff and its resources – in the conditions it faces. Issuing impossible orders, setting conflicting targets, demanding results without the necessary resources, refusing to use the expertise of those who have skills and experience, all result in failure. It is as damaging to allow an organisation to become slack and inefficient because no one at the top takes any interest in what is happening until a scandal or a disaster occurs. Pouring money into an organisation without specifying where the money should go or what results should be achieved, is as culpable as starving it of funds. Poor industrial relations are a consequence of bad and inadequate management. All these are errors committed by senior civil servants and Ministers who have ignored the responsibility they have for the organisations they so eagerly seek to lead.

This is not a new revelation. 'Reformers' in the United Kingdom have repeatedly drawn attention to the lack of management expertise in the senior Civil Service. Both the Fulton Report and the Next Steps Report identified the lack of relevant skills in the senior Civil Service as a serious weakness. Fulton said in 1968 'too few civil servants are skilled managers. Since the major managerial role in the Service is specifically allocated to members of the Administrative Class it follows that this criticism applies particularly to them.' Twenty years after the Fulton Report, the Next Steps Report said much the same: 'Although at the most senior levels Civil Servants are responsible for both policy and service delivery, they give a greater priority to policy . . . because that is the area in which they are on familiar ground and where their skills lie' and recommended that senior officials should have experience in both management and policy to be able to link the two effectively.

The Next Steps Report went one stage further than Fulton and drew attention to the serious confusion over the role of Ministers and Permanent Secretaries – the top officials in departments, even though Fulton had emphasised: 'there should be one man who has overall responsibility under the Minister for all the affairs of the Department and he should continue to be the Permanent Secretary'. Although both reports were accepted in full by the governments of the day, the problem that Fulton and the Efficiency Unit both described was not resolved.

Criticism of the inadequate skills and experience of the senior Civil Service continued. In 1994 William Plowden, a former senior civil servant himself and Director of the Royal Institute of Public Administration, in an IPPR publication *Ministers and Mandarins*, analysed the experience of the current Permanent Secretaries, six years after Next Steps and twenty-six years after Fulton. Only one Permanent Secretary had spent more than a year outside a government organisation (in Tanzania), two had been in Brussels at the UK Representation and the European Commission, the other 18 in his sample had 'no significant experience of working in any non government environment'. Plowden commented: 'Government means government at the centre; it is not the custom for high flyers destined for the top to spend time in the gritty milieu of a department's regional office'.

Even more significantly for the next century, the Senior Appointments Committee, which was responsible for appointments to the most senior posts in 1993 had among its six members, one who had entered the Treasury late in his career. The remaining five had one year of non Whitehall experience *between them* (Plowden, 1994).

A group of ex-civil servants who had left the service in the 1980s raised similar concerns in a paper circulated to ministers in the Major Government and discussed at a series of private meetings in 1993, with, among others, Michael Heseltine, then Deputy Prime Minister, and Robin Butler, then Head of the Civil Service and Cabinet Secretary. Their view was that the Civil Service within a decade – by 2004 – should be 'able to provide the highest quality possible policy advice and management to those areas of government which provide services'. The Civil Service should be small, flexible, open and 'expert in the contracting functions which achieve optimum delivery'.

The Institute for Public Policy Research returned to the charge more than a decade later, in 2006. In *Whitehall's Black Box* Guy Lodge and Ben Rogers argued that there were inadequacies in the way Whitehall – the senior Civil Service – was governed. Their recommendation was for reforms 'in the way it is directed and held to account'. Their investigation into the Civil Service reiterated many points that were familiar to a member of the Next Steps scrutiny team. They noted a Cabinet Office publication of 2005 which recorded that in 2004 60% of the respondents to a staff survey in the senior Civil Service had a policy background (Cabinet Office, 2005). They observed: 'the senior Civil Service it seems has not lost all its bias against management and operational delivery' (Lodge and Rogers, 2006). They described 'a governance vacuum' at the top of the Civil Service.

The think tank 'Reform' reiterated the IPPR findings in rather blunter terms: 'the same people are expected to provide and implement solutions for system failure when they themselves are products of a system that is part of the problem' (Darwell, 2005).

Sir Kenneth Stowe in an article for Public Administration in 1992 (Stowe, 1992) explained the reaction of the Civil Service to the criticisms made by Fulton. Of the Fulton Report he said: 'the first chapter of the Fulton Report is a perfect example in our own United Kingdom experience of how to destroy a good case: by stridently anathematising the existing civil service managers at the highest levels, it alienated them and they were never committed to reforms which were really needed'. In other words, the Civil Service, whose values included carrying out the wishes of the government of the day, would not do so if those wishes applied to them and they did not like it. 'Stridently anathematising' are strong words for the polished phrases of the Fulton Report written, we should not forget, by the senior civil servants in the secretariat of the Commission. The squabbles within the Fulton commission about their first chapter have been described by Richard Wilding, one of the secretariat, in a memoir of his time as a civil servant (Wilding, 2006). He describes the Commission as 'quarrelsome, suspicious and disagreeable from start to finish'. Much of the argument focused on the degree of criticism of the Civil Service to be included in the first chapter. The dissenting reservation by Lord Simey argued that the skills and judgement of the existing Civil Service were 'an asset which it would be utterly foolish to discard. Its potentialities provide a more than adequate basis for any reforms that may be necessary.'

In a series of essays published by the Civil Service Commission to celebrate its 150th anniversary nearly forty years after Lord Simey's defence, senior members of the Civil Service assure the reader that all is well. 'I am confident', writes the Head of the Civil Service 'that the civil service is well placed to adapt to continuing change' (Office of the Civil Service Commissioners 2005). The criticisms of the very top of the Civil Service continue, despite the commitment to change. Darwell argued that 'it is a self selecting, in-bred system that promotes people who care about public service and are conditioned to be more comfortable making suggestions than taking responsibility . . . change has to come from the top' (Darwell, 2005).

The Blair government went one significant step further than its predecessors had done by removing much of the traditional policy function from the job description of many civil servants. The Civil Service was to be responsible for 'delivery'. Unfortunately this was the part of their job description that most senior civil servants were least prepared for. The contempt with which some senior officials treated Mrs Thatcher's strictures appeared to have been inadequate to deal with politicians who simply left civil servants out of policy discussions. By 2006 the relationship between Ministers and senior officials had plummeted. Civil servants spoke publicly in a way unthinkable twenty years before when a modest leak of information to one of the Whitehall journalists would have been as far as they would go. The replacement of some senior civil servants as policy advisers with political advisers, the conferring of power on named political appointees to give directions to career civil servants and the intervention of Ministers in the carefully guarded process of appointments to Civil Service posts had all destabilised a once ordered system.

One view of what had changed could be gleaned from the reports of the first 'Capability Reviews' which were conducted in the main departments of the central government in the United Kingdom during 2005–2007. Each published review included the views of a distinguished team of assessors, the response of the head of the Department and the action plan to deal with any deficiencies that had been pointed out. But there is something odd about the language. It is stilted and clichéd. It refers to 'relentless sharpening' and 'igniting passion'. It is the language of private sector management speak. There are few references to the political dimension which dominates the work of central government or to the resource issues which drive difficult choices about priorities. It reads as though broad generalisations about 'leadership' or 'communication' are all that is necessary to run a successful Department. The analysis implies that the 'management task' can be divorced from the central function of the Department. It is as though management is a separate activity – another policy – not the way in which the whole organisation should be run. The annex describing the 'model of capability' gives the game away. There are no references to the priorities or preoccupations of Whitehall; it is inadequate as an analytical tool for the public service. Using the tools of a different culture can be an interesting and often valuable way of testing, adapting and discussing how a Department works, but the report and the model read like a poor adaptation of something produced for another purpose.

POLITICIANS

Politicians are in an unenviable position. The operations of government are not working well, the voters are turning away from the political process, Members of Parliament sit in an essentially unreformed House of Commons. If they chose to, they could insist on reform of the Civil Service, they could run a decent modern Parliament, they could have an electoral system which is free from corruption and worth voting in – but they have not done so.

Ministers have not only onerous tasks but also an impossible role. They must work through the political establishment to qualify for appointment or election to a political job. The pinnacle of their careers is a job for which they can have little or no experience. There could be few more unsuitable preparations for a senior political position in a government than the legal, academic, political party or trade union background from which many Members of Parliament come. Of the six contenders for election to the post of Deputy Leader of the Labour party in the summer of 2007, four were Cabinet Ministers, one a junior minister in the Blair government. Before their election as Members of Parliament and their appointments as Cabinet Ministers, two had spent much of their career as officials in the Labour Party, two as officials in a trade union, one had been a solicitor in local government and one had worked in a civil liberties pressure group. None of them had any senior experience in management, in the public or private sector.

The working relationship between politicians and officials should balance the experience of Ministers with the expertise of officials in the workings of government developed over a career. They are, or should be, professional equals with complementary skills, each needing the other for successful action and each understanding the constraints and pressures of the others' task. That understanding grows with experience but while some civil servants have a modest training in the political world of Ministers as private secretaries, most politicians have little experience of government to guide them on taking office. They have little time to acquire expertise as they are moved from one senior post to another. They have to survive on native wit and good material from their officials. Ministers are surrounded with professional experts, some are political appointments, others are career professionals but their skill is essential in making it possible for a Minister to be effective. They are not 'servants' as the traditional title miscalls them. Too many politicians are misled into discourtesy and offensiveness by assuming that senior officials are part of their personal staff and at their disposal once they have become Ministers, rather than expert colleagues with whom they need to work as equals.

The perks of office do not help good working relationships. Senior Ministers are provided with lavish accommodation, expensive cars, computers and country houses. Their official counterparts have slightly less lavish offices, definitely less lavish cars and no houses at all. Painstaking deference surrounds the Minister, which bears no relation to how they are referred to outside the office door. It is easy for an inexperienced Minister to assume that the deference is attached to themselves rather than to their role. Many Ministers fall into the trap of thinking that since they are at the top of the hierarchy the rules do not apply to them. The bizarre United Kingdom tradition designed to emphasise where responsibility lies, and much beloved of old style civil servants, is to refer to their Minister as 'my master'. The uninitiated believe that they mean it.

IMMUNITY TO CHANGE

Most modern democracies have had a revolution or two, an invasion or two, a serious war or independence which provoked rethinking about their structure of government. While no one would argue that these events are an essential foundation for a modern democracy, they do shake the institutions of government and at least provide an opportunity for rethinking or reshaping how government institutions might work – and they tend to remove one oligarchy from power. England has had none of these advantages; Scotland, Wales and now Northern Ireland have a better chance to develop genuinely democratic institutions.

There is nothing new about crises and changes in government. For the past fifty years in the United Kingdom there have been fitful attempts to improve the workings of the Houses of Parliament, the relations between Parliament and the executive and the structure of government that underpins it. The structure and functions of local government have been reshaped on several occasions, both comprehensively and piecemeal. Different authorities have been constructed, functions transferred, names changed and large buildings constructed at high cost. There have been parishes, shires, counties, shire counties, district councils, districts, municipal authorities, boroughs, unitary authorities, two tier authorities, regions and regional government. There have been Royal Commissions, studies, reviews and endless discussions. At the same time the powers of local authorities have been constantly eroded as the grip of central government over local policies and services has been extended.

While Britain may not have had the benefit of a revolution for over three hundred years it has invented and discarded ways of governing with rapidity. It has responded to corruption, terrorism, Europe, new political parties, major shifts in immigration, social patterns, working habits and new technology, rethinking the boundaries and the policies of the major political parties. Parliament has made modest changes to itself, with a great deal of complaint: hours of work, television, life peerages, fewer hereditary peers, a few more women, badges, security and concrete blocks around the entrances. Its Select Committees grow in expertise and public stature and the chairmen of Committees cross examine the Prime Minister twice a year – politely it is true – but it does happen. Government has absorbed a new career structure for many civil servants, executive agencies, contracting out, privatisation, political advisers and much more.

The senior Civil Service and the members of the House of Commons, responsible for many of these changes, eager to plan and impose changes on virtually all parts of the system of government, taking decisions which involve spending 40% GDP and affecting the lives of everybody living in the United Kingdom, appear reluctant to accept any but the most modest change to themselves. The capacity of these two powerful groups to respond to what is happening appears to be severely limited, despite the evidence of what is wrong. There is no institution to force change on them, they have to do it for themselves. In 1968 the Fulton Report recommended radical changes to the composition of the senior Civil Service. It was, the report said, restricted, inexperienced and drawn from a very limited pool. The Next Steps Report, twenty years later, described the Civil Service in similar terms.

Twenty years on, the Civil Service's own capability reviews contain similar criticisms. The senior Civil Service looks much the same in education and background, in gender, in ethnicity and, according to the 'Capability Reviews', in its capacity to manage. On each occasion, acceptance of the recommendations of a report has meant accepting the changes recommended for other parts of the system but not those that apply to the top.

All the current senior Civil Service is post-Fulton, most of them were relatively junior when the Next Steps Report was introduced, but the same criticisms are made now as then. In the Cabinet Office in 2006 'building capability' and 'delivery' were areas, in the jargon of the Capability Review which were 'urgent development areas'. The capability reviews are not alone in their familiar criticisms of the Civil Service, the IPPR put together an assessment of the senior Civil Service in the familiar terms – undertrained, inexperienced and disillusioned. Even members of the Civil Service itself, in private, make the same points. The problem is simple – the senior Civil Service has not changed, while the world changes round it.

The same pattern can be observed in the House of Commons. It passes more and more complicated legislation, imposing and requiring changes to every aspect of national life, it has made major constitutional changes to other parts of the United Kingdom and even to the Upper House at Westminster but it remains obstinately nineteenth century in its procedures, its pace of working, its composition, its behaviour and its attitude to government.

The ultimate symbol of government, the Houses of Parliament, is not designed for democracy. Its entrances are unwelcoming and mean and its interiors a hymn to the struggles of an oligarchy for power. It was designed for a governing group which had little interest in democracy and represented a small minority in the population defined by gender and property. The institutions by which the British population is governed today are just as much a reflection of that governing group and of the assumptions of the mid-nineteenth century.

By the start of the twenty-first century the House of Commons appeared weak and inadequate. Its procedures are controlled by its own appointees, most of the organisation and management of its business is in the hands of a committee chaired by a Minister of the Government of the day. In its most visible manifestation, on the television news, the benches in the chamber are almost empty for any but the most major event or the knockabout entertainment of Prime Minister's Questions. Only the Select Committees demonstrate some independence, even though their membership is controlled by the majority party. Their criticisms of the executive are remarkably even-handed and becoming more so. But the House of Commons has even accepted the Labour Government's refusal to face the serious democratic anomaly of its own making: the ability of Scottish, Welsh and Northern Ireland members of parliament, with separate parliaments for their national domestic affairs, to legislate for the domestic affairs of England and to act as ministers on solely English matters. Ironically the House of Lords, an even greater anachronism from the past which has had much needed changes in its composition forced on it in recent decades, is regarded as expert and effective in its role of considering and intervening in incompetent or unsuitable legislation which the Commons has passed.

To the visitor the Houses of Parliament reflect some of these attitudes. Visitors stand in the rain in queues. They are passed through an unwelcoming security check where the employees of the House work under cover searching chilled or dripping visitors and their umbrellas. Visitors then pass bored policemen and are waved into the dim entrance called, bewilderingly 'St Stephen's', which consists of a steep flight of stairs. It is less welcoming than an international airport in the throes of a security scare; there is no shred of a suggestion that this is a democratic institution, 'our' House of Commons. It is a private institution to which the public are admitted on sufferance, at restricted times. As the public scuffle in queues under the dreary murals of improbable and long forgotten events, the only entertainment is the swiftly passing figures in dark suits who obviously do belong, and are greeted obsequiously by the ornately dressed functionaries who wave the queues onwards with little explanation. The setting reeks not of democracy but of private and exclusive power. Most of the insiders who wield the power carefully use another door lest they be caught by someone with an awkward question, and disappear into the large sections of the building which are reserved for 'members' only.

CRACKS IN THE RELATIONSHIP: ANTAGONISTS, NOT COLLEAGUES

The secrecy which used to surround the working relationships at the top of government is being pushed aside as Ministers ignore the Civil Service and civil servants find themselves outside the centre. Ministers and political advisers are free to write and speak openly about what happens when decisions are made. Civil servants, no longer part of the charmed circle, feel increasingly free to talk themselves. *DC Confidential*, a chatty record of life in the Foreign Office by a retired ambassador was regarded as treachery by politicians, who appeared to regard many of their civil servants as Buckingham Palace regarded the nanny to royal children, definitely in the servants' wing and muffled by what they described as 'loyalty' (Meyer, 2005). A head of the security services, pushed into the public eye by a government anxious to give the spies a human face was similarly regarded as 'disloyal' and ostracised by her erstwhile colleagues when she published a harmless book of personal reminiscences (Rimmington, 2001).

The clearest sign of the breakdown of relationships at the most senior level in government was evident during the summer of 2007 when the Prime Minister's role passed to Gordon Brown on Tony Blair's retirement. A chorus of complaint from senior civil servants was recorded in the press and the media. A senior Cabinet Office official, Sir Stephen Wall, and a number of other senior officials commented publicly and unfavourably on the working habits of Ministers, and of Brown in particular. Damage to the co-ordinating role of the Cabinet Office and the system of allocating public expenditure were cited as consequences of secretive working methods which made the normal process of government business difficult to operate.

The challenges to the working methods of Ministers, including poor interpersonal skills and inability to understand how to behave as a senior Minister in charge of a major Department of State, were serious charges enough, but refusing to work within the system used to co-ordinate government policy, timing interventions to the point of maximum damage, and ignoring the process of working with colleagues made much of government activity difficult to manage properly. The civil servants who made these charges and talked openly about what had been happening were breaking with the long standing professional requirement for discretion (Channel 4, *Dispatches*, May 14 2007). No senior civil servant had spoken so openly and critically 'on the record' about working with a current government in power before.

An unprecedented comment by Lord Turnbull, a retired Head of the Civil Service, about the serving Chancellor of the Exchequer, criticising his behaviour, his attitude to his staff and disregard of his colleagues and describing him as Stalinist, was but one of a number of opportunities taken by civil servants to protest at the Government's treatment of them (*Financial Times*, April 2007). The 'Capability Reviews' demonstrate the aridity of the relationship between Ministers and Civil Servants and the degree to which the working methods of the past have broken down. The 'model of capability' does not mention policy at all. The 'most crucial areas of capability' are 'Leadership, Delivery and Strategy'. The senior Civil Service appears to have lost much of its primary professional function of working with politicians to develop policy. In doing so it will have lost its capacity to provide Ministers with impartial advice and Ministers will have lost access to that advice.

Ministers will also have lost access to any expertise in the management of the government machine. If policy is increasingly developed as Lord Turnbull suggested in *Changing Times* 'off line', 'in dedicated strategy units', information about what is practical and possible will be even less available (OCSC, 2005). The gulf between the development of policy and the management of government, which Next Steps tried to address, will become wider and policies less effective in consequence. The impartial policy capacity will atrophy and with it the skills of managing the political business of government. External recruits can be brought in to manage the big executive functions of government, skills which most senior civil servants lack, but the Whitehall system, that 'Rolls Royce' which steered inexperienced Ministers through the many difficulties of working in Westminster and Whitehall, will have disappeared for good.

These defects in the Whitehall system are more serious than the day to day problems of politics and poor interpersonal skills. They reflect serious constitutional failures which can only become more acute if they are not dealt with. British constitutionalists are fond of referring to the checks and balances of the system. They are less clear about what those checks and balances are but at the heart of them are what are called 'conventions' about what is or is not an acceptable way to govern. Ministers are responsible for policy, but the convention was that their decisions were based on judgement informed by independent advice from Civil Service advisers that was taken seriously, however negative Ministers might feel the Civil Service to be.

One of the essential checks and balances was supposed to be the senior Civil Service, part of whose job was, in that phrase popular with those who don't have to do it: 'to speak truth to power'. It becomes impossible to do when 'power' refuses to listen and is inclined to dismiss you or ruin your career for doing so. Over the past decade there have been strong signs that this has been happening, as in the final years of the Thatcher administration. There are a decreasing number of civil servants who see independent advice on policy proposals as part of their role and few politicians prepared to accept the necessity for such advice. Too many civil servants now define their role as 'doing what the Minister wants', as one senior official in the Home Office did in a discussion in the mid-1990s. The virtues of independent policy advice had already slipped from their view of their professional role.

What has been happening recently is that the oldest check and balance of all is coming into play – whistle blowing. Government has become far more messy but more open at the same time. Appeals for changes tend to try to stem the tide rather than look for new routes. It is possible that the time is approaching when what is needed is a new approach to government and democratic accountability rather than what Peter Drucker once described as the 'patch and spot welding' of the old (Drucker, 1995).

The classic solution to the inexperience at the top of government would be more of the same. The solutions for the senior Civil Service that have

been promised in the past keep recurring. Secondments, outside appointments, better training are repeatedly promised as if they had not been
thought of before. There will not be a solution to the problems in the politics and political institutions of the United Kingdom by tinkering with the
relationships between the senior Civil Service and Ministers. Both groups
are victims of the expectations of the system they work in. The Civil Service
appears unable to cope with the change in its traditional function of advising Ministers and unable to reinvent itself. Ministers appear lost as well,
making poor political decisions, lying earnestly about what is happening,
complaining and alienating their staff and spending an inordinate amount
of time on petty politicking.

Too many opportunities have been lost to introduce the necessary
improvements and the habit of slow and modest alterations at the pace of
the slowest is inadequate to the task. New politicians are needed who can
look forward, not back; new civil servants are needed who reflect the community around them and have a shared understanding of their role. The
driving force should be to achieve more effective government.

RADICAL CHANGE – NEW PEOPLE, NEW SKILLS

In this book discussion has focused on the crucial relationship between
career officials and politicians in government. It is a curious relationship,
not least because many of those involved speak warmly of their colleagues
and assert they have no problems. The senior Civil Service still has strengths
which are important. Financial corruption is very rare, nepotism was
unheard of – although the Blair Government created a new form known as
'cronyism': the appointment of people to public office with the sole
qualification of being a friend of the Minister concerned. In many countries this would be considered the natural action of a government in power;
that is becoming the case in Britain.

Some of the Civil Service's strengths are also its weakness. Many people
dealing with senior civil servants speak almost with awe about the quality
of intellectual ability which is evident. They are right; there are many highly
able people in Whitehall, selected in their extreme youth on the basis of
their intellectual capacity as demonstrated in universities, and trained
solely within the senior Civil Service. This is the pattern which has been virtually unchanged, except at the margins for nearly a hundred and fifty
years. Most of the senior Civil Service at the beginning of the twenty-first
century have come through this system. For more than fifty years there has
been advice from distinguished commentators urging changes to the senior
Civil Service so that they are able to deal with modern Britain. The changes

that have occurred have not dealt with the problem. Plans are made for training courses, exchanges and for more management experience but they seldom happen, and they are not enough.

The people and the jobs they do have to be different. Senior civil servants have to have experience of being adults in a world where they take responsibility, and they have to have a grasp of the consequences of what they do. Undergraduate life is no preparation for working in government. Recruitment should change. For example, two attributes should be required for entry to the senior Civil Service: at least five and preferably ten years experience outside the Civil Service with at least two years relevant professional training, some of it outside the United Kingdom. The Civil Service should develop intensive professional training for the public service, lasting at least a year and concluding with examinations. In the United Kingdom every other serious professional group does so; it is extraordinary that the Civil Service does not. Successful candidates could then begin to specialise in finance, management, policy making, and continue training to a higher professional level. The objective would be to develop a skilled profession of the kind originally described by Fulton and implied by almost every review since then, which could deal with all aspects of the public service. The break with the past would be in age, recruitment and training. No longer would the inexperienced be selected and trained solely by those who had been trained by their predecessors in habits of thinking and working going back decades.

The functions undertaken by the senior Civil Service should be rethought. So far names have been changed, some newer management tasks have been devised, advisory 'boards' have been appointed but the underlying responsibilities remain much the same. The 'policy' civil servant has been joined by political appointees in an often uncomfortable relationship; their function should not be to edge out political appointees but to bring experience of how a policy might work to the discussion. At the policy level, civil servants should be able to demonstrate expertise which is valuable enough to hold its own with the urgency of political commitment. The expertise has to extend to experience of what happens, not merely writing papers. 'Focusing on delivery' is something policy makers have to understand as well as executive managers. If the two are divorced the policy is likely to flounder. A civil servant has to have training and experience in both. Most senior jobs should have a period of three to six months for preparation and training and be expected to last for five years at least. The Civil Service fondness for a 'hand over' which consisted of a maximum of two days for discussion, a quick look at current problems, a friendly lunch and the transfer of the office keys should be abolished.

The professional generalist has to disappear. Too often the traditional civil servant has too shallow a grasp of the detail of anything apart from how the Whitehall system works. Those who have been recruited as generalists can too easily sound as amateur as their political colleagues and raise questions about the distinctiveness of their contribution. The professional training has to be good enough and rigorous enough to transmit what is of importance and to open minds to new approaches. The training has to be relevant in the job to be done at the end of the course or much of the benefit will be lost. Senior civil servants should have retraining and sabbaticals; they should do regular and serious reviews of policy or organisation to keep their professional knowledge up to date, and their capacity to find solutions, as well as difficulties, refreshed. There should be experts within the Civil Service as well as outside it.

The politicians have to change too. The same criticisms made of the Civil Service can be made of them. They remain generalists, heirs of the nineteenth-century traditions of the knowledgeable amateur. As a new Prime Minister, Gordon Brown moved or replaced almost the entire membership of the cabinet with one exception, as though Ministerial offices were simply a series of labels. The role of a politician in power is difficult and challenging if he or she is to be responsible and effective. All politicians need a deep understanding of the workings of the government they aim to run and the Department they are to lead, and of the impact of their policies on what happens across the social and economic life of the country in the short and long term. Without that breadth of understanding they will make inadequate and incompetent decisions and fail to understand the potential and the limitations of what they can achieve; they will be too dependent on their officials and their advisers for ideas and decisions.

The emotional commitment of many politicians to improvements in economic and social welfare has to be enhanced by a professional recognition of what can and should be done in practice. The leaders of political parties have a responsibility to ensure that their colleagues as well as they themselves recognise the need to become expert in government, not only in politics, both to perform their current function and to be able to move to effective government. Politicians should aim to become expert in the practicalities of what a government could or should do and in what it should not do as well as in the theory.

THE ROLES OF MINISTER AND OFFICIAL

Wider experience and some formal training would improve the quality of government, if it is relevant and applied. Politicians and officials who fully understand the scale and the implications of what they try to do should be able to do more and do it better. But better training and the recruitment and appointment of more experienced people will only be effective if the tasks they are given are well defined and their responsibilities and accountability are understood and respected by all involved. The training should support a more fundamental change. British government needs an open and accepted statement of the roles and responsibilities of Departmental Ministers and the senior officials in Departments and agencies.

There has been confusion about the boundaries between Minister and official for decades. The confusion is compounded by the new language of leadership and the more overt roles of senior civil servants in 'delivery'. There has been an ingrained reluctance to define the roles of politicians; responsibilities at the top of many Departments simply reflect the capacity and the interests of those concerned. The evidence of Fulton, the Efficiency Unit and the IPPR raised the question repeatedly. While the issue has gone unresolved, the scale of what Departments do, the numbers they employ and the resources they consume have grown. It is not enough for Ministers to do what interests them and leave the rest to be handled by someone else. It is not appropriate for junior advisers and officials to be taking decisions that should be the responsibility of a more senior person or the converse – the dragging up of modest decisions to a level which is unnecessary. The application of the principles of leadership and capability should mean that there is a formal solution to this long standing muddle, however uncomfortable it may be.

Greater clarity about responsibilities will only work if those who take on the roles bring the necessary skills and expertise to them. Ministers will need the capacity to take difficult decisions, to tolerate the frustrations and limitations of what is practical and to bring a sufficient understanding of how the system works to be able to judge what is and what is not significant. They have to have an informed understanding of government and the principles which underpin public administration as well as their understanding of politics and the political world. Only then can they know when to insist on political priorities which demand major changes in policy and when to temper their objectives to what can be more easily achieved.

The Civil Service and politicians will need to ensure that all aspects of government are covered in the definition of roles at the top of departments. There is a fundamental question about the new role of the Civil Service which should not be ignored. The old 'Whitehall' system had three critical components: the development of independent advice on policy, protection of the public face of their Ministers, and responsibility for the implementation of policy. The majority of what the senior Civil Service did was taken up with the first two tasks and it was there that their skills lay. Most senior civil servants also considered that they had a wider responsibility to the quality of public administration, its honesty, truthfulness and its freedom from corruption and political interference. This has been further interpreted as a responsibility for the constitutional assumptions about the way in which political decisions are taken: the importance of independent advice, the legality of decisions and the proper use of public funds. Uncomfortable and inconvenient as these principles may be in individual instances they have been assumed to be an important part of the fabric of government, which can get ignored in specific instances, but which should underpin how governments work.

The role of independent advice and protection of the Minister has always been seen as distinct and more significant than the executive management task, no matter how large the organisation or its budget. The risk in giving greater prominence to the executive tasks of officials is that the strengths and the capacity of the policy 'Whitehall' official are undervalued and lost in the rush for the 'delivery' role. When executive agencies were introduced the Efficiency Unit regarded the unfinished business as being the reconstruction of the 'policy role' of the Civil Service. That remains an important task and is now an urgent one. The civil servant in the British Government in the twenty-first century needs far wider experience and skills than his or her predecessor. Intelligence is not enough. It must be combined with knowledge of government, experience of other parts of the economy and other ways of working and with specific professional skills in their own area. They should also develop the professional self confidence of the expert whose advice is sought and heeded.

A decline in the role and in the value attached to the contribution of the policy civil servant appears in the extent of poorly drafted legislation, as constantly changing Finance Bills, Criminal Justice Bills and immigration rules have demonstrated. There have been ill thought out policies and wasted resources as Health Service 'reforms' and frequent changes to education policy have shown. The responsibility still lies with senior officials and Ministers in making poor or hurried decisions which cause repeated changes to legislation, missed opportunities and damage to individuals.

Once Ministers and Civil Servants accept that what they are trying to do is exceedingly difficult, that each can and does bring relevant and valuable skills to the task and that they need both approaches to achieve their objectives, it might be possible to improve the quality of government and, as a consequence, the services that are provided. Both need to develop a higher degree of specific professional skill for their distinctively different tasks and to respect each others capacities. Both need to have sensible jobs with defined roles: Ministers to provide political direction and to understand when to hand over to professionals to understand the implications of what they are asking for and to recognise sensible advice about what is possible or affordable or where the consequences may be unexpected or unfortunate. In the structure in which they work, politician and official will often pull in different directions. The outcome will often be unsatisfactory, their task will be to understand and value both viewpoints so that the solution is as good as possible. It will seldom be ideal.

THE DIFFICULTY OF CHANGE

Ministers and officials must also understand and never lose sight of that other part of the government which they seldom see, described in the first chapter, the thousands whose work is directed by their decisions and on whom they depend totally for the implementation of their policies. Ministers should always remember that those are the people who provide the results they are seeking. In government there is seldom a simple management task; the web of management, policy and politics has to be mastered by politicians and officials alike if they are to perform their functions effectively.

It is not easy for the senior Civil Service or politicians to change themselves, and it is not a change that can be achieved easily or quickly or one which will yield rapid results. Civil servants and Ministers may recognise the problems but they have not moved with the necessary perception, innovation or determination to deal with it. Both groups cling to the past. Many might find the changes too uncomfortable. But politicians and public officials need to be ready for the more radical political change which will face them, in a way that retains the virtues of the older system with the imperatives of the new. The old certainties are becoming more fluid as the structure of government in the United Kingdom changes. The nascent federalism of 'devolution', together with the crisis in voting patterns and the spread of proportional representation will, over time, mean that ways of working and making policy will change.

Politicians will face a very different policy environment in which they have to work. The relentless pressure from media reporting with close scrutiny of every action requires care and knowledge in the choice and development of policy as well as its presentation. They need to make fewer mistakes and they will need professional help to do so. They will need to be sufficiently self confident in their judgement and their grasp of what they are trying to achieve to be able to deal with external pressure, particularly from the media, without being deflected from their objective. Civil servants will need the self confidence and the flexibility to work with a spread of different power structures, interest groups and ways of making things happen. Their political independence and their skills in developing policy which works and has been well thought out will become more not less important. Civil servants should be competent experts on the public sector, with a grasp of the techniques of their trade: economics, law, social sciences and management and politics as they affect the private as well as the public sector. The expertise of the public official should be overt and unquestioned, they should be partners in government not 'servants', answerable for what they do and responsible for the outcome.

POLICIES AND IMPLEMENTATION

New solutions to improve the workings of the public sector do not appear obvious when one considers how many times politicians and governments have tried. Christopher Hood observed that debates about how best to do public management 'tend to throw up the same fundamental ideas in different times and places' (Hood, 1998). After the experience of Next Steps and its implementation, I would argue that it is in fitting together what is wrong with a constructive answer that the best chance of making progress lies. The solution has to solve the problem, not just be a bright idea which deals with a current fashion. The difficulty lies in making the solution happen, not in having the good idea. History, as Hood argues, does have some important lessons and one of the most useful is to remember that the last reformers were as well intentioned as the current ones – it is also useful to remember that it is much easier to tell other people to reform than to reform oneself.

The experience of past efforts at reform has demonstrated how significant the failure to understand the complexities of the implementation of difficult changes has been. Centralisation has made the problem more serious because the problems are frequently invisible until they become acute. The Efficiency Unit, in the Next Steps Report, argued that centralisation had reduced the Civil Service to a serious level of administrative incompetence. The same is true of many governments whose systems make it possible for a small group of politicians and officials to believe that they can oversee and control all that happens within government. If politicians want to see the policies on which they were elected introduced, to oversee what is happening and be able to report sensibly on the outcomes, they need to understand the principles of genuine delegation, the mechanics of their 'delivery organisation' and what the limitations of their position are. They have to have realistic expectations of what can be done and what their part should be in that process. In the short term the system can stagger on; it is to the credit of those working in it that it continues to function. But those responsible have neither the skills nor the capacity to deal with the scale of the issues which face governments in the twenty-first century. The question for the United Kingdom is whether the senior Civil Service and the politicians in power can develop the skills and the experience they need to run a modern government – can they reform themselves without a revolution?

11. Politics and management: can they co-exist?

In most political systems there is a recognisable gulf between Ministers and their immediate circle of advisers and officials and the senior managers responsible for the government machine. The pattern varies from country to country; senior managers can be anyone from the General in charge of the military to the doctor in charge of public health or a career official who has run the same part of the government for years, the President of a university or the chief executive of the Institute of National Heritage. The issues that perplex them will be partly specific to their country and their role but all of them will talk about budgets, priorities, staffing and, above all, about their relationship with the politicians who direct them.

Politicians in office have a similar but not identical list of issues: political priorities, political pressures, what the President wants, what the press are saying, budgets and operational problems that are said to prevent the implementation of policy. Some Ministers have their own answers to the issues and want reassurance that they are right, others are confused and unsure which direction to take or whether anything can be done. For many, their horizons are limited to the problems they are dealing with immediately whether of policy or a serious politically charged system failure. Longer term strategic issues are constantly knocked aside by the immediate pressures. Senior officials at the Budget ministry, the Health ministry or the Accountant General are likely to be more professionally self-confident. They can handle their subject, they know their range of skills and they can delegate without losing face or control. But they too seldom know what goes on in their local offices or beyond their immediate concerns.

One of the themes of the Next Steps Report was the scale and size of what government was trying to do in the 1980s. In most countries that scale has grown considerably over the intervening twenty years. There have been substantial political and economic policy changes, national and international, the effects of population change, the age profile of populations and the impact of migration and immigration, environmental, health and economic issues have all contributed to increasing the scope as well as the scale of government. While the activities of governments have been changing, the profiles of politicians have much the same mix of backgrounds and experience. American politicians, like their United Kingdom and other European Union counterparts have similar backgrounds as their colleagues from earlier generations. University, law school, the military, academia, trade unions and business provide many of the figures who appear at senior levels in government. South America provides a wider range of backgrounds as does Africa but there are few examples of experience of senior and large scale management. That is hardly surprising; the process of achieving political power leaves little time for a serious management career in the public or private sector. Early experience as a mayor, a governor, or a lawyer may provide a partial view of the role of government but as a background for senior political office it is not sufficient to equip a politician for the responsibilities of most Ministerial jobs. Most politicians learn on the job. 'Mega' government has to deal with bigger issues, larger budgets and more complex problems; the people involved in government have to be competent to deal with the scale of the decisions they make.

Most politicians who make a career of politics will be involved at some stage with the provision of public services, but it is not inevitable. There are spectacular examples of lack of experience of the bedrock of government in most countries. While in the USA the route to national political office is most frequently through state politics with relative closeness to reality and to the electorate, in the United Kingdom it is possible to have a government, like the Blair administration between 1997 and 2007, where neither of the two most senior politicians – the Prime Minister and the Chancellor of the Exchequer – had any experience of direct responsibility for the provision of public services before taking over the most senior offices in government.

Politicians are easy to blame. There is little incentive for them to become expert in the mechanics of how government works. The only real pressure on them comes from the risk of electoral defeat or a hounding by the media. In some systems, one of the recognised functions of civil servants has been to protect weak or incompetent ministers from the public consequences of their mistakes. Errors in public management are not only a consequence of naïve political involvement or poor decision taking; politicians can find themselves powerless to change rules dictated by central regulation or wider policy imperatives which affect their capacity to fulfil their own objectives.

Resolving the different interests and balancing conflicting priorities are central to the role of a minister and the officials advising him or her. It is seldom an easy task. The task is made more difficult for those involved if they do not know enough about the organisation they are using to carry out policy directly or indirectly. Unforeseen or unintended consequences can wreck the best intentioned plans; misunderstandings about responsibilities, outcomes and costs can be disastrous. An arms length relationship between a politician and a public service can be productive provided that it is genuinely arms length. The problems arise when ministers who do not understand the complexity of what has to be done assume a quasi managerial role and use their ministerial authority to take decisions about the detail. As public institutions become larger and public policy more complex, such interventions can be disproportionately damaging.

The policy role of Ministers is essential, not only for democratic legitimacy and the implementation of political objectives but also to challenge accepted ways of managing and existing policy assumptions in a manner which can provide a stimulus to improvement. A new approach can be invaluable whether it is in the detail or the whole policy direction. But erratic policy changes or sudden shifts in political priorities can also be more damaging than the benefits they bring. A balance has to be struck between political imperatives and the way in which an organisation is run to achieve its objectives. Most organisations need some policy stability to perform well. Erratic and frequent political appointments can be seriously damaging. As one ex-Home Secretary in England replied grimly to an interviewer on being asked why, when in office, he had not dealt with a very difficult issue, 'I did, it was all under way . . . when I left office'. The following pause did not need to be filled, his successor had changed the priorities again.

I have argued that both politicians and officials have a responsibility to recognise that modern government needs better and more relevant expertise than even twenty years ago, better procedures and clearer responsibilities. The increased involvement of governments in the lives of their citizens, the size of public expenditure and the regulation of economic life makes the quality of decision taking and implementation more significant. Ill considered and broad directives do not translate into effective policies. Peter Drucker who had seen many governments come and go argued that 'the new political theory we so badly need will have to rest on an analysis of what does work rather than on good intentions and promises of what should work because we would like it to', a weary rebuttal of the over optimism of political promises, based on little understanding of what was possible and practical (Drucker, 1995).

Academics and consultants have tried to bridge the gap between what is wanted and what is possible. There have been serious attempts to bring a new understanding of what happens in government and what is going on. Academics and experts have entered government service, bringing their perception of how government does or should work with them. The old academic departments of public administration have been swept away to be replaced by centres of political science, governance, bureaucratic studies and politics. New terminology has been invented: Reform agendas, Leadership, Capability. 'Reform' has been popular for thirty years and each wave of enthusiasts produces an expensive new initiative and a new jargon.

Public services have not been immune to the fever of new reforms. Analysis of what happens is exhaustive. But analysis of why it happens is less extensive. The reasons for the strengths and weaknesses of the British National Health Service (NHS) or Medicare in the USA lie deeper than local failures in management, not enough money or the machinations of national politicians. Within the vast range of public services there can be good and bad under similar regimes. Parts of the NHS are excellent, some welfare schemes in the States run smoothly and competently, transport links in most of Europe work well. There is no simple model which would always work or we would have found it. It is not for lack of looking. The management and business schools still struggle to find answers. The solutions have been seen in training, reorganisations, more money, less money, devolution, centralisation, computerisation, privatisation, contracting. Nothing has proved to be infallible, nor will it. The public sector is far too complicated to be described by a single solution.

Even when priorities are sorted out, finances allocated and policies formulated the process of providing a service and running it has not yet begun. One innocent theorist argued that 'to have good performance what you need is a good policy'. On that basis the world should be in perfect order. Policy, like intelligence is not in short supply. Public offices are full of high level intellects, expensive think tanks and bought in experts. But what is undervalued, by officials as much as by politicians, is the scarcest skill of all: making an idea happen. It is at the point of turning policy into practice where all public sectors have so often failed to learn from the private sector.

One significant reason for the failure is where high level public sector management comes from. In effective companies, a little research demonstrates that many senior directors will have spent some time working on the shop floor, running a small part of the business, serving behind the counter, building the IT platform or packing pies. One chairman of a major international bank said he had never forgotten running a small engineering firm in his first two years with the company where he spent most of his career. 'I had to make a profit or I'd be fired – profit is the first question I ask about, even today.' Few senior civil servants or politicians have started life running a small business or even working in one, or paying out benefits, or delivering the post. While a spell at Harvard or in ENA may provide all the intellectual training possible it cannot provide experience of the constant effort of running an organisation, persuading people to do what they may not agree with and facing the intolerable frustration of a public servant who can see what is needed to provide the expected service, but is ignored behind mountains of instructions, forms and demands for immediate action on the latest initiative.

The solution may not be found where the politicians and the advisers hope – in better ideas, more money or faster response times. It may be found in looking again at the problem, understanding where the difficulty lies and why it appears so difficult for the political elites to understand it. Most public policy is made top down – the policy driven by the politics of place, party and time. The consequences of that approach are slowly becoming recognised. The solution is seldom looked for in something as simple as the answers to the question of what is stopping the policy from happening. From this question the Efficiency Unit in 1987 constructed a new approach to public management. The significant question is what is preventing the people concerned from carrying out the existing policy, or why is it not working where it matters? The answers to those questions, of course, will not be found in Washington or Delhi or even in the Town Hall; they will be found in the local school, the roadside, the clinic or the military depot. The answers can only be found by observing what is happening on the ground and asking those who are doing it what is going wrong.

MANAGING THE MISFIT

Public services are essential to a well ordered society; they are an important part of the responsibility the electorate gives to politicians. They absorb a major proportion of most government revenues; they pose some of the most challenging issues of social welfare, economic development and domestic security. If a simple way of improving the performance of public services is to be found, it will not be in the attempts of the past quarter century, where experts, reforms, change management, revolutions in care, in policing, in health policy litter the field. They will probably not be found in elaborate new policies, however well researched – or even sensible and realistic changes. None of these have produced more than marginal changes for disproportionate cost.

The process of improving public services might more constructively be regarded as one of steady improvement rather than dramatic change, managed with care and diligence over longer periods of time, learning from mistakes, testing and developing new approaches, with a constant focus on the service supplied to the individual citizen either directly or indirectly. If the argument for long and patient improvement is valid, it is manifest that for politicians this analysis is wholly unsuited to their time horizons. Politicians do not have 'long periods of time' unless they are secure and unelected dictators. The optimum time scale for an improving public service is not going to be one which will fit with those who have democratic accountability for running it. There is an organisational misfit which can not – and does not – work and has to be faced.

This is the complex problem at the heart of public management: What governments try to do is almost always beyond their capacity to deliver, in time, in money and in capability. The priorities of politics and management have to be developed in partnership between politicians and officials if they are not to impede effective delivery. Some public services work well and some countries manage to run competent services. There are factors which make it possible to run good services. Size may be important: not too big, not too small. Consensus about the service objectives may be significant. The degree of control over quality may be a necessary but not a sufficient condition. Analysts have tried to find a common thread and most admit failure. It is also possible that the attempt to find a common thread across all public services is bound to fail because there are so many differences between them. Apart from the fundamental issue of what constitutes success and who assesses it, there are some common conditions which contribute to the desired outcome – sustained political support, clear objectives, a reasonable budget and a minimum of changes once the plans and budgets have been agreed are all themes that recur.

The role of a politician in government is challenging. So is that of a senior official. The size and scale of any public sector is huge, the impact its policies and management have on social and economic life is vast, and the responsibility and accountability for it rests with a group chosen for their role for a wide range of reasons, most of them nothing to do with the management responsibility they acquire as Ministers or top officials.

What is increasingly evident is that the consequences of the responsibilities Ministers accept in taking the strategic decisions for the public sector impose on them not merely an obligation but a necessity to understand fully what they are doing. Effective strategic decision taking requires an underpinning of detailed and expert analysis of options and consequences. Officials have to be capable of providing informed and professional judgements; Ministers have to be prepared to listen, to understand and to accept even uncomfortable advice supported by evidence. The responsibility for executive management may lie elsewhere particularly as government becomes more complex, but understanding what is involved in management has to be part of the professional skill set of senior civil servants and Ministers both to determine the policy and to oversee the executive or contracted tasks. Failure to acquire and use these skills results in poor decision taking and ineffective performance. It can have a serious effect on the economic and social wellbeing of the nation.

The Next Steps team in the United Kingdom found that most senior officials and Ministers did not know how to deal with management with serious consequences for the way the United Kingdom government was run. The democratic argument for political oversight of public services is obvious; what is equally obvious is that if politicians take the ultimate responsibility for those services, they must also equip themselves to do it properly. In the previous chapter we looked at some of the issues which face the government in the United Kingdom in adapting and equipping the senior Civil Service, Ministers and politicians to carry out their responsibilities. Other governments face similar issues. Modern government is complicated; it is probably impossible to manage to an optimum level of effectiveness. There are serious mistakes and expensive errors: people suffer. The objective should be to aim for realism about what is possible, equitable and affordable and to achieve what is promised.

In the last chapter I argued for specific professionalism in the career Civil Service in the United Kingdom. I also argued for a similar but different expertise for politicians. This is not only true for the United Kingdom Government. In any government officials should understand the practical possibilities of the issues facing them including public service developments and service quality together with a good grasp of the legal, economic and social welfare implications of policy. Politicians should understand the way institutions behave, the structures of organisations and the reactions of people. They should respect the expertise of their advisers. Both sides would then be able to discuss, develop and decide on policies which were realistic, possible and affordable within a political framework.

The solutions would never be easy; with greater knowledge they might be less unrealistic and have a better chance of working. No system can force constructive working between different groups in government. Democratic accountability imposes a constraint on what can be done which requires those involved in government to find a sensible solution. It is not their money they are spending, it is seldom their lives they are directly affecting. The relationship between politicians and officials is a difficult one. It is conducted under conditions which are frequently stressful, it can go very wrong or it can be constructive and creative. It cannot flourish under master and servant conditions, nor under bully and victim relationships. Both sides need the other too badly for such absurdities.

Many new democracies are impatient of incompetent government but many are endemically corrupt. Balanced and incorrupt management of the machinery of the state and the public sector both provides much of the structure of modern life and a bastion between a peaceful existence and disaster. In some countries disaster is close and palpable. In April 2007 the London *Times* newspaper interviewed the Environment Minister of the Government of the disaster ridden Somalia in a hotel lobby in Mogadishu. 'We asked if he had any civil servants. "No", he replied cheerfully, "but we have guns." ' In many countries Ministers and civil servants are working perilously close to that situation.

In other countries the problems are merely the bickering of the highly privileged and comfortable, seeking to extend their personal power and ignoring the consequences, or just unable to understand what they are doing. Co-operative, constructive and informed co-existence between politician and official, both policy maker and manager, is essential if modern government is to work. The responsibility lies with politicians and senior officials to acquire the skills that will make them effective. They should accept that responsibility and ensure that they themselves are equipped for their tasks. An informed and professional relationship between decision takers and managers is essential if all parties to the political compromise including the users of public services are to be benefit from modern government.

Annex

EFFICIENCY UNIT

IMPROVING MANAGEMENT IN GOVERNMENT: THE NEXT STEPS

Report to the Prime Minister

by
Kate Jenkins
Karen Caines
Andrew Jackson

LONDON: HMSO

CONTENTS

1 INTRODUCTION

1. As a result of initiatives taken since 1979, the management of government business is much improved, especially in those parts of government where there are clear tasks to be performed and services to be delivered. But there is still a long way to go; in particular there is insufficient sense of urgency in the search for better value for money and steadily improving services. There is wide agreement in departments themselves that substantial further improvement is achieveable, but that this depends heavily on changing the cultural attitudes and behaviour of government so that continuous improvement becomes a widespread and in-built feature of it. This report makes recommendations on the structure and management needed for the better delivery of services both to the public and to Ministers, the experience that staff need to be given and how sustained pressure for improvement can be developed. This should bring the changes needed in attitudes and behaviour and with them progressive improvement in performance.

2 FINDINGS

2.   As part of this scrutiny we have spent three months
in discussions with people in the Civil Service throughout the country. We have also reviewed the evidence
from other scrutinies in the central programme since
1979 and looked at earlier reports on the management
of the Civil Service. The themes which have emerged
during the scrutiny have followed a broadly consistent
pattern, whether in discussions in a small local benefit
office or in a Minister's room. Some are also common
themes in earlier scrutinies and in reports on the Civil
Service (see Appendix A to Annex B). There are seven
main findings.

3.   **First, the management and staff concerned with the
delivery of government services (some 95 per cent of the
Civil Service) are generally convinced that the developments towards more clearly defined and budgeted management are positive and helpful.** The manager of a
small local office in the north east said that for the first
time in 20 years he felt that he could have an effect on
the conditions under which his staff worked and therefore on the results they produced. But this kind of
enthusiasm is tempered by frustration at constraints.
Although there is a general acceptance of the importance of delegating meaningful authority down to
the most effective level, diffused responsibility still
flourishes, especially in offices away from the sharp end
of delivery of services to the public. Middle managers
in particular feel that their authority is seriously circumscribed both by unnecessary controls and by the
intervention of Ministers and senior officials in relatively minor issues. People who had recently resigned
from the Civil Service told us that frustration at the
lack of genuine responsibility for achieving results was
a significant factor in encouraging them to move to
jobs outside.

[3]

4. **Second, most civil servants are very conscious that senior management is dominated by people whose skills are in policy formulation and who have relatively little experience of managing or working where services are actually being delivered.** In any large organisation senior appointments are watched with close attention. For the Civil Service the present signals are, as one senior Grade 2 told us, that 'the golden route to the top is through policy not through management'. This is reflected in the early experience and training of fast-stream recruits. This kind of signal affects the unwritten priorities of a whole organisation, whatever the formal policy may be.

5. Managing large organisations involves skills which depend a great deal on experience; without experience senior mangers lack confidence in their own ability to manage. Although, at the most senior levels, civil servants are responsible for both policy and service delivery, they give a greater priority to policy, not only because it demands immediate attention but because that is the area in which they are on familiar ground and where their skills lie, and where ministerial attention is focused. A proper balance between policy and delivery is hard to achieve within the present framework, even though taxpayers are becoming increasingly conscious of what they should expect from public expenditure on health, education and other services and hold Ministers to blame for their deficiencies.

6. **Third, senior civil servants inevitably and rightly respond to the priorities set by their Ministers which tend to be dominated by the demands of Parliament and communicating government policies.** In this situation it is easy for the task of improving performance to get overlooked, especially where there is, as we observed, confusion between Ministers and permanent secretaries over their respective responsibilities for the management of service delivery. This confusion is made worse when short-term pressure becomes acute. Nevertheless the ability of Ministers supported by their senior officials to handle politics and political sensitivities effectively is a crucial part of any government's credibility. Changes in

the mangement process should therefore aim to increase rather than diminish this crucial skill.

7.   **Fourth, the greater diversity and complexity of work in many departments, together with demands from Parliament, the media and the public for more information, has added to ministerial overload.** Because of other pressures on Ministers, and because for most of them management is not their forte and they don't see it as their function, better management and the achievement of improved performance is something that the Civil Service has to work out largely for itself. It is unrealistic to expect Ministers to do more than give a broad lead. Most Ministers who are worried about overload are of the view that while changes in management that reduced the ministerial load would be welcomed, provided they entailed no major political risks, Ministers themselves do not have the time or the experience needed to develop such changes.

8.   **Fifth, the pressures on departments are mainly on expenditure and activities; there is still too little attention paid to the results to be achieved with the resources.** The public expenditure system is the most powerful central influence on departmental mangement. It is still overwhelmingly dominated by the need to keep within the levels of money available rather than by the effectiveness with which that money is used.

9.   **Sixth, there are relatively few external pressures demanding improvement in performace.** The Prime Minister has given a valuable lead and holds seminars to discuss value for money in individual departments. Her Adviser on Efficiency and Effectiveness has annual discussions with Ministers about their priorities for getting better value for money. These are useful but occasional rather than continuous pressures. Pressure from Parliament, the Public Accounts Committee and the media tends to concentrate on alleged impropriety or incompetence, and making political points, rather than on demanding evidence of steadily improving efficiency and effectiveness. This encourages a cautious and defensive response which feeds through into

management. On the positive side, the Treasury and the National Audit Office (NAO) are developing work on value for money. But the process of searching for improvement is still neither rigorous nor sustained; it is not yet part of the basic institution of government.

10. **Seventh, the Civil Service is too big and too diverse to manage as a single entity. With 600,000 employees it is an enormous organisation compared with any private sector company and most public sector organisations.** A single organisation of this size which attempts to provide a detailed structure within which to carry out functions as diverse as driver licensing, fisheries protection, the catching of drug smugglers and the processing of Parliamentary Questions is bound to develop in a way which fits no single operation effectively.

11. At present the freedom of an individual manager to manage effectively and responsibly in the Civil Service is severely circumscribed. There are controls not only on resources and objectives, as there should be in any effective system, but also on the way in which resources can be managed. Recruitment, dismissal, choice of staff, promotion, pay, hours of work, accommodation, grading, organisation of work, the use of IT equipment, are all outside the control of most Civil Service managers at any level. The main decisions on rules and regulations are taken by the centre of the Civil Service. This tends to mean that they are structured to fit everything in general and nothing in particular. The rules are therefore seen primarily as a constraint rather than as a support; and in no sense as a pressure on managers to manage effectively. Moreover, the task of changing the rules is often seen as too great for one unit or one manager or indeed one department and is therefore assumed to be impossible.

12. In our discussions it was clear that the advantages which a unified Civil Service are intended to bring are seen as outweighed by the practical disadvantages, particularly beyond Whitehall itself. We were told that the advantages of an all-embracing pay structure are breaking down, that the uniformity of grading frequently inhibits effective management and that the concept of

a career in a unified Civil Service has little relevance for most civil servants, whose horizons are bounded by their local office or, at most, by their department.

3. CONCLUSIONS

13.   The main themes which have emerged from our discussions in the course of the scrutiny suggest that the changes of the last seven years have been important in beginning to shift the focus of attention away from process towards results. The development of management systems, particularly those which cover programme as well as administrative areas, forces senior and junior management to define the results they wish to achieve. But this also produces frustrations because of the lack of freedom to vary the factors on which results depend. The new systems are demonstrating how far attitudes and institutions have to change if the real benefits of the management reforms, in the form of improvement in the way government delivers its services, are to come through. It was striking that in our discussions with civil servants at all levels there was a strong sense that radical change in the freedom to manage is needed urgently if substantially better results are to be achieved.

14.   Five main issues have emerged from the scrutiny. *First*, a lack of clear and accountable management responsibility, and the self confidence that goes with it particularly among the higher ranks in departments. *Second*, the need for greater precision about the results expected of people and of organisations. *Third*, a need to focus attention on outputs as well as inputs. *Fourth*, the handicap of imposing a uniform system in an organisation of the size and diversity of the present Civil Service. *Fifth*, a need for a sustained pressure for improvement.

15.   These are serious problems which need leadership, and commitment to change, from Ministers and the senior Civil Service if they are to be dealt with. Our conclusions are that to begin the process of change three main priorities are necessary:

[7]

First: The work of each department must be organised in a way which focuses on the job to be done; the systems and structures must enhance the effective delivery of policies and services.

Second: The management of each department must ensure that their staff have the relevant experience and skills needed to do the tasks that are essential to effective government.

Third: There must be a real and sustained pressure on and within each department for continuous improvement in the value for money obtained in the delivery of policies and services.

These three priorities apply equally to all aspects of government. In our recommendations we apply them to the delivery of services, the tasks of departments and the centre of Whitehall. Simultaneous action is needed on all three.

16.   It is important to recognise that the changes implied by these conclusions, although straightforward, are quite fundamental in the overall impact they will have if carried forward as we suggest. Some fairly radical decisions and a tightly-knit timetable will be required if the necessary momentum for change is to be built up. But the process, although it must be quite rapid to maintain that momentum, will need to be evolutionary so as to gain full advantage from the favourable climate we observed, and to build on moves of the right kind already taking place in some departments. It will also need to be tightly managed so that the acute problems of transition are properly handled, and so that the drive for more positive management and more freedom for local decision is not undermined by vested interests or lack of confidence.

4 RECOMMENDATIONS

Focusing on the job to be done

17. Greater priority must be given to organising government so that its service delivery operations function effectively. This must be backed by supporting changes in the attitudes and day-to-day behaviour of Ministers and their officials.

18. Changes of the kind we are proposing are so fundamental that they can be brought about only with the lead and support of Ministers. Without this lead they will falter partly because of the inertia of any very large organisation and a natural tendency for fine details to be discussed at length, but partly because it is Ministers who will have to explain, promote and defend them in Parliament as and when the difficulties are encountered.

The delivery of services

19. **We recommend that 'agencies' should be established to carry out the executive functions of government within a policy and resources framework set by a department.** An 'agency' of this kind may be part of government and the public service, or it may be more effective outside government. We use the term 'agency' not in its technical sense but to describe any executive unit that delivers a service for government. The choice and definition of suitable agencies is primarily for Ministers and senior management in departments to decide. In some instances very large blocks of work comprising virtually a whole department will be suitable to be managed in this way. In other instances, where the scale of activity is too small for an entirely separate organisation, it may be better to have one or even several smaller agencies within departments.

20. These units, large or small, need to be given a well defined framework in which to operate, which sets out the policy, the budget, specific targets and the results to be achieved. It must also specify how politically sensitive issues are to be dealt with and the extent of the delegated authority of management. The management of the agency must be held rigorously to account by their department for the results they achieve.

[9]

21.   The framework will need to be set and updated as part of a formal annual review with the responsible Minister, based on a long-term plan and an annual report. The main strategic control must lie with the Minister and Permanent Secretary. But once the policy objectives and budgets within the framework are set, the management of the agency should then have as much independence as possible in deciding how those objectives are met. A crucial element in the relationship would be a formal understanding with Ministers about the handling of sensitive issues and the lines of accountability in a crisis. The presumption must be that, provided management is operating within the strategic direction set by Ministers, it must be left as free as possible to manage within that framework. To strengthen operational effectiveness, there must be freedom to recruit, pay, grade and structure in the most effective way as the framework becomes sufficiently robust and there is confidence in the capacity of management to handle the task.

22.   Once the framework had been set the head of the agency would be given personal responsibility to achieve the best possible results within it. He or she must be seen to be accountable for doing so. In due course formal accountability, before the Public Accounts Committee for example, might develop so that for significant agencies the Permanent Secretary would normally be accompanied by the head of the agency. The Permanent Secretary's role would be to justify and defend the framework; the manager would have to answer for his or her performance within that framework.

23.   Placing responsibility for performance squarely on the shoulders of the manager of an agency also has implications for the way in which Ministers answer to Parliament on operational issues. Clearly Ministers have to be wholly responsible for policy, but it is unrealistic to suppose that they can actually have knowledge in depth about every operational question. The convention that they do is in part the cause of the overload we observed. We believe it is possible for Parliament, through Ministers, to regard managers as directly

responsible for operational matters and that there are precedents for this and precisely defined ways in which it can be handled. If management in the Civil Service is truly to be improved this aspect cannot be ignored. In view of its importance it is considered in more detail in Annex A, where it is suggested that to achieve changes in the arrangements for formal accountability would generally require legislation and that in suitable instances this should be considered.

24. The detailed nature of the relationship between a department and an agency will vary with the job to be done or the service to be delivered. The agency structure could be used to cover a substantial proportion of the activities of the Civil Service. It is clear from our discussions with Permanent Secretaries that some departments are already moving towards this concept. What is needed is a substantial acceleration and broadening of this trend through a major initiative. Ultimately some agencies could be in a position where they are no longer inside the Civil Service in the sense they are today. Any decision of this kind should be taken pragmatically – the test must always be adopting the structure which best fits the job to be done.

The tasks for departments

25. The setting up of agencies has substantial implications for the staff of departments, for Ministers, and for Parliament. Departments have two main functions – ministerial support including policy development and evaluation, and managing or influencing the delivery of government services. Where departments are directly responsible for service delivery their task will no longer be the detailed prescription of operational functions: it will be the definition of a rigorous policy and resources framework within which the agency management is set free to manage operations, and is held to account for results.

26. The setting of a policy and resources framework is needed not only for agencies but also in situations where the department has to proceed by influence rather than by direct control. It applies therefore to the relationship with any organisation which is providing

services for which the department carries some responsibility, whether agency, nationalised industry, local authority, or public body, although the detail and the structure will vary with the precise relationship and the job that has to be done.

27. In any of these relationships the department's task is to set a framework, tailored to the job to be done, which specifies policies, objectives, the results required, and the resources available. It will also need to ensure that indicators of effective performance are developed and used for regular monitoring. For directly managed agencies, Ministers and civil servants must then stand back from operational details and demonstrate their confidence in the competence of their managers and the robustness of the framework by leaving managers free to manage.

28. Although setting a framework is not a new task for government departments, it is one which has not generally attracted the attention it deserves. To do it successfully requires a balanced expertise in policy, the political environment and service delivery which too few civil servants possess at present. Operational effectiveness and clarity need to be given a higher priority in the interpretation of policy objectives and the thinking of Ministers.

29. We have already emphasised that, for the successful operation of any agency, politically sensitive issues must be handled effectively. Ministers and departments will have to ensure that this happens if difficulties are to be sorted out without shattering the position and confidence of executive managers. Unless the inevitable political crises are handled well, while safeguarding the effectiveness of the agency, the benefits of giving more independence to management and so getting better performance will not emerge. In some instances legislation may be necessary to establish a framework within which the agency can operate with sufficient independence on behalf of the Secretary of State.

30. In order to direct the tasks of a department effectively, senior management will need the same kind

of flexibility that we consider necessary for agencies. In particular they must have greater freedom about how the department is staffed and structured to ensure that they are able to give priority to the main tasks for which the department is responsible.

31.   We have concentrated on the role of departments in relation to their service delivery agencies, but the management of the policy areas of departments, although on a smaller scale in terms of the staff numbers employed, is no less important than managing the big executive areas. Precision about the results required and the resources involved is crucial when large programme resources are at stake.

The centre of government

32.   The identification of agencies and providing the necessary framework within which they can be managed effectively are essentially tasks for departments, but the cultural changes implicit in these simple ideas will only take place if a strong lead is given from the centre. Moreover the centre has to have confidence in the new pattern before it can responsibly start relinquishing some of the present constraints on departments. We are convinced that our recommendations can be implemented successfully only if the centre takes a leading role in managing the change.

33.   It is important to distinguish the task of managing change, from the longer term role of the centre, when the new situation has been brought about. Once the change has been established we see four continuing tasks for the centre which no one else can do. *First*, to allocate resources; *second*, to ensure there is rigorous external pressure on departments continually to improve results; *third*, to ensure that the overall shape of the Civil Service continues to respond to changes in the needs of government and the country; *fourth*, to set and police essential rules on propriety for the public service in carrying out its essential functions. The centre has to be authoritative, demonstrably efficient and low cost, and a helpful resource to departments, not a handicap. Our specific recommendations are given at paragraphs 40–42.

The right people

34.   Our first recommendation – the establishment of agencies for government services – has implications for the functions and organisation of departments and may need a legislative framework in some instances. Its success depends critically on the people working in departments and the skills they bring to the task. **We recommend that departments ensure that their staff are properly trained and experienced in the delivery of services whether within or outside central government; the staff will then be in a position to develop and interpret government policy and manage the agencies in a way that can maximise results**.

35.   Departments must ensure that they have people who have the managerial skills necessary to run agencies. This will mean that experience of managing the delivery of services must be built up at all levels in a department. It is most important that there should not be two classes of people in departments – those in agencies and those at the centre. The aim must be to have senior managers who at more junior levels have had substantial experience of the skills and practical reality of management as well as effective experience of the political and policy aspects of work in a department. They must be prepared to show real qualities of leadership, the ability to back their judgement and to take and defend unpopular decisions. Hitherto relatively few civil servants have had an opportunity to learn or exhibit these skills. A wide range of new arrangements will be needed, including training and secondments to give the required experience, and the promotion of some younger people.

36.   One of the benefits that will come as senior managers in departments obtain greater experience of management is that the policy areas of departments will also become better managed. There will be an increasing need for these senior managers to have greater freedom about how the department is structured and staffed to ensure that they can give effective priority at any time to the most important tasks.

Pressure for improvement

37.   The aim of our first two recommendations is to ensure that the organisational structure and the skills

of the Civil Service are adapted to deliver government services as effectively as possible. The radical changes entailed for departments will not happen without some pressure external to the organisations directly involved. That pressure must be both for change and for continuous improvement in the delivery of services.

38. The responsibility for setting the management strategy for the Civil Service and ensuring that there is pressure for change and improvement inevitably rests with the Prime Minister and the Head of the Civil Service. They need the commitment of Ministers and of permanent secretaries to ensure that the changes are pursued with urgency and are not sacrificed to other priorities. The pressure for change from within the government must also be sustained by understanding and support from Parliament for the long-term benefits which are being sought.

39. For each of these groups – for Parliament, for Ministers and for civil servants – a precise means of ensuring their support needs to be developed. The Civil Service must own the changes as they evolve; it must not feel that ill-considered change is being thrust on it. Ministers must be confident that they can influence political aspects of the changes, and that one of the benefits will be their being able to concentrate more on their main political task. Further consideration needs to be given to what arrangements would best ensure that each group plays the right role in directing and sustaining the changes.

40. However, pressure at the highest level will only be effective if the centre of the Civil Service is organised with certain essential characteristics. It must be authoritative and able to ensure that its authority is recognised and acted upon. It must be 'slimline': the development of a new bureaucracy would be disastrous. It must be seen to be competent and helping rather than obstructing the delivery of effective service by operational departments. It must be cohesive and not as apparently diverse and fragmented as at present.

41. Our recommendations on changes in the way departments operate are fundamental and radical. They will only be introduced successfully if there is an extremely senior official who has unequivocal personal responsibility for achieving the change. The Head of the Civil Service has to be personally committed to the change; but with his other responsibilities he cannot be expected to devote the time and energy to managing the change that the task demands. **We recommend that a full Permanent Secretary should be designated as 'Project Manager' as soon as possible to ensure that the change takes place**. He will need to work with the authority of the Prime Minister and the Head of the Civil Service, to whom he should report.

42. The Project Manager will be responsible for planning and supervising the process of change. The Prime Minister will regularly receive reports from him, via the Head of the Civil Service, on the progress made by departments in setting frameworks for their agencies and on the timetable for relaxing the constraints on management. The Project Manager will also have to ensure that departments have enough flexibility to handle their tasks effectively. To do this, he will have to make certain that obstacles to change are removed and that the totality of the centre is helpful to the management of change. The need to have a very high level project manager cannot be overemphasised. A more junior project manager will not carry weight with departments. The slow rate of progress on so many of the changes since 1979, even with ministerial support and an abundance of small units, is ample evidence of this.

5   THE NEXT STEPS

43.   This report is concerned with identifying the fundamental changes needed to achieve a further major step forward in the delivery of services and the mangement of government. We have avoided detailed prescription because so much depends on the individual tasks of different departments. Generalised solutions have been the bane of previous attempts at reform and have led to the structural rigidities that are now part of the problem. It will be the job of the Project Manager to check that each department develops these concepts in the way that best suits its particular needs, and to indicate how far and how fast the changes are progressing.

44.   The aim should be to establish a quite different way of conducting the business of government. The central Civil Service should consist of a relatively small core engaged in the function of servicing Ministers and managing departments, who will be the 'sponsors' of particular government policies and services. Responding to these departments will be a range of agencies employing their own staff, who may or may not have the status of Crown servants, and concentrating on the delivery of their particular service, with clearly defined responsibilities between the Secretary of State and the Permanent Secretary on the one hand and the Chairmen or Chief Executives of the agencies on the other. Both departments and their agencies should have a more open and simplified structure.

45.   The early changes should be in the management tasks at the centre. The first new feature should be a Project Manager working on the planning and early implementation of the service-wide changes. As these come about, the management function at the centre will diminish. The Cabinet Secretariat and the expenditure functions of the Treasury will remain and there will still need to be provision at the centre for determining directions, keeping up pressure on departments, and

setting standards. Many of the detailed management functions now carried out at the centre will disappear, though transitional arrangements will be needed. For example, the central responsibility for pay and conditions of service, and the associated negotiations with national Trade Unions, will be progressively and substantially reduced, though pay determination will be carried out within running cost controls. The aim will be to pursue as rapidly as possible an evolutionary approach, so that the Project Manager harnesses those developments which are already taking place in some departments and which are in line with what is now proposed.

46. Within two years at the most, departments should have completed identification of areas where agencies are the most effective way of managing and should have changed their own internal structures to implement this change. In some cases legislation may be necessary to effect the change. Departments will need to move, train and promote their staff far more flexibly and, where necessary, develop their specialised management skills while reducing the existing establishments and finance functions, as the agencies take full management responsibility.

47. Once these changes have taken place, Ministers and senior civil servants should have enough confidence in the system they have set up to be able to concentrate on their proper strategic role of setting the framework and looking ahead to plan policy development. Greater freedom to manage should be delegated progressively to individual agencies, depending on the robustness of the framework and their capacity to put the freedom to good use.

48. It is difficult to put a figure on the benefits which should become available from our recommendations but the potential is obvious. Five per cent of Civil Service running costs amounted to £630 million in 1986–87, and experience elsewhere certainly indicates that when good management has the opportunity to perform well, percentage improvements larger than

this are achieved. Where accountability on the lines we suggest is in place, substantial and quantifiable benefits are coming through. But a primary aim of the recommended changes is to improve the delivery of services both to the public and to Ministers. With total programme expenditure of £128 billion (1985–86), there is an immense opportunity to go for substantial improvement in outputs, with better delivery of services and reduced delays as an alternative to savings.

49. The recommendations we have made should ensure that authority and responsibility for operations will be clear and Ministers will know who is accountable to them. The confusion we observed about the role of Ministers in management should be substantially resolved. Inevitably and rightly it is open to a Minister to get involved in any part of his or her department's business, but in a well managed department this should normally only be necessary by exception.

50. The substantial gain we are aiming for is the release of managerial energy. We want to see managers at all levels in the public service:
- eager to maximise results,
- no longer frustrated or absolved from responsibility by central constraints,
- working with a sense of urgency to improve their service.

ANNEX A

Accountability to Ministers and Parliament on Operational Matters

1. Evidence we gathered in the scrutiny suggested that when individuals had to answer personally to Parliament, as well as to Ministers, their sense of personal responsibility was strengthened. The accountability of permanent secretaries to the Public Accounts Committee, as Accounting Officers, is long established. It includes direct personal accountability for financial propriety. Another instance of officials having specific functions which may require them to answer directly to Parliament (though on behalf of their Minister) is the case of principal officers, and of bodies with independent or delegated authority, answering to the Select Committee on the Parliamentary Commissioner for Administration.

2. In paragraph 23 we point out that if the concept of agencies developed in the report is to succeed, some extension of this pattern of accountability is likely to be necessary. The principal reasons are, first, that the management of an agency is unlikely in practice to be given a realistically specified framework within which there is freedom to manage if a Minister remains immediately answerable for every operational detail that may be questioned; and second, that acceptance of individual responsibility for performance cannot be expected if repeated ministerial intervention is there as a ready-made excuse.

3. The precise form of accountability for each agency would need to be established as part of drawing up the framework for agencies. Any change from present practice in accountability would, of course, have to be acceptable to Ministers and to Parliament. It is axiomatic that Ministers should remain fully and clearly accountable for policy. For agencies which are government departments or parts of departments

[17]

ultimate accountability for operations must also rest with Ministers. What is needed is the establishment of a convention that heads of executive agencies would have delegated authority from their Ministers for operations of the agencies within the framework of policy directives and resource allocations prescribed by Ministers. Heads of agencies would be accountable to Ministers for the operations of their agencies, but could be called – as indeed they can now – to give evidence to Select Committees as to the manner in which their delegated authority had been used and their functions discharged within that authority. In the case of agencies established outside departments, appropriate forms of accountability to Ministers and to Parliament would need to be established according to the particular circumstances.

4. There is nothing new in the suggestion that Ministers should not be held answerable for many day-to-day decisions involving the public and public services. Apart from services delivered by local authorities, there are large numbers of central government functions carried out at arm's length from Ministers. The main categories are:

- decisions on individual cases, where these need to be protected from the risk of political influence, e.g. tax cases, social security cases;
- some management and executive functions, e.g. in Customs and Excise, Regional and District Health Authorities, Manpower Services Commission (MSC);
- quasi-judicial or regulatory functions, e.g. Office of Fair Trading, Immigration Appeals;
- nationalised industries.

5. A variety of different structures exists to cover these functions, for example:

- Customs and Excise and the Inland Revenue are non-ministerial departments with boards which have defined statutory responsibilities;
- the MSC and the other main bodies in the Employment Group (Health and Safety Executive, and ACAS) are non-departmental

public bodies. The Chairman of the MSC is Accounting Officer for the MSC's expenditure;
– HMSO and some other internal service bodies (e.g. Crown Suppliers) are established as trading funds and work on a commercial basis;
– the PSA, the Procurement Executive and the NHS Management Board are agencies within departments;
– a range of quasi-judicial functions is carried out by statutory tribunals (e.g. Rent Tribunals, Industrial Tribunals).

6. Agencies outside departments generally operate within a statutory framework which lays down the constitution of the particular agency and the powers of Ministers in relation to it. In answer to Parliamentary Questions about matters within the control of the agency, Ministers often preface their reply by saying 'I am advised by the Chairman of the Board that . . .'. Most operations currently carried out within departments operate under statute. Where it is necessary to change the arrangements for formal accountability for operations currently carried out within departments, legislation (normally primary legislation) would generally be required, and in instances where this is needed it should be considered. Provided that the objective of better management is clearly explained and understood, and that an appropriate form of accountability to Ministers and to Parliament is retained, the government should be able to present such proposals in a positive light.

7. As regards the Public Accounts Committee, as explained in paragraph 22 of the report, the modification of accountability we propose should not immediately affect accountability to the PAC. This would remain, as now, with the Accounting Officer, who may still be, but need not be, the Permanent Secretary. (Of the 76 Accounting Officers appointed by the Treasury, only 18 are First Permanent Secretaries.) However, the practice might develop of the Accounting Officer being accompanied at a PAC hearing by the manager of the agency. The Accounting

Officer would answer questions about the framework within which the agency operated; the manager would answer questions about operations within the framework. This would give the PAC the ability to question in detail the person who had firsthand knowledge of the particular operation. It would also in the process put a clear pressure on the agency head to be responsible for his or her agency and to strive for good value from his or her spending.

8. In the case of other Select Committees it is existing practice for officials with operational responsibility to give evidence before them. It would be normal in the future for the agency head to give evidence before a Select Committee about operational matters within his or her responsibility.

9. The powers of the Parliamentary Commissioner for Administration could continue to apply to agencies.

10. Quite apart from the issue of improving Civil Service management, there is a good case for trying to reduce the degree of ministerial overload that can arise from questions about operations, as distinct from policy. For example, Social Security Ministers receive about 15,000 letters a year from MPs, many of which are about individual cases. In the future, MPs could be asked to write about operational matters directly to the Chairman of the Board or the local office manager. Arrangements of this sort could be promulgated by a letter from the relevant Minister or the Leader of the House to all MPs. (In the past the Chancellor of the Exchequer has written to all MPs asking them to refer questions about constituents' tax to local tax offices, and the Secretary of State for Social Services has written similarly about referring social security cases to DHSS local office managers.) If an MP writes to an operational manager about matters which are essentially political, it is already normal practice for the manager to refer the letter to the Minister.

11. It would be part of the framework drawn up between the department and the agency to have specific targets for promptness in dealing with correspondence

with MPs. It should be possible for MPs to get a quicker answer when dealing direct with the responsible person, because the intermediate stage of a headquarters branch calling for a report from a local manager before drafting a reply for the Minister will have been cut out.

ANNEX B

Findings

1. This annex sets out the main findings from our fieldwork.

2. Our terms of reference asked us:
   - to assess *progress* in improving management
   - to identify *successful measures* in changing attitudes and practices
   - to identify *obstacles* to better management and efficiency that remain
   - to report to the Prime Minster on what *further measures* should be taken.

I. Summary of Findings

3. Our main findings are that:
   - some progress has been made: civil servants are now more cost conscious, and management systems are in place;
   - budgeting systems and manpower cuts are the two measures which have been most effective in changing attitudes and practices;
   - but substantial obstacles to further progress remain:
     - there is insufficient focus on the delivery of government services (as opposed to policy and ministerial support), even though 95 per cent of civil servants work in service delivery or executive functions;
     - there is a shortage of management skills and of experience of working in service delivery functions among senior civil servants;
     - short-term political priorities tend to squeeze out long-term planning;
     - there is too much emphasis on spending money, and not enough on getting results;
     - the Civil Service is too big and too diverse to manage as a single organisation.

[21]

- while the introduction of systems is a start, real changes in attitudes and institutions are needed to get the full benefits of better management.

4. The findings from our fieldwork about obstacles to progress are consistent with the main themes which come out of earlier scrutinies. They also echo the findings of some earlier reports on the Civil Service, e.g. the Fulton Report (Appendix A).

II. Detailed Findings

5. We held extensive discussions with civil servants in London and the regions. A list of those we saw and where we went is in Annex C.

A. Progress in improving management

6. Everybody we talked to said that there had been progress. Most people were enthusiastic about measures which gave them more responsibility and some control over how they did their job. They welcomed the principles of the Financial Management Initiative (FMI), if not always the way the principles were applied.

7. A striking impression we got was that most civil servants now know how much their activities cost. The local office manager has at his fingertips his staffing, accommodation and other costs; the headquarters policy Grade 5 can tell you the cost of his unit.

8. When asked what they meant by progress, most people identified FMI and the systems developed under it (top management systems and budgeting systems) as the main difference. They also commented on changes in personnel management systems, particularly linking open appraisal of performance with the achievement of objectives.

Top Management Systems

9. All departments now have Top Management Systems. These systems are intended to force management at all levels to take clear decisions about the direction of activities in a department. Strategic objectives can then be translated down the line to provide individuals with personal objectives.

10. Our evidence suggests that Top Management Systems are seen as having more relevance in executive functions and in the regions, than in headquarters or policy functions. One good example we saw was the use of MINIS in Department of the Environment regional offices. The system is precise and directed towards things which matter in the outside world (not just internal bureaucratic processes). There are good systems of delegation to go with it. The Grade 7 in a regional office handling claims for derelict land grant has a minute from his Permanent Secretary telling him precisely what his delegated authority is. One Grade 7 we talked to said 'having a personal minute from the Permanent Secretary really brought it home to me that I was responsible'.

11. There was more scepticism in some headquarters and policy divisions about the value of Top Management Systems as they were being operated. Very few people said to us that setting objectives did not apply to policy work. However, in many departments it was not clear how far the use of management systems had become an integral part of the work of policy divisions, rather than a one-off form filling exercise. A number of people commented on the weight of paper surrounding the systems and the number of forms to be filled in – or as one person said 'typical Civil Service: management has been bureaucratised'. We heard trenchant views in some departments, especially from Grades 5–7, about the absence of feedback from top management, and the failure of top management to face the decisions which the systems confronted them with.

Budgeting systems

12. All departments now have budgeting systems which delegate financial responsibility to specified levels of authority in the hierarchy. This gives managers some control over how they spend the money allocated to them. Over 7,000 line managers now manage budgets which account for about three quarters of the Civil Service's running costs.

13. The range of costs covered and the flexibility allowed within budgets vary from department to

department. For example, Customs and Excise
Collectors have authority over 96 per cent of their
running costs and authority to switch money between
one item and another. In practice, however, staffing
costs amount to about 70 per cent of running costs and
the margin in which managers have immediate flexibility
is very small. A persistent complaint of budget holders
was the inflexibility caused by the annuality rule, and by
restrictions on their ability to move money between
different items. (These are dealt with in paragraphs 46
and 49 below.)

14.   Budgeting has been applied mainly to administrative expenditure (some 13 per cent of total public
expenditure). Its spread into programme spending has
been slow.

Personnel
management
systems

15.   The main changes in personnel management in
the last five years have been:
  a.   the introduction of an open appraisal system
       based on reviewing performance against per-
       sonal objectives;
  b.   the development of performance-related pay;
  c.   the prospect of a new pay agreement with pro-
       fessional civil servants which offers much
       greater flexibility;
  d.   more delegation of clerical recruitment to local
       office managers;
  e.   the introduction of unified grading down to
       Grade 7 (Principal) level.

16.   Appraisal systems are now based on *performance*,
not on the possession of particular intellectual qualities. Everybody we spoke to welcomed this. Most
people like having a clear set of objectives which tells
them what they are there to do and having their performance judged against whether they achieved these
objectives – not against some hidden agenda in their
manager's bottom drawer. Open reporting encourages
managers to talk about an individual's performance
face-to-face.

17.   Two schemes for relating pay to performance have
been developed. First, an experimental performance

bonus scheme was introduced in 1985. A formal evaluation after the first year showed that while the bonus scheme in its present form had not been successful, 70 per cent of civil servants supported the principle of rewarding good performance with better pay. Second, the Treasury and the OMCS are now developing proposals for discretionary pay for staff at all levels.

B. Measures effective in changing attitudes and practices

Manpower cuts

18. The two measures which have had most effect in altering the climate and the way the Civil Service works are manpower cuts and budgeting.

19. As a result of government policy, the Civil Service was reduced in size by nearly 15 per cent between 1979 and 1984. It had been reduced by nearly 20 per cent by 1 April 1987. The cuts were imposed as simple outline targets. Departments then had to decide how to reach the targets. There is evidence that in some departments top management was forced to take hard decisions about whether to continue particular activities, and to think about different ways of doing things. So the cuts were useful in making some departments 'think the unthinkable'. In other departments, however, cuts were imposed across the board, without regard to the functions affected. A view we heard in a number of departments was that the manpower cuts had 'taken the fat out of the system' and that further large reductions would harm the quality of services delivered by government.

20. Controls on running costs were introduced in 1985–86 on top of manpower controls. We saw a number of examples where the control on staff in post on 1 April together with controls on cash were causing distortions. One local office manager was running down his staffing levels at the end of the year by 12 people to meet his 1 April headcount limit. In early April he planned to recruit another 10 people. He had enough money in his budget to have kept 6–7 people on over the year end.

21. In the course of our scrutiny the Treasury announced that from 1 April 1988 formal controls on manpower would be lifted, and the main control on departments would be exercised on running cost totals.

Budgeting   22.   Where budgeting systems are working well there
systems   is evidence that they change the way people behave.
Specifically they enable budget holders to save money
or make better use of money; and encourage forward
planning of activities and spending, and setting of
priorities.

C. Obstacles   23.   The main concern of most people we met was
to further   with the obstacles which stood in the way of manage-
progress   ment improvement.

a) Top management is dominated by the policy and political support tasks

24.   The business of top managers in many departments is still dominated by the policy and political
support tasks. However 95 per cent of civil servants
(about 570,000, costing some £12 billion a year) are
involved in collecting taxes, paying benefits, providing
support to the armed forces and other executive functions. Some of the operations are very large. In DHSS,
for example, over 80,000 staff are involved in paying
benefits. It was made clear to us that these organisations need highly skilled top managers who can devote
most of their time to the business of running them.
One top manager of a very large executive organisation
told us that at present 90 per cent of his time was spent
dealing with Ministers and other pressures from the
top and only 10 per cent on managing the organisation.

25.   The skills of top civil servants are still policy ori-
ented. Promotion to senior jobs is given to those whose
main skills and experience are in policy and ministerial
support. Very few have had direct experience of management in large executive organisations. This is
reflected when senior civil servants are suddenly put in
positions which do have management responsibilities.
Either they neglect management, because the immediate pressures are to deal with day-to-day ministerial
business; or they go about the management task in a
way which lacks confidence and conviction. Many
people commented to us that too few senior civil servants showed the qualities of leadership which would

be expected from top managers in organisations outside the Civil Service.

26. The Top Management Programme, a six week training course, is an attempt to change the balance of skills of those entering the senior ranks of the Civil Service. But it is not a substitute for real experience of running an organisation. At middle levels the Senior Management Development Programme sets out a range of individual 'competencies' which should be developed through job experience and training. The first two core competencies are management of resources/organisations and the management of staff. There are few indications so far that the perception that middle ranking civil servants should get management experience has affected the way departments post their staff.

27. The younger staff we spoke to told us that they wanted to get experience of management. The FDA confirmed that ATs and HEODs were clamouring for management jobs. Departments agreed in principle that younger staff and fast streamers should get management experience, but said that in practice they could not spare their good staff from policy jobs. There is an automatic assumption that fast streamers go into Private Office jobs, but no equivalent assumption that they should also do management jobs. The majority of the next generation of senior civil servants will still not have been tested in or gained experience from working in large service delivery organisations.

b) Responsibilities for management at the top of departments are unclear

28. Most Ministers told us that they were answerable for both the policy and the management of their departments. But they said that in practice they were so overloaded that they looked to their Permanent Secretaries to do the management. A few said candidly that they did not have the skills to manage their departments. The government has accepted the recommendation of the Third Report of the Treasury and Civil

Service Select Committee (1982) that the relationship between Ministers and permanent secretaries on the management of departments should be clarified, but has not yet acted on it.

c)   The main pressures at the top are short term

29.   The main pressures on Ministers stem from Parliament and coping with crises. Together with routine business from departments this creates an extremely heavy workload. In addition Ministers have Parliamentary and constituency duties. The resulting overload tends to squeeze out the ability to look to the long-term. Some Ministers said to us that they would like to be able to spend more of their time dealing with longer term strategy, but just did not have the time to do so.

30.   The pressures on Ministers are reflected onto top civil servants, who may have to spend much of their time giving policy and presentational advice to their Ministers.

31.   It was suggested that while there were some tasks which Ministers could not delegate to officials, there were others where this could be done. One example was dealing with correspondence from MPs. Correspondence about individual cases could in many cases be dealt with effectively by local office managers.

d)   Outputs are neglected

32.   While the introduction of management systems has helped make civil servants cost conscious, there is less consciousness about results. Departments regard the major central influence on them as the PES process. However, many people told us that the PES system gave the wrong signals. They felt that the emphasis was on inputs, not outputs or value for money.

33.   This is not surprising. The Treasury has two goals with the PES round: to ensure that public spending does not exceed a specified total and to press departments to achieve maximum output from the resources

they are allocated. The two are not mutually exclusive, but as the PES round progresses, attention inevitably focuses on the absolute levels of spending. Furthermore, at the later stages, the debate is about spending at the margin of the total bid. The combination of these two factors – emphasis on inputs and 'marginality' – leads departments to feel that although increased stress is being put on results and outputs, it is inputs which still really matter.

34. There are, however, encouraging signs of change. The 1986 Public Expenditure White Paper included 1,200 output measures; the 1987 White Paper cites some 1,800 measures of output. The April 1987 guidelines for PES asked departments to provide the Treasury with a full statement of output and performance measures to support their baseline expenditure. These will be discussed between the Treasury and departments. Any proposals for additional resources must be supported by information on what indicators and targets for outputs will be used to evaluate their use.

35. There are also some signs in particular areas of government of an increasing awareness of the importance of outputs. For example, in 1986 the Foreign and Commonwealth Office undertook a scrutiny of existing output measures to see to what extent they could be improved and applied systematically to the full range of work of the FCO at home and overseas.

36. It is apparent that the closer staff are to the sharp end, the more conscious they are of outputs. In many areas staff are strongly motivated by a wish to serve the public. A common source of frustration in many local offices is the inadequacy of the service staff feel they are giving. Our evidence suggests that very few departments set themselves formal targets for improving the quality of service to the public.

e) There is little support or pressure for value for money

37. Most pressures on government are to spend money, not to get good value from it. Parliament and the media often reinforce this by judging the

government on how much money goes in, not what comes out (e.g. more hospitals, or better education). The National Audit Office (NAO) now has a specific remit to do value for money investigations. For example, it has looked at value for money in the National Health Service. However, the response of departments to the NAO and the Public Accounts Committee tends to be cautious and defensive, probably because the main role of these bodies is seen as being to find fault with what has happened in the past rather than to apply pressure for improvement for the future.

f)   The organisation at the centre of government is fragmented

38.   Many of those to whom we spoke, particularly Permanent Secretaries, told us that the centre of government was fragmented. They complained that the centre, either the Treasury, the OMCS, or the various central units, pursued their own initiatives without regard to departments' own priorities; and that sometimes the messages from the centre conflicted. There was no single voice of authority.

39.   At the same time the centre created little effectice pressure on departments to deliver better results. Some people suggested to us that the centre's reliance on detailed control of the way departments organised and managed themselves was totally at odds with the principles of good delegated management as set out in the FMI.

g)   The Civil Service is too big and too diverse to be run as a single rigid organisation

40.   The Civil Service is vast (600,000 people), and the diversity of activities which civil servants peform is immense. Yet it is run as one organisation with common rules for financial management and personnel management.

41.   One problem inherent in trying to bind a very large and diverse organisation in one set of central

rules is that the rules fit no particular part of the organisation. For example, a service-wide pay agreement to give certain computer specialists an extra allowance may be what one department needs to retain those specialists, but simply an unwelcome addition to running costs for another which has no difficulty at all in keeping them.

42.   Civil Service-wide grading and promotion structures create problems for some departments. For example, there is no direct recruitment above EO level. The structural needs of some departments are to take staff in at a higher level.

43.   All recruitment above clerical level is conducted centrally by the Civil Service Commission (with the exception of some limited experiments in direct recruitment of Executive Officers by departments). The personal qualities which DHSS requires for its Executive Officers, who may be dealing with the public in a local office or investigating benefit fraud, are very different from the qualities required of an EO for a Whitehall policy job. Some departments told us that central recruitment prevented them from getting the staff they wanted, though the Civil Service Commission is now attempting to distinguish the different types of quality needed among recruits at EO level.

44.   The justification for service-wide terms and conditions has traditionally been in terms of ensuring fairness between different groups of people doing the same work, and making it possible for people to move easily between departments. Evidence we gathered suggests that many groups of staff in the Civil Service are doing very different types of work; and that most staff spend their career within their own department.

h)   Central rules take away the flexibility managers need to manage

45.   Many managers told us that central rules were acting as a constraint on good management and taking away their scope to do things which would be sensible in terms of their own organisation.

46.   One example of a rule constraining good management which was mentioned to us by nearly all budget holders we met was annuality – the lack of flexibility at the end of the financial year to carry unspent money over or to anticipate next year's spending. This has two effects. First, there is often a major effort to spend money in the final months of the year so as not to be underspent. Last minute spending often means spending on things which are useful, but not a top priority. Second, a huge management effort goes into coming in on budget. In 1985–86 Customs and Excise underspent a budget of £400 million by only £40,000.

47.   Most people accept that controls on departments' running costs are effective and necessary. However, the reliance on gross running cost controls has caused problems for some fee-earning businesses: when demand has grown for their services, they have been prevented from taking on more staff to cope with demand, even though the extra cost would have been met from increased fee revenue. This is an area where it has been shown possible to change the controls. For example, from 1 April 1987 the Driver Testing and Training Organisation of the Department of Transport moved to a new financial regime which will enable the Department to recruit more examiners to cope with the increased demand. One effect in the past of being unable to take on extra staff to meet increased demand was queues for driving tests of six months or more in some areas.

48.   A further problem mentioned to us was that of hidden controls. The best example is the use by the Treasury of an inadequte assumption for pay increases when setting running cost totals. In the last six years the Treasury has reached the pay settlement after the start of the financial year, and in each year the actual settlement has been at least 1.3 per cent higher than the pay assumption. Departments have had to fund the difference.

49.   Sometimes the 'central' rules about which man-

agers complained to us are rules imposed by the centre of their own departments (for example Finance Branches), not rules imposed by the Treasury or OMCS. For example, there are marked differences in the flexibility which budget holders in different departments have to move money from one item to another. The main rule imposed by the Treasury is that there should be no movement of money from non-running costs to running costs. Rules about moving money between different running costs items are generally imposed by departments themselves.

i) Delegation is not always happening

50. Most people we met welcomed delegation where it was happening. However, many pointed out to us the strong pressures which acted against effective delegation:

- the public accountabilities of departments through Ministers to Parliament tend to suck up decisions on matters of detail;
- central controls, whether from the centre of the Civil Service or the centre of departments, restrict people's ability to operate (e.g. a manager may have money in his budget to buy a photocopier, but a central branch in his department has laid down rules which prevent him from having the machine);
- civil servants are generally reluctant to risk delegating and do not understand that interference in detail destroys effective delegation. We saw examples in the budgetary field, where at the first sign of trouble in a particular area the reaction of the centre of the department had been to draw back responsibility from all budget holders instead of getting the difficulties of the individual area sorted out.

j) The culture of the Civil Service is cautious and works against personal responsibility

51. The culture of the Civil Service puts a premium on a 'safe pair of hands', not on enterprise. It does not

reward the person who says 'I have saved money'. It does not penalise the person who ignores the opportunity to get better value.

52. There will always be limits on individual ownership when civil servants are fulfilling their ministerial support function. However, more could be done within the existing framework to encourage personal responsibility. The group of people who had left the Civil Service all told us that while pay was an important reason for leaving, as important was the fact that they had little personal responsibility, and saw little prospect of getting more as they rose through the hierarchy.

k) Working and career patterns have changed relatively little

53. The working patters of departments have changed relatively little in the last seven years. Chains of command still tend to be long; little use is made of special task forces to cut across hierarchies and to take policies forward in a given timescale; the emphasis on consultation across various interests in a department is always time consuming and often leads to compromise decisions; the system is still paper dominated; there is insufficient awareness of the possibilities of information technology in Whitehall departments.

54. Departments have paid insufficient attention to managing relationships with organisations who are delivering services. In some cases the relationship is direct; in other cases indirect (as with local authorities). In both cases departments have the ability to control or influence the delivery of services. A number of departments are beginning to take this task more seriously. In the DHSS a Division, headed by a Grade 3, is responsible for managing the relationship with the National Health Service. This includes, for example, performance reviews with Regional Health Authorities.

55. The career pattern of civil servants is relatively predictable through the hierarchy. In practice seniority is usually a requirement for promotion at certain levels

(for example, very few people are promoted to Grade 5 under the age of 35). It is almost unheard of for people of that age to be promoted to the top grades in the Civil Service. One Permanent Secretary argued to us that the Service should have the courage and the flexibility to promote the occasional outstanding young person very fast.

III. Conclusions

56. The changes which civil servants are most aware of are the introduction of systems. There is enthusiasm for the benefits the systems can bring in terms of greater flexibility, more personal responsibility, and more precision about what the job is they are there to do. At the same time many civil servants question whether the underlying assumptions which mould the way in which government does its business have changed sufficiently to realise the benefits. The key themes which emerge as obstacles in the way of real change are:

    a.   the lack of focus of top management on the service delivery and executive functions of government;

    b.   the effects of treating the Civil Service as a single organisation;

    c.   the lack of effective pressure to get better results.

APPENDIX A

Previous Reports on the Civil Service

General

1.   The Northcote-Trevelyan Report (1854) identified for the first time some of the principles which underlie the development of the modern Civil Service. Its main recommendations fell into four categories:
   a.   recruitment by competitive examination rather than patronage;
   b.   a division between intellectual and mechanical work;
   c.   promotion by merit;
   d.   measures to unify the Civil Service, including a common basis of recruiting across departments.

2.   It took nearly 20 years to implement open competition. The other principles of the Report were not fully developed and applied until the 1920s. Commissions after Northcote-Trevelyan up to 1931[1] and the Reconstruction Period immediately following the First World War established the basis of the Civil Service for the next 45 years. These developments included uniform systems of recruitment; the class division of officials; Whitley machinery; and the central power of the Treasury over the Civil Service.

3.   From 1931 until the establishment of the Fulton Committee in 1966, there was no major Commission on the Civil Service as a whole (the Priestley Commission in 1953–55 was largely concerned with pay).

4.   The Fulton Report (1968) recognised the need for the Civil Service to change in line with the changed external world. Its opening words were: 'The Home Civil Service today is still fundamentally the product of the nineteenth-century philosophy of the Northcote-Trevelyan Report. The tasks it faces

[1]   The Playfair Commission (1874–75); The Ridley Commission (1886–90); The MacDonnell Commission (1912–15); The Tomlin Commission (1929–31).

today are those of the second half of the twentieth century'.

5.   The Committee noted six main deficiencies which it attributed to the fact that the structures and practices of the Civil Service had not kept up with changing tasks:
- the Service was based on the philosophy of the amateur;
- the division into classes made for a cumbersome structure;
- specialists had no authority;
- too few civil servants were skilled managers;
- Whitehall had too little contact with the outside world;
- there were deficiencies in personnel management.

6.   The Report set down one basic principle, which was intended to ensure that the Civil Service should keep up with the changing world:

'One basic guiding principle should in our view govern the future development of the Civil Service. It applies to any organisation and is simple to the point of banality, but the root of much of our criticism is that it has not been observed. The principle is: look at the job first. The Civil Service must continuously review the tasks it is called upon to perform and the possible ways in which it might perform them; it should then think out what new skills and kinds of men are needed, and how these men can be found, trained and deployed. The Service must avoid a static view of a new ideal man and structure which in its turn could become as much of an obstacle to change as the present inheritance.'

7.   Fulton recommended that the principles of accountable management should be introduced into the Civil Service, and recommended further study of 'hiving off' functions as a means to ensuring accountable management. In the meanwhile the report made proposals:

'a.   to distinguish those within departments whose primary responsibility is planning for the future, from those whose main concern is the operation of existing policies or the provision of services;

'b.   to establish in departments forms of organisation and principles of accountable management, by which individuals and branches can be held responsible for objectively measured performance.'

8.   Other significant Fulton recommendations were for the creation of a Civil Service Department and the Civil Service College; and unified grading between administrators and professional groups.

9.   The major reports on the management of the Civil Service after Fulton were the Eleventh Report for the Expenditure Committee (1977) and the Third Report of the Treasury and Civil Service Select Committee *Efficiency and Effectiveness in the Civil Service* (1982). Lack of accountable management was a common theme of both these reports.

ANNEX C

Terms of reference

Terms of Reference and Working Method

1. The terms of reference for the scrutiny were:
    - to assess the progress achieved in improving management in the Civil Service;
    - to identify what measures have been successful in changing attitudes and practices;
    - to identify the institutional, administrative, political and attitudinal obstacles to better management and efficiency that still remain; and
    - to report to the Prime Minister on what further measures should be taken.

2. The scrutiny was carried out under the supervision of Sir Robin Ibbs by three members of the Efficiency Unit (Kate Jenkins, Karen Caines and Andrew Jackson). Other members of the Unit (Graham Cawsey, David Tune and Richard Hirst) joined in the fieldwork and specific studies.

3. The Action Manager for the scrutiny was Sir Robert Armstrong (now Sir Robin Butler).

Timetable

4. The scrutiny started on 3 November 1986 and was completed on 20 March 1987 (90 working days).

Method of working

5. The evidence on which the report is based is derived from:
    - interviews with Ministers and a wide range of officials;
    - field visits to regional and local offices, and some major installations outside London;
    - a cross section of past scrutinies undertaken with the help of the Efficiency Unit;
    - studies of three organisations outside government and discussions with a number of outside observers of Whitehall.

Interviews

6. We conducted over 150 individual interviews with Ministers and officials in Whitehall, including:

[33]

- Twenty-one Ministers;
- Twenty-six Permanent Secretaries (or equivalent), including all Permanent Secretary heads of major departments;
- Twenty-six Grade 2s (one or two in most departments).

7.   In addition we held a number of group discussions:
- Five for Grade 3s (involving 35 people);
- Seven for Grades 5–7 (involving over 50 people);
- One for Heads of Treasury Expenditure Groups.

8.   We talked to a group of people who had left the Civil Service recently.

Field trips to regional and other offices

9.   We talked to meetings of Regional Directors of the following Departments:
Departments of Environment and Transport
Property Services Agency
Department of Employment
Manpower Services Commission
Department of Health and Social Security
Department of Trade and Industry
Inland Revenue

10.   Members of the Efficiency Unit made a series of visits to regional and local offices in Birmingham, Manchester and Leeds.

11.   In our visits to Birmingham and Manchester we talked to staff at various levels in the regional offices of the following departments:
Departments of Environment and Transport (Manchester)
Property Services Agency (Birmingham)
Department of Employment (Birmingham)
Department of Health and Social Security (Birmingham)
Customs and Excise (Manchester)

12.   In Leeds we talked to the Regional Directors of departments to get a view of the links between departments. We visited the following offices:
Departments of the Environment and Transport
Property Services Agency

Department of Employment
Manpower Services Commission
Department of Health and Social Security
Department of Trade and Industry
Lord Chancellor's Department
Ministry of Agriculture, Fisheries and Food
Export Credits Guarantee Department

13.   We visited the following local offices and talked widely with staff:
DHSS ILO (Erdington)
Inland Revenue (Birmingham, Newcastle)
DE Unemployment Benefit Office (Birmingham, Newcastle)
Customs and Excise (Birmingham Airport)
Manpower Services Commission (Birmingham)

14.   We visited the following large installations outside London and talked to staff at all levels:
Inland Revenue, Telford Development Centre
DHSS North Fylde Central Office
DHSS Newcastle Central Office
RAF Support Command Headquarters (RAF Brampton)

Scrutinies

15.   Over 300 scrutinies have been conducted since 1979. Their reports provide valuable evidence about change in the Civil Service over the last seven years and a detailed view of some of the workings of particular aspects of individual departments. A special survey of a cross section of 50 scrutinies was undertaken to draw out the lessons for this scrutiny.

Organisations outside government

16.   Members of the Unit visited the following organisations to look at major management changes which had been brought about in the last few years. Each organisation is essentially a career organisation:
British Rail (Network SouthEast)
Halifax Building Society
ICI Fibres Division

Central reports

17.   The Unit has kept closely in touch with developments in the Treasury and Cabinet Office (OMCS), in particular over progress on personnel management changes and the implementation of the Wilson report

on Budgeting. We have also examined previous reports on the management of the Civil Service.

Trade unions

18.   We held two formal meetings with the Council of Civil Service Unions.

Cost of the scrutiny

19.   The estimated cost of the scrutiny was £50,000.

* Printed in the United Kingdom for Her Majesty's Stationery Office. Dd 290517, 6/88, C10, 405, 5673, 20141.

Bibliography

Barberis, Peter (ed.) (1996) *The Whitehall Reader*, Buckingham: Open University Press.

Barzelay, Michael (1992) *Breaking through Bureaucracy*, Berkeley, LA, California: University of California Press.

Bogdanor, Vernon (ed.) (2005) *Joined-Up Government*, Oxford: Oxford University Press.

Brazier, Alex (ed.) (2004) *Parliament, Politics and Lawmaking*, London: Hansard Society.

Brazier, Alex, Flinders, Matthew and McHugh, Declan (2005) *New Politics, New Parliament?*, London: Hansard Society.

Brazier, Alex and Ram, Vidya (2006) *The Fiscal Maze, Parliament, Government and Public Money*, London: Hansard Society.

Brown, George (1971) *In My Way*, London: Victor Gollancz.

Campbell, Colin and Wilson, Graham K. (1995) *The End of Whitehall: death of a paradigm?*, Oxford: Blackwell Publishers.

Castle, Barbara (1993) *Fighting all the Way*, London: Macmillan.

Centeno, Miguel Angel (1994) *Democracy Within Reason*, Pennsylvania: Pennsylvania State University Press.

Chapman, Leslie (1978) *Your Disobedient Servant*, London: Chatto and Windus.

Coyle, Andrew (1991) *Inside, Rethinking Scotland's Prisons*, Edinburgh: Scottish Child.

Crofts, Freeman Wills (2000 [1942]) *Death of a Train*, London: House of Stratus.

Darwell, R. (2005) *The Reluctant Managers*, London: KPMG.

Day, Patricia and Klein, Rudolf (1987) *Accountabilities, Five Public Services*, London: Tavistock Publications.

Donahue, John D. and Nye, Joseph S., Jr (2003) *For the People, Can we Fix the Public Service?*, Washington DC: The Brookings Institution Press.

Drewry, G. and Butcher, T. (1991) *The Civil Service Today*, Oxford: Blackwells.

Drucker, Peter (1955) *The Practice of Management*, Oxford: Heinemann.

Drucker, Peter (1995) *Managing in a Time of Great Change*, Oxford: Butterworth, Heinemann.

Eliassen, Kjell and Kooiman, Jan (1993) *Managing Public Organisations*, London: Sage Publications.

Exworthy, Mark and Halford, Susan (1999) *Professionals and the New Managerialism in the Public Sector*, Buckingham: Open University Press.

Faulkener, David (2001) *Crime, State and Citizen*, Winchester: Waterside Press.

Ferlie, Ewan, Ashburner, Lyn, Fitzgerald, Louise and Pettigrew, Andrew (1996) *The New Public Management in Action*, Oxford: Oxford University Press.

Finer, Herman (1937) *The British Civil Service*, London: The Fabian Society and George Allen and Unwin.

Finer, Samuel (1950) *A Primer of Public Administration*, London: Muller.

Foster, Christopher (2005a) *Why Are We So Badly Governed?*, London: Public Management and Policy Association.

Foster, Christopher (2005b) *British Government in Crisis*, Oxford: Hart Publishing.

Foster, Christopher and Plowden, Francis (1996) *The State Under Stress*, Buckingham: Open University Press.

Fraser, Sir Angus (1992) *Making the Most of Next Steps*, London: Efficiency Unit, HMSO.

Fry, Geoffrey (1995) *Policy and Management in the British Civil Service*, Hemel Hempstead: Prentice Hall, Harvester Wheatsheaf.

Fulton, Lord, Chairman (1968) *The Civil Service, Volume 1 The Report of the Committee*, Command 3638, London: HMSO.

Geddes, Barbara (1994) *Politician's Dillemma, Building State Capacity in Latin America*, Berkeley California: University of California Press.

Giddings, Philip (ed.) (1995) *Parliamentary Accountability: a Study of Parliament and Executive Agencies*, London: Macmillan.

Goldsmith, M.J. and Page, E.C. (1997) 'Farewell to the British State', in Lane, J-E (1997) *Public Sector Reform*, London: Sage Publications.

Goldsworthy, Diana (1991) *Setting up Next Steps*, London: HMSO.

Gray, Andrew and Jenkins, William (1985) *Administrative Politics in British Government*, Brighton: Wheatsheaf.

Greer, Patricia (1994) *Transforming Central Government: The Next Steps Initiative*, Buckingham: Open University Press.

Hart, Jenifer (1998) *Ask Me No More*, London: Peter Halban.

Healey, Denis (1989) *The Time of My Life*, London: Michael Joseph.

Heclo, Andrew and Wildavsky, Aaron (1974) *The Private Government of Public Money*, London: Macmillan.

Hennessy, Peter (1989 and 2001) *Whitehall*, London: Pimlico/Secker and Warburg.

Hogwood, Brian (1993) 'Restructuring central government; the "next steps" initiative in Britain', in Eliassen, K. and Kooiman, J. (eds) (1993) *Managing Public Organisations*, London: Sage Publications.

Hood, Christopher (1976) *The Limits of Administration*, London: John Wiley.

Hood, Christopher (1998) *The Art of the State*, Oxford: Oxford University Press.

Hunt, G. (1998) *Whistle Blowing in the Social Services*, London: Hodder Headline Group.

Jackson, Eric, W. (1961) *Local Government in England and Wales*, London: Penguin.

James, Oliver (2003) *The Executive Agency Revolution in Whitehall*, London: Palgrave, Macmillan.

Jenkins, K.M., Morris, Brian, Caplan, Charlotte and Metcalfe, Les (1984) *Consultancy Inspection and Review Services in Government Departments*, London: The Efficiency Unit, HMSO.

Jenkins, K.M., Oates, Graham, and Stott, Andrew (1985) *Making Things Happen. A Report on the Implementation of Government Efficiency Scrutinies*, London: The Efficiency Unit, HMSO.

Jenkins, K.M., Caines, K. and Jackson, A. (1988) *Improving Management in Government: The Next Steps*, London: The Efficiency Unit, HMSO.

Jenkins, K.M. and Plowden, W. (1995) *Keeping Control: the Management of Public Sector Reform Programmes*, London: The British Council.

Jenkins, K.M. and Plowden, W. (2006) *Governance and Nationbuilding: The Failure of International Intervention*, Cheltenham, UK and Northampton, MA, USA: Edward Elgar.

Jenkins, S. (2004) *Big Bang Localism. Policy Exchange*, London: Localis.

Jenkins, S. (2006) *Thatcher and Sons*, London: Penguin Books.

John, Peter (1998) *Analysing Public Policy*, London and New York: Continuum.

Jordan, Grant (1994) *The British Administrative System*, London: Routledge.

Kellner, P. and Crowther Hunt, Lord (1980) *The Civil Servants, an Inquiry into Britain's Ruling Class*, London: Macdonald General Books.

Kemp, Peter (1993) *Beyond Next Steps, a Civil Service for the 21st Century*, London: Social Market Foundation.

Kemp, Peter and Walker, David (1996) *A Better Machine, Government for the 21st Century*, London: European Policy Forum.

Kirton, Claremont (1992) *Jamaica, Debt and Poverty*, Oxford: Oxfam.

Lane, Jan-Erik (1993) *The Public Sector: Concepts, Models and Approaches*, London: Sage Publications.

Lane, Jan-Erik (1997) *Public Sector Reform*, London: Sage Publications.

Lawson, Nigel (1992) *The View from No 11*, London: Bantam Press, Transworld Publishers.

Lodge, Guy and Rogers, Ben (2006) *Whitehall's Black Box*, London: Institute for Public Policy Research.

Mandelson, Peter and Liddle, Roger (1996) *The Blair Revolution*, London: Faber.

Marquand, David and Seldon, Anthony (1996) *The Ideas that Shaped Post War Britain*, London: Fontana.

Marsh, David and Rhodes, R.A.W. (eds) (1992) *Implementing Thatcherite Policies*, Buckingham: Open University Press.

McCourt, W. and Minogue, Martin (2001) *The Internationalisation of Public Management*, Cheltenham, UK and Northampton, MA, USA: Edward Elgar.

Meyer, C. (2005) *DC Confidential*, London: Weidenfeld and Nicholson.

Minogue, Martin, Polidano, Charles and Hulme, David (eds) (1998) *Beyond the New Public Management*, Cheltenham, UK and Northampton, MA, USA: Edward Elgar.

Oakeshott, Michael and Fuller, T. (ed.) (1996) *The Politics of Faith and the Politics of Scepticism*, New Haven and London: Yale University Press.

OECD (1993) *Public Management Developments*, Survey, Paris: OECD.

OECD (1994) *Responsive Government: Service Quality Initiatives*, Paris: OECD.

Osborne, D. and Gaebler, T. (1992) *Reinventing Government*, Reading, MA: Addison-Wesley Publishing Company.

Oxfam: Kirton, Claremont (1992) *Jamaica, Debt and Poverty*, Oxford: Oxfam.

Parsons, Wayne (1995) *Public Policy*, Cheltenham, UK and Northampton, MA, USA: Edward Elgar.

Paxman, Jeremy (1990) *Friends in High Places*, London: Penguin Books.

Peters, Thomas and Waterman, Robert, H. Jr. (1982) *In Search of Excellence*, New York: Harper Collins.

Plowden, William (1994) *Ministers and Mandarins*, London: Institute for Public Policy Research.

Pollit, C. and Harrison, S. (1992) *Handbook of Public Services Management*, Oxford: Blackwells.

Pressman, J.L. and Wildavsky, A. (1973) *Implementation; the Oakland Project*, Berkeley, California: University of California Press.

Priestley, Clive (1988) in *The Independent*, 26 February 1988, London.

Ponting, Clive (1989) *Whitehall, Changing the Old Guard*, London: Fabian Society.

Richards, Sue and Metcalfe, Les (1987) *Improving Public Management*, London: Sage Publications.

Rimmington, S. (2001) *Open Secret*, London: Hutchinson.

Rosenblatt, Gemma (2006) *The New MP*, London: The Hansard Society.

Roseveare, Henry (1973) *The Treasury, 1660–1870*, London: George Allen and Unwin Ltd.

Sisson, C.H. (1989) *On the Lookout*, Manchester: Carcanet Press.

Sorensen, Rune (1993) 'The efficiency of public service provision', in Elaissen, K.A. (ed.) *Managing Public Organisations*, London: Sage Publications.

Stewart, John and Stoker, Gerry (eds) (1989) *The Future of Local Government*, Basingstoke and London: Macmillan.

Stiglitz, Joseph E. (2002) *Globalisation and its Discontents*, London: Penguin.

Stiglitz, Joseph E. (2003) *The Roaring Nineties*, New York: W W Norton.

Stoker, Gerry (2006) *Why Politics Matters*, Basingstoke and London: Palgrave Macmillan.

Stowe, Kenneth (1992) *Public Administration*, vol 70, Autumn, Oxford: Blackwells.

Sweden (1997) *Papers on Public Sector Budgeting and Management in Sweden, Volume 3, Public Sector Productivity in Sweden*, Budget Department, Stockholm: Swedish Ministry of Finance.

Tanner, J.R. (1928) *English Constitutional Conflicts of the Seventeeth Century*, Cambridge: Cambridge University Press.

Thatcher, Margaret (1993) *The Downing Street Years*, London: Harper Collins.

Titmuss, Richard, M. (1968) *Commitment to Welfare*, London: George Allen and Unwin.

Tomalin, Claire (2002) *Samuel Pepys, The Unequalled Self*, London: Viking, Penguin.

Waldegrave, William (1993) *Public Service and the Future*, London: Conservative Political Centre.

Wedgwood, C.V. (1938) *The Thirty Years War*, London: Penguin.

Weir, Stuart and Beetham, David (1999) *Political Power and Democratic Control in Britain*, London: Routledge.

Weller, Patrick and Davis, Glyn (1996) *New Ideas, Better Government*, St Leonards NSW: Allen and Unwin.

Wildavsky, A. (1980) *The Art and Craft of Policy Analysis*, London: Macmillan.

Wilding, Richard (2006) *Civil Servant, a Memoir*, County Durham: The Memoir Club, Stanhope Old Hall, Weardale.

Williams, Walter (1988) *Washington, Westminster and Whitehall*, Cambridge: Cambridge University Press.

Williams, Walter (1990) *Mismanaging America, the Rise of the Anti-analytic Presidency*, Kansas: University Press of Kansas.

Wilson, Harold (1976) *The Governance of Britain*, London: Weidenfeld and Nicholson, Michael Joseph.

Wilson, James, Q. (1989) *Bureaucracy: What Government Agencies Do and Why They Do It*, New York USA: Basic Books, Harper Collins.

Winetrobe, Barry (1995) in Giddings, Phillip (ed.) (1995) *Parliamentary Accountability: A Study of Parliament and Executive Agencies*, London: Macmillan.

Woodward, Bob (2002) *Bush at War*, New York, London: Simon and Schuster.

Woodward, Bob (2004) *Plan of Attack*, New York, London: Simon and Schuster.

Woodward, Bob (2006) *State of Denial*, New York, London: Simon and Schuster.

Young, Hugo (1993) *One of Us*, London: Pan.

Zeigler, Phillip (1993) *Wilson*, London: Wiedenfield and Nicholson.

Zifcak, Spencer (1994) *New Managerialism: Administrative Reform in Whitehall and Canberra*, Buckingham: Open University Press.

UK GOVERNMENT PUBLICATIONS

In Place of Strife (1969) A Policy for Industrial Relations, Cmnd 3888, London: HMSO.

The Reorganisation of Central Government (1970) Cmnd 4506, London: HMSO.

Central Policy Review Staff:

   (1975) *A Joint Framework for Social Policies*, London: HMSO.

   (1977) *Review of Overseas Representation*, London: HMSO.

   (1977) *Population and the Social Services*, London: HMSO.

Efficiency and Effectiveness in Government (1982) London: HMSO.

Cassells, J.S. (1982) *Review of Personnel Work in the Civil Service*, Report to the Prime Minister, London: HMSO.

Financial Management in Government Departments (1983) (Cmnd 9058), London, HMSO and *Progress in Financial Management in Government Departments* (1984) (Cmnd 9298), London: HMSO.

National Audit Office (1986) *The Financial Management Initiative*, HC 588, 1985–6, London: HMSO.

National Audit Office (1986) *Report on the Rayner Scrutiny Programme*, London: HMSO.

Treasury and Civil Service Select Committee Reports: Fifth Report, Session 1988–89 HC 348, London: HMSO.

Audit Commission (1994) *Watching their Figures: a Guide to Citizen's Charter Indicators*, London: Audit Commission.

The Citizen's Charter (July 1991) Cmnd 1509, London: HMSO.

Questions of Procedure for Ministers (1992) London: Cabinet Office.

A Code of Conduct and Guidance on Procedures for Ministers (1997) London: Cabinet Office.

Office of the Civil Service Commissioners (2005) *Changing Times*, London: OCSC.

Efficiency Unit reports

    Jenkins, K.M., Morris, Brian, Caplan, Charlotte and Metcalfe, Les (1984) *Consultancy Inspection and Review Services in Government Departments*, London: The Efficiency Unit, HMSO.

    Jenkins K.M., Oates, Graham and Stott, Andrew (1985) *Making Things Happen. A Report on the Implementation of Government Efficiency Scrutinies*, London: The Efficiency Unit, HMSO.

    Jenkins, K.M., Caines, K. and Jackson, A. (1988) *Improving Management in Government: The Next Steps*, London: The Efficiency Unit, HMSO.

    Fraser, Sir Angus (1991) *Making the Most of Next Steps*, London: The Efficiency Unit, HMSO.

Improving Management in Government: The Next Steps Agencies, Review 1990, Cm. 1261, London: HMSO.

Improving Management in Government: The Next Steps Agencies, Review 1991, Cm. 1760, London: HMSO.

The Next Steps Agencies, Review 1992, Cm. 2111, London: HMSO.

Next Steps Review (1995) Cm. 3164, London: HMSO.

Next Steps Report (1997) Cm. 3889, London: The Stationary Office.

Cabinet Office (2005) *Report for Senior Civil Service: Overall Senior Civil Service Leadership and Skill Survey, 2004*, London: HMSO.

NEXT STEPS DOCUMENTS

Next Steps Quarterly Briefing Notes: September 1988–September 1998, London: Cabinet Office.

Framework Documents

Companies House (1988)
National Weights and Measures Laboratory (1989)

Historic Royal Palaces (1989)
Royal Mint (1990)
The Employment Service (1990)
The Forensic Science Service (1991)
The Medicines Control Agency (1991)
The United Kingdom Passport Agency (1991)
Wilton Park (1991)
Inland Revenue North West, an Executive Office (1992)
The Public Record Office (1992)
The Royal Parks (1993)
The Pesticides Safety Directorate (1993)
The Child Support Agency (1993)
H M Prison Service (1993)
The Highways Agency (1994)
Historic Scotland (1994)
Driver and Vehicle Licensing Agency (1995)
The Court Service (1995)
The Intervention Board (1995)
Veterinary Medicines Directorate, a 'Simpler' Agency (1995)
HM Land Registry (1996)

Ministry of Defence Agencies

The Meteorological Office (1990, 1996)
Naval Aircraft Repair Organisation (1992)
The Pay and Personnel Agency (1993)
Army Base Repair Organisation (1993)

Index